£44·10 - Amazon.

IOWA

IOWA CLASS BATTLESHIPS

THEIR DESIGN, WEAPONS & EQUIPMENT

ROBERT F SUMRALL

DRAWINGS BY TOM WALKOWIAK

CONWAY
MARITIME PRESS

© Robert Sumrall 1988

First published in Great Britain 1988 by
Conway Maritime Press Ltd
24 Bride Lane, Fleet Street,
London EC4Y 8DR

IBSN 0 85177 479 2

The drawings in the appendices can be obtained from
The Floating Drydock
c/o General Delivery
Kresgeville, PA 18333
USA

Designed by John Mitchell
Typeset by Witwell Ltd, Southport
Printed and bound in Great Britain by The Bath Press

CONTENTS

Chapter 1

THE FAST BATTLESHIP

With the evolution of the modern, or steel navy, battleships and battlecruisers were considered the primary combatants in all navies, being the most heavily armed and the best protected ships of the fleet. They were, in a sense, the projection of national power.

As the world's navies continued to develop battleship and battlecruiser types, the concept of a fast battleship began to take shape from a desire to combine the best features of both. While both types were about equal in displacement and carried the same heavy main battery, they differed with regard to speed and protection.

In theory, battleships were protected by heavy armor plate against weapons comparable to their own main battery guns. This armor was spread over a considerable length of the vessel's side in order to protect machinery rooms, magazines and other vital spaces. Much of the deck area was also armored to protect against shells coming in at steeper angles.

On the other hand, battlecruisers were considerably faster, but were protected by much lighter armor plate. The weight saved on armor was invested in additional machinery to achieve higher speed. This greater speed was intended to compensate, at least in part, for the battlecruiser's inferior armor. However, with the rapid development of gun fire control, the increase in gun caliber and the improvement in ballistic efficiency, battle ranges began to increase and the speed advantage of the battlecruiser steadily declined against the battleship as an opponent.

The battlecruiser's place in a fleet became one of scouting with advanced forces, or detached as a powerful raider. In the latter role she was capable of overpowering cruisers and any other covering force except another of her type or a battleship.

As naval planners considered a variety of new ship designs, they returned repeatedly to the idea of a vessel with the heavy protection of the battleship and the great speed of the battlecruiser that could

The British Royal Navy introduced the *Invincible* class battlecruisers in 1906. They mounted eight 12in/45cal guns and were rated at 25 knots. The *Invincible*, shown here about 1914, actually made 26.6 knots on a measured mile course.

perform the functions of both. It became an increasingly attractive prospect, even though combining speed and the protection of heavy armor in the same vessel meant a considerable increase in size and weight. A fast battleship would be much larger and heavier than either of the existing types.

The first American studies of a battlecruiser/fast battleship type were undertaken in 1912. The United States was a late-comer in the battlecruiser construction race that had begun when the British Royal Navy introduced the *Invincible* class battlecruisers in 1906 and Germany countered with its *Von der Tanns*. The precipitating event for the American action was Japan's entry into the race with its order of the *Kongo* from Britain's Vickers Armstrong shipyard in 1910 and disclosure of subsequent plans to lay down three more of the class by mid-1911.

The thought that an American force of armored cruisers might no longer be able to protect United States commercial interests in the Pacific was indeed disturbing. The battlecruiser studies were shelved,

existing battle fleet. The battlecruisers, however, were to have a top speed of 33.25 knots and they were clearly intended to be among the fastest ships afloat.

THE WASHINGTON TREATY

In 1921, not only the United States, but all of the major naval powers were still engaged in their massive building programs, even though the German High Seas Fleet had been dismantled after World War I. All of the countries that had been involved in the 'Great War' were facing the problems of post-war recession and it was obvious that the enormous financial outlay for naval construction could not be continued much longer; some countries indeed were on the brink of financial disaster. In the United States, there was little hope that the Congress would continue to fund the ambitious building program already underway, certainly not in its entirety, after a costly 'war to end all wars'.

however, due mainly to austerity in naval construction and long-standing US Navy doctrine that favored firepower and protection over speed. In 1915, after the outbreak of World War I, the studies were revived and by 1918 several designs had been developed. The United States was by that time involved in the war and interest in the battlecruiser as a type remained high, even after the actions at Jutland. Battlecruisers were considered necessary to counter the tactical situations presented by countries possessing them.

Conventional battleship design progressed on a parallel course and, by the end of World War I, the US Navy was in the midst of a huge expansion program. Under construction were six 43,200 ton battleships mounting twelve 16in guns and a further six 43,500 ton battlecruisers carrying eight 16in guns. The battleships were to be capable of 23 knots, only a knot or two faster than the ships in the

The six battleships of the first *South Dakota* (BB 49) class were laid down in 1920–1921. They were to mount twelve 16in/50cal guns in the main battery and were to have a speed of 23 knots. None were completed and all were cancelled and broken up in accordance with the Washington Treaty of 1922. (Paul Bender.)

The practical solution was negotiation, the outcome of which was the Washington Treaty signed by Great Britain, the United States, Japan, France and Italy on 6 February 1922. The Treaty effected a 'building holiday' for ten years. It also restricted the total tonnage that each country could build and it further specified the maximum displacement and gun caliber of each type of combatant that could be built.

The total tonnage limitations imposed were:

Great Britain – 580,450
United States – 500,320
Japan – 301,320
France – 221,170
Italy – 182,000

This allocation was referred to as the '5–5–3' ratio and established the following requirements for capital ships:

Maximum displacement was fixed at 35,000 tons
Maximum gun caliber was fixed at 16in
Age was determined to be twenty years, and a new replacement was not permitted before that time
Reconstruction was permitted, but limited to improvements against aerial and underwater attack

battlecruisers *Lexington* and *Saratoga* which were reordered and completed as aircraft carriers. As a result of the curtailment of the building program, the existing battlefleet was still only capable of 21 knots which was not inconsistent with US Navy doctrine of firepower over speed. The problem would be that the Treaty allowed potential adversaries to retain capital ships with high-speed capabilities.

Japan was permitted to retain the *Nagato* and *Mutsu* of 32,700 tons carrying eight 16in guns. Both vessels were completed just before the Treaty was signed. The United States could keep the *Maryland*, also completed just before the Treaty went into effect, and complete her two sisters the *Colorado* and *West Virginia*. These 32,000 tonners were armed with eight 16in guns. Great Britain was allowed to design and construct two battleships in accordance with the new regulations. The result was the *Nelson* and the *Rodney*. Both were completed in 1927, displaced 33,950 tons and mounted nine 16in guns. Both France

Improvements were limited to a displacement increase of 3,000 tons
The term 'standard displacement' was established and defined as the weight of the vessel complete, fully manned and ready for sea including ammunition, provisions, potable water and all other items carried in war but excluding fuel and reserve feedwater
Displacement weight was defined as 2,240 pounds per ton

Some vessels under construction at the time the Washington Treaty was signed were allowed to be completed if they met all of the Treaty restrictions. Most new construction, however, had to be scrapped in order to comply. It was also necessary to dispose of many older vessels in order to reach the adjusted allotments.

The negotiations during the conference produced a great deal of discord among the participants. The most bitter disagreement was over the question of displacement and type allocation. Japan was never satisfied with the '5–5–3' ratio established for the top three powers. She felt forced into a position of inferiority and by 1936 had withdrawn from participation in continuing treaty negotiations.

The battleship and battlecruiser programs of the United States both fell victim to the Washington Treaty. All construction underway was cancelled and the hulls were broken up on the ways except for the

Six battlecruisers of the *Lexington* (CC 1) class were also laid down in 1920–1921. They were to carry eight 16in/50cal guns and be capable of 33.25 knots. Construction was cancelled in compliance with the Washington Treaty. The *Lexington* and her sister *Saratoga* (CC 2) were redesigned and completed as aircraft carriers. The *Lexington*s would have been the first fast capital ships in the US Navy. (Paul Bender.)

and Italy were experiencing such severe financial difficulties that they had abandoned all hope of completing any of their wartime construction. When the conference convened in Washington, only the French *Bearn* had survived and she was eventually completed as an aircraft carrier. As compensation, special clauses in the Treaty permitted the French and Italian navies enough tonnage to build two capital ships each, of comparable size and strength to those of the other countries.

THE LONDON TREATIES

The Washington Treaty had provided for a conference to be held at London in 1930, a year before the expiration of the 'building holiday'. By the late-1920s, the post-war recession had worsened and the financial atmosphere was hardly conducive to the beginning of

The *Nagato* on trials in 1920. The Washington Treaty allowed Japan to keep the *Nagato* and her sister, the *Mutsu*, which were completed before the treaty was signed. Their main armament was eight 16in/45cal guns. A very well-kept secret for many years was their 26.75 knot speed.

another naval arms race. Yet those countries not at par with Great Britain and the United States wanted equity, even if they couldn't afford it. Their prestigious floating fortresses were viewed as symbolic of a nation's industrial capability and scientific achievement. Another interesting aspect (very seldom mentioned in this regard) is that most of the Treaty signatories were engaged in some manner of colonialism. As these colonies were exploited financially to aide their motherlands, control of the sea lanes became even more important in the projection and maintenance of national power.

The League of Nations attempted to assume control of naval arms limitations by sponsoring a conference at Geneva in 1927. Even though the United States was not a member nation, the League was confident that, if an arrangement could be worked out, the United States would be a party to the resulting treaty. By the time of the conference, the Japanese, French, and Italians had nurtured dissatisfactions with the original agreement in Washington to the point where discussions proved useless. Great Britain would not yield in her position and the Americans were not there. The conference was a failure.

As provided for, the second naval arms limitation conference was duly convened at London in 1930. The same grievances that had ruined the talks at Geneva foreshadowed the assembly with the participants seemingly even farther apart. It was undoubtedly the hope and intent of Great Britain and the United States to continue to negotiate their naval superiority. Conditions were on their side for by 1930, the recession had become a depression and spread throughout the world. Most of the signatory nations were not in a position to expend funding necessary for capital ship construction at the expense of their nation's economic survival. The state of the world economy was probably the most compelling factor in bringing about an eventual, though limited, agreement and extending the 'building holiday' for another five years.

In 1929, however, Germany had laid down her first major warship since the Great War. German naval construction was regulated by the Treaty of Versailles, which formally ended World War I, but was not bound by any other agreement. A limit of 10,000 tons per vessel was imposed and a maximum gun caliber of 11in was allowed. Coast

Above: Germany was not a participant in the Washington Treaty. She was bound only to the Treaty of Versailles which ended World War I. Limited to 10,000 tons displacement and an 11in gun size, Germany produced the *Deutschland* class. The class was capable of 28.5 knots and mounted six 11in/54.5cal guns. The *Deutschland* was commissioned in 1933 and is seen here in the mid-1930s. She was renamed *Lutzow* in 1939.

Below: The Washington Treaty allowed the United States to keep the *Maryland* (BB 46) and complete two sisters, the *Colorado* (BB 45) and *West Virginia* (BB 48). A fourth ship of the class, the *Washington* (BB 47), had to be disposed of. The *Maryland* is shown on builder's trials on 21 June 1921, a month before her commissioning. The class carried eight 16in/45cal guns in their main battery, but their speed was only 21 knots.

defense ships and heavy cruisers would be tolerated but nothing more. The design which was selected in 1927 resulted in the *Deutschland* (later renamed *Lutzow*) with a displacement of 10,000 tons (actually 11,700 tons), mounting six 11in guns and capable of over 26 knots. Officially referred to as a *panzerschiffe* (armored ship), the *Deutschland* soon became known as a 'pocket battleship'. The Germans had intended her to be used as a commerce raider and not as a capital ship in the sense of operating in a battle line like battleships and battlecruisers. She was certainly more than a match for a heavy cruiser, except in speed, and could be feared as a raider. It was not until the test of battle that the weaknesses of this type became known. The greatest impact of the pocket battleship was, undoubtedly, the psychological effect it had on naval strategy and tactics.

The agreement reached at London in 1930 was, therefore, not without a price. France refused to ratify, putting forth as justification the fact that Germany had laid down the *Deutschland* and intelligence indicated that at least two more ships, possibly even larger in size,

down in 1934. Officially described as 35,000 tonners, they were actually over 40,000 tons, carried nine 15in guns and were capable of 30 knots. The Italians also undertook a massive reconstruction program for the two *Conte di Cavour* and two *Caio Duilio* class ships which, arguably, in effect made them new battleships. These were by far the most extensive battleship reconstructions ever made, including the Japanese *Kongo*s and any US Navy wartime modernizations.

Germany had, indeed, planned to build more pocket battleships. Construction on the *Admiral Scheer* began in 1931 and on the *Admiral Graf Spee* in 1932. Plans called for a total of six *panzerschiffes* in all and ordnance and material for the next three were ordered. With the appearance of the *Dunkerque* class, consideration was given to increasing the size of the last two units to accommodate a third 11in turret. The need for additional speed and protection made the idea impractical and a new battlecruiser design emerged which was comparable to the *Dunkerque*s. The last three *panzerschiffes* were cancelled and two units were ordered to the new battlecruiser design.

were about to be laid down. France's vital link to North Africa had to be maintained. New ships without restrictions were necessary as a countermeasure. Italy refused to support the treaty, as expected, claiming that if France built new capital ships Italy's position in the Mediterranean would be threatened. Japan, still unhappy with her capital ship allotment, revelled in the discontent, but agreed to the five year extension at the expense of other concessions.

The French had designed a battlecruiser in the late-1920s and planned to construct two as allowed by the Washington Treaty. They were never laid down because of the poor economic conditions. Although France was primarily concerned with the Italian Navy in the Mediterranean, the design was revived and revised to counter the *Deutschland*. Construction began on the *Dunkerque* in 1932 and the *Strasbourg* in 1934. They were handsome vessels of 26,500 tons, mounted eight 13in guns and made over 30 knots on their trials

The *Dunkerque* class had made an impression on the Italian designers. They started with a fresh battleship design in 1930, almost completely laying aside the design work they had done in the previous two years. The first two units, the *Littorio* and *Vittorio Veneto*, were laid

The Washington Treaty provided for the British to construct two new battleships, the *Nelson* and *Rodney*, to offset the Japanese *Nagato*s and American *Colorado*s. The first capital ships designed and built under Treaty restrictions, they joined the fleet in 1927 and were indeed unique, with their main battery of nine 16in/45cal guns all located forward in three turrets. Their top speed was 23 knots. The *Nelson* is shown here during the mid-1930s.

Work on both the *Scharnhorst* and *Gneisenau* started in 1934, but they were not actually laid down until 1935. The displacement was originally stated to be 26,000 tons, but they were actually 31,800 tons when completed and could do over 31 knots. The six 11in turrets planned for the cancelled *panzerschiffes* were used to arm each new battlecruiser with nine 11in guns.

The Japanese, in the meantime, had given the statutory two years' notice that they did not intend to renew the Treaty when it expired, claiming the right to build as they considered necessary for their national interests. While not having started any work, Japan was thought to have designs with which to immediately begin construction.

With the introduction by France of the *Dunkerque* class,
Germany cancelled the last three *Deutschland*s. A full-
sized battleship was designed, but the armament for the
last three 'pocket battleships' was used; however,
provision was made in the design for re-gunning with
15in guns at a later date. The *Scharnhorst* and
Gneisenau were completed with nine 11in/54.5cal guns.
Their speed was 31 knots. The *Scharnhorst* sports her
new Atlantic bow in late-1939. (Courtesy Erich Groner.)

The French replied to the *Deutschland* class with the
Dunkerque and *Strasbourg*. These two handsome
vessels had their main battery of eight 13in/52cal guns
concentrated forward in two turrets. On sea trials in
1936, the *Dunkerque* reached a speed of 31 knots. She is
seen here during the naval review at Spithead in 1937.

The *Deutschland* had a significant impact on the world's naval powers, at least politically, for it disturbed the calculated capital strength of the Washington Treaty. It can also be said that the *Deutschland* touched off the second naval arms race which was well under way when the next naval arms limitation conference met at London in 1936 as scheduled. Against this gloomy outlook, the remaining signatory powers inserted an 'escalator clause' which would allow them to increase tonnage and gun caliber to match any increase by non-participants. It was required that other signatories be consulted if any escalation was to be undertaken but this was only a formality. As for the original hopes at Washington in 1922, the Treaty did work for ten years.

In the United States, the building holiday effectively froze all capital ship design. Any advancement in technology could only come through the improvements which were allowed to be made on existing ships. The oldest ships were modernized first, anticipating that they would

The Italian Navy began work on a new battleship design to counter the *Dunkerque*s being built in France. The first two units of the new class, the *Littorio* and *Vittorio Veneto*, were laid down in 1934. They were much more heavily gunned than the French ships, having a main battery of nine 15in/50cal guns. Their rated speed was 30 knots and on trials they made slightly over 31 knots. The *Vittorio Veneto* is shown here at Taranto in 1940, shortly after her commissioning. (Courtesy Aldo Fraccaroli.)

be the first to be retired. In the late-1920s, the Bureau of Construction and Repair resumed battleship studies but did not engage in any serious capital ship design. The US Navy was eagerly awaiting the appearance of the Royal Navy's *Nelson* and *Rodney* for they would likely set the standard for future capital ship design and replacement under the Treaties. Serious design work on battleships did not resume until Spring 1935 for the first replacements allowed under the Treaties.

After World War I, the US Navy began to station major portions of the fleet on the West Coast and in the late-1930s conducted full-scale fleet maneuvers, including specific battle problems, between the West Coast and the area around the Territory of Hawaii. A portion of the main battle line is shown during maneuvers in 1938. In the foreground is the battleship *Tennessee* with the *Nevada* just beyond.

Chapter 2

DESIGN BACKGROUND

The United States emerged from the nineteenth century as a world naval power. Fresh from a victory over Spain, she was suddenly in control of a number of island areas which ranged from the Caribbean to the Western Pacific. In 1893, Hawaii had asked to become a part of the United States and was finally annexed in July of 1898 during the Spanish-American War. Guam, Wake and Midway Islands were also occupied during that war and became American territory. In the ensuing treaty, ratified in 1899, Spain ceded to the United States most of her colonial empire which included Cuba, Porto Rico and other smaller islands in the Caribbean and the Philippine Islands in the Pacific. The United States also finally assumed sovereignty, after several years of trouble, over the islands of Samoa in 1900.

With this 'flash of empire' there also came responsibilities. Territorial governments and lines of communications had to be established and maintained. More simply put, these new areas had to be cared for and protected. On the other hand, they were a network through which endless trade opportunities existed; a look at a map will quickly show how important and strategically located these new possessions were.

The United States was still primarily involved with the European powers, both financially and culturally, and development of the Pacific possessions was slow. The political scene in Europe was tense and in 1914 finally boiled over in the Great War. Eventually America was drawn into World War I from which she emerged as a great naval power, second only to Great Britain.

The four *Kongo*s were overhauled and refitted in the late-1920s, as the *Kongo*, photographed in August 1932, shows. Their 26 knot speed was an important tactical factor in the games played at the Naval War College. The battlecruisers could be detached from the main battle line to operate independently or to assist their carriers on strike operations.

Four Japanese battleships are seen here at anchor in Tankan Bay in the Kuriles during the early-1930s. The Japanese conducted many exercises and maneuvers out of Tankan Bay. The Pearl Harbor strike force was assembled there. From front to rear are the *Nagato*, *Kirishima*, *Ise* and *Hiuga*. In the background is a light cruiser of the *Sendai* class.

After World War I, United States national interests gradually shifted to the Pacific where the development of trade with countries in the Far East offered countless commercial opportunities. In the mid-1920s, the US Navy began to station major portions of the fleet on the West Coast and strategic planning was directed toward protecting American possessions and commercial interests in the vast Pacific area. It was essential that trade routes and lines of communication remained intact.

Naval strategists assumed that America's next war would be with Japan for the domination of the Pacific and that the US Navy would play a decisive role in any such struggle. Recalling the '5–5–3' ratio allowed by the Washington Treaty, the US Navy was allowed fifteen capital ships and the Imperial Japanese Navy only nine. Many battle problems were staged at the Naval War College based on the various expected Japanese war plans and options for their imperial expansion. It was anticipated that the Japanese would try to reduce the numerical superiority of the US Navy by attrition before any major confrontation where they would have to commit their battle line.

It seemed the most likely target of attack would be the Philippine Islands, America's major possession in the Western Pacific. In the event of such an attack, American forces would have to steam west in relief of the islands. The great distance to be covered would put them at a logistical disadvantage. In addition, they would have to pass through a chain of islands which had been mandated to the Japanese. By the early-1930s, intelligence estimates suggested that these 'mandated islands' were being fortified. With a heavy concentration of air and naval forces operating from these bases, Japanese submarines and fast surface ships such as aircraft carriers and heavy cruisers could attack American advance units and attempt to sever their long lines of communications. The American ships would again come under attack when they came within range of land-based aircraft operating from the Japanese held islands. As the American advantage was reduced to more favorable odds, the Japanese could then commit their battle line to a decisive engagement.

A very important factor in the games played at the Naval War College was the tactical use of the three Japanese *Kongo* class battlecruisers. The class consisted of the *Kongo*, *Haruna* and *Kirishima* mounting eight 14in guns and capable of 26 knots. A fourth ship of the class, the *Hiei*, had been demilitarized under the terms of the Treaty and was serving as a training ship. These units could be detached from the Japanese main battle line to operate either independently or to assist their carriers and cruisers. In either case, American scouting forces, composed primarily of carriers and cruisers, were no match for the 14in guns of the Japanese, nor could the units of their 21 knot battle fleet chase down the faster Japanese in order to bring them to action.

As indicated in Chapter 1, the Treaty allowed a limited amount of reconstruction for capital ships. The Japanese viewed the Treaty as a conspiracy to relegate them to the status of a second-class naval power and began a reconstruction and modernization program deliberately and carefully planned to exploit the Treaty to the fullest. It was their intent to have the finest vessels possible, within the agreed limitations, and extract the maximum fighting capabilities from each.

The reconstruction and modernization program for the Japanese battle fleet was common knowledge, but details concerning the new characteristics of the rebuilt vessels was kept top secret. The *Kongos*, in fact, were reconstructed twice before the attack on Pearl Harbor and, at the time of the second modernization, the *Hiei* was secretly remilitarized and brought up to the standard of her sisters. After their second refitting the *Kongo* class ships were rerated as battleships and their speed was increased to 30.5 knots. Another very well kept secret was the fact that the *Nagato* and *Mutsu*, both mounting eight 16in guns, were capable of 26 knots. By the mid-1930s, United States intelligence suspected that designs were in preparation for new capital ships so that construction might begin immediately after the Treaty expired.

The US Navy was also in the midst of a reconstruction and modernization program. It was not, however, nearly as extensive as that undertaken by Japan. America was still suffering from the effects of the Great Depression and the US Navy preferred to use its major resources for new construction which the over-age replacement allowance of the Treaty provided for.

The Secretary of the Navy was responsible for determining the characteristics for new naval vessels. His decisions were based primarily on the recommendations of the General Board and the Chief of Naval Operations (CNO). The General Board was a group of senior naval officers that advised the Secretary of the Navy on fundamental naval policy in regard to strategy, tactics and the shipbuilding program. It reported directly to the Secretary and served to coordinate the various bureaus under the CNO. The Board was effective in this role, but could exercise no direct authority over the CNO or any of the bureaus.

The Department of the Navy was made up of a number of powerful bureaus which in turn reported to the CNO. Those bureaus directly related to the shipbuilding program were: the Bureau of Construction and Repair (Bu C & R), responsible for hull design and general arrangement; the Bureau of Ordnance (Bu Ord), which designed all of the weapons and armor; and the Bureau of Engineering (Bu Eng), that provided design and arrangement of all of the machinery. The 'bureau system', as it existed at the time when the *Iowa* class was designed, was rather loosely coordinated at the level of the CNO, and each bureau operated with almost complete autonomy.

There was a great deal of rivalry between the General Board and the office of the CNO and its various bureaus. Although the Board

The *Mutsu* is shown in May 1936 nearing the completion of her modernization at Yokosuka. The *Mutsu* and her sister *Nagato* were extensively rebuilt during this period. They were fitted with bulges and a triple bottom and they were re-boilered and re-engined. The new boiler arrangement required only one stack which changed their silhouette considerably.

Top: This view of the *Nagato*, photographed at Tsingtao, China about 1937, shows the clean silhouette of her 1936 modernization. The fact that the *Nagato* and *Mutsu* were capable of 26 knots was a very well-kept secret and until the *North Carolina* class became operational they were the fastest 16in gunned battleships in the world.

Above: The *Hiei* was modernized between 1936 and 1939. The refit was somewhat more extensive than that of her sisters. New fire control systems were installed in the superstructure area which were the prototypes for the *Yamato* class. Here, the *Hiei* is making 30 knots during speed trials on 5 December 1939. The refit was completed in January 1940.

had no direct authority over the bureaus, the seniority of its members within the command structure of the US Navy usually resulted in their actions and recommendations being decisive.

THE *North Carolina* CLASS

Design work on new United States battleships began in May 1935 when the General Board asked the Bu C & R for design sketches of a battleship armed with 14in or 16in guns and capable of steaming at 30 knots. The somewhat ambiguous instructions concerning gun caliber reflected the uncertainty of the upcoming treaty negotiations scheduled for London in 1936. The US Navy felt that the performance of the 14in/50cal gun would be comparable to any of its contemporaries and, therefore, adequate. Japan had already announced her intention to withdraw from further treaty negotiations and it was hoped that, if the Treaty participants did not increase the gun caliber, neither would the Japanese. In good faith, battleship design proceeded accordingly.

A 30 knot design was prepared, but within the 35,000 ton limit only nine 14in guns in three 3-gun turrets could be worked in. After some consideration, the design was rejected. The main battery was considered inadequate compared to that of the *Tennessee* and *California* which carried twelve 14in guns in four 3-gun turrets and could make

21 knots on a displacement of 32,600 tons. Since firepower and armor had always been favored over speed, the reduction in firepower seemed a high price to pay for 9 knots. The requirement for higher speed, however, remained. The Bu C & R reworked the basic configuration to add three additional 14in guns. The new design featured twelve 14in guns mounted in three 4-gun turrets. The additional guns were not without a price, for in order to stay within the 35,000 ton limit, a reduction in speed to 27 knots had to be accepted. The design was finalized and became the *North Carolina* class.

Work began on the *North Carolina* on 3 June 1936, the same day that construction authorization was passed in the Congress; however, the keel was not actually laid until 27 October 1937. Long lead items such

The 30 knot design for the *North Carolina* class could only accommodate nine 14in/50cal guns. Although the 14in gun was considered a good weapon, the battery was considered inadequate compared with that of the *Tennessee* class. The *Tennessee* and *California* were considered to have a well-balanced battery of twelve 14in/50cal guns. A smaller battery for new battleships was rejected. The *North Carolina* design finally adopted had twelve 14in/50cal guns in three quadruple turrets but the speed had to be reduced to 26 knots. The *North Carolina* was laid down on 27 October 1937, the *Washington* on 14 June 1938. Here, the *Washington* begins to take shape on 6 January 1939 at the Philadelphia Navy Yard. The progress on the double and triple bottoms can be seen and the bulkheads for machinery space No. 2 have been erected. Framing for the tunnel of the twin skeg stern is also visible.

as armor and machinery had to be ordered well in advance of any keel laying. The procurement of armor alone could take as long as nine months (see Chapter 8). It was also the first heavy armor to be produced since the cancellation of the battleship and battlecruiser programs in 1922, and allowances had to be made for industry retooling. Finally, a new and improved 14in/50cal gun was planned.

While contract plans for the *North Carolinas* were being completed, the second London Treaty was signed on 25 March 1936. At that time, the Japanese formally withdrew from the treaty. They also refused to state that they would not adopt 16in guns in their new designs. This is what the General Board had feared when they issued the dual instructions to the designers in 1935 regarding gun caliber. The 'escalator clause', permitting tonnage and gun caliber to increase if non-signatories failed to observe the established limits, had been inserted in the Treaty for just such a situation.

Actually, matters were even worse than imagined at that time for the Japanese had begun work on the 69,500 ton *Yamato* with nine 18.1in guns. The actual size and gun caliber of the *Yamato* did not become known until 1945.

By mid-1937, the US Navy had decided to adopt a 16in gun caliber

Carolina, design studies were begun for the next generation of battleships. It was the general consensus of the designers that the *North Carolina* represented the maximum vessel that could be attained on 35,000 tons, and that she was even badly compromised in regard to armor protection when the gun caliber was increased to 16in. Nevertheless, the General Board asked for two more *North Carolinas* for Fiscal Year 1938. The CNO objected strongly to two additional under-protected battleships. His arguments prevailed and a new battleship design was begun in March 1937. Referred to as 'battleship 1939' it became the *South Dakota* class.

The design of 'battleship 1939' presented a technical challenge to the Bu C & R. The 16in 3-gun turret of the *North Carolinas* had become

As completed the *North Carolinas* mounted nine 16in/45cal guns. Consideration was made in the design to switch from three quadruple 14in turrets to three triple 16in turrets if the gun caliber was increased under the 'escalator clause' of the second London Treaty of 1936. Construction was well along when the larger caliber gun was adopted and her armor protection could not be increased to protect her against the heavier weapon. The *North Carolina* is shown during her shakedown cruise in 1941.

for all new construction including the *North Carolina* class. The Bu Ord was asked to design a 16in 3-gun turret to replace the 14in 4-gun turret. The new battery of nine 16in guns would be comparable to the heaviest batteries then afloat—those in the Royal Navy ships *Nelson* and *Rodney*.

The decision to increase the gun caliber would prove to be a wise one. It was too late, however, to protect the new ships against the heavier gun (see Chapter 8). All of the heavy armor was either nearing completion or already delivered and the date for keel laying was near at hand. Even if the armor thickness could have been increased it would have put the displacement well over the weight limit. Treaty obligations were taken seriously, and this situation would have been unacceptable.

THE *South Dakota* CLASS

Immediately upon completion of the contract plans for the *North*

the standard main battery ordnance for new battleships and the designers were tasked with protecting the vessel against the new shell and retaining the 27 knot speed, all on the same 35,000 ton limit. It was obvious from the beginning that a radical new approach was necessary for the armor arrangement and the machinery since the design hinged on these two areas. Protection, of course, was the most important consideration which meant an increase in weight per foot of protected length. To stay within the 35,000 ton limit, therefore, meant that the new ship had to be reduced in overall length. The shorter length would require more horsepower if the 27 knot speed was to be retained. There had really been no weight margin in the *North Carolina* design and at this point the spill-over complications from one change to another begin to become appreciated.

The design solutions were as radical as the new approach had implied. Some basic comparisons between the *North Carolina* and *South Dakota* designs clearly show how drastically the design actually changed:

	North Carolina	South Dakota	
Waterline Length	714ft	666ft	–48ft
Protected length	440ft	372ft	–68ft
Main machinery length	176ft	160ft	–16ft
Total machinery length	228ft	216ft	–12ft
Shaft horsepower	121,000	130,000	+9,000

It is remarkable, then, that the *South Dakota*s were armed with nine 16in guns, protected against the 16in shell, made 27.8 knots and did not exceed 35,000 tons.

The above figures indicate a saving of 68ft of protected length. The protected length of a battleship included all vital spaces such as magazines, machinery, plotting rooms, etc. (see Chapter 8). This armored box or citadel was enclosed by the side belt armor, and the forward and aft armored bulkheads and was covered over by the armor deck. The reduction in protected length allowed the savings in weight to be invested in a new arrangement of armor which was the key to the success of the new design. The designers were so pleased with the new arrangement that it would eventually be incorporated in the *Iowa* class as well.

The *North Carolina*s had an external main belt 12in thick with an average depth of 16ft. The lower third of the belt was knuckled and tapered to 6.6in at the bottom. It was bolted to a 0.75in thick special treated steel (STS) plate which was inclined outboard at 15 degrees. This arrangement was designed to resist the 14in shell but did not allow for shells falling short and following an underwater trajectory.

The keel of the *South Dakota* was laid on 5 July 1939 and by late that year considerable progress had been made. Here, the double bottom is being plated over and a portion of the holding bulkhead up to the triple bottom is in place. Framing for the outboard wing tank is being worked aft and the bulkheads for the forward auxiliary machinery are being erected.

This seems to have been an afterthought and only nominal protection was provided locally in the magazine areas by armoring Torpedo Bulkhead No. 5, the holding bulkhead.

The armor arrangement in the *South Dakotas* was entirely different. It was necessary to increase the main belt thickness to 12.2in, the backing plate to 0.875in and the slope to 19 degrees to provide resistance against the 16in shell. The question of underwater trajectories was also addressed in the new design. The outcome was a lower belt of armor below the main belt tapering from 12.2in at the top to 1in at the bottom. By increasing the slope of the armor belt from 15 to 19 degrees, an external belt became impractical. The maximum allowable beam, as dictated by the locks of the Panama Canal, was 108ft. An external belt on such a restrictive beam would have cut away a considerable waterplane area. Initial stability would have been greatly reduced and a wider area at the top of the belt would have required armor. Although not considered ideal, the solution was to locate the belt internally. In this new arrangement, the armor was placed at Torpedo Bulkhead No. 3. The 10ft 8in deep

Now that the machinery was fitted into the new arrangement, it would be necessary to attain an additional 9,000 horsepower. With the steam conditions set at 570psi and 850 degrees (*North Carolina* used 575 degrees at 850psi), it was accepted that the new machinery had to be designed to the latest state-of-the-art technology. From the beginning, the turbine nozzles, blading and piping were designed to extract the maximum efficiency from the steam cycle and the reduction gearing received similar attention for maximizing the mechanical transmission of power. The goal of 130,000 shaft horsepower was easily met with an overload capacity to 135,000.

With an acceptable armor system and machinery arrangement, the primary goals had been met and final design work could proceed. The armored citadel (protected length) had been shortened some 68ft which had to be taken up in the superstructure. In addition, the new third deck arrangement forced many living spaces and store rooms, normally located in that area, to be relocated higher up or in the ends of the ship. To save superstructure length, all uptakes were trunked into a single funnel which was combined with the forward fire control

upper belt was hung to the extension of the bulkhead between the second and third deck and the 28ft deep lower belt actually formed Torpedo Bulkhead No. 3 from the third deck down to the inner bottom within the armored citadel.

The other primary area of concern was the main machinery. The shorter hull required an additional 9,000 shaft horsepower to maintain the 27 knot speed and in the new design the length allotted to the main machinery spaces was reduced by 16ft. The propulsion machinery was very similar to that installed in the *North Carolinas*. There were four combination fire room, engine room spaces, with each space containing the machinery for one shaft. With each machinery space being 4ft shorter, a drastic rearrangement of the spaces was necessary. Two boilers were located on one side, and the turbines and reduction gears were located opposite, in each of the four spaces. The arrangement alternated with each space. The boilers were placed above the shaft from the space ahead and up through the third deck. The alternating spaces opposite the boiler compartments on the third deck became magazines and handling rooms for the 5in battery. This arrangement was under the second, or armor deck, and was entirely within the protection of the armored citadel.

The armor system for the *South Dakota* class was designed to protect against the 16in/45cal gun. A number of changes had to be made in the machinery arrangement to accommodate the additional armor weight and retain the 26 knot speed on the same tonnage as the *North Carolinas*. The armor system for the *Iowa* class was patterned after the *South Dakotas*' system and is very nearly identical. The *South Dakota* leaves the Philadelphia Navy Yard on 4 June 1942 for her shakedown cruise in the Atlantic.

tower. The dual conning station on the bridge was also changed. The unarmored pilot house was eliminated and the ship was operated from the armored conning tower. This resulted in a severely cramped superstructure arrangement as compared to the *North Carolina*. The primary objective, however, was not comfort but to fight the ship and this it could do very well.

The preliminary design for 'battleship 1939' was completed in August 1937 and after preparation of the contract plans and specifications, the *South Dakota* was laid down on 5 July 1939. Given the restrictions of the Washington and London Treaties, the *South Dakotas* were the most successful of any of the 'treaty battleships'. Many of their unique features, in particular their system of protection, would later be applied to the *Iowa* class design.

Chapter 3

THE IOWA CLASS DESIGN

The question of how to proceed with capital ship development during the mid-1930s was perplexing. There seemed to be a lack of meaningful United States intelligence information concerning Japanese naval construction and fleet operations. The situation in January 1938 was still one of uncertainty as the Bu C & R continued its battleship studies. Only six months earlier, the US Navy had invoked the 'escalator clause' of the second London Treaty and adopted the 16in gun for all new construction. This included the *North Carolina* and *Washington*, already on the ways, and 'battleship 1939', the *South Dakota*, which was in the contract design stage. Reports had been circulating since the previous November that the Japanese had laid down as many as three large battleships. It seemed certain that the United States would again use the 'escalator clause', this time to increase displacement to 45,000 tons.

The battleship studies proceeded with two different approaches as to how to utilize the expected 10,000 tons. Using the *South Dakota* as a starting point, the first approach was to increase the armament and protection, while the second was to attain high speed. The two studies were referred to as the 'slow battleship' and 'fast battleship' of 1938.

At this point, a review of the design and construction process used by the US Navy is helpful. The Bu C & R was responsible for the design of all new vessels which proceeded in three distinct phases: preliminary design, contract design and detail design. The first phase was handled by the Preliminary Design section which prepared design sketches based on various requirements initiated by the General Board. Upon approval by the General Board and the Secretary of the Navy, the next phase was the development of the contract drawings and specifications by the Contract Design section. Prospective shipbuilders based their bids on this material. In the final phase, the selected shipbuilder or the designated design agent was responsible for the preparation of the detail working drawings and finished plans. The Supervisor of Shipbuilding, assigned to the building yard,

When the Japanese withdrew from the second London Treaty in 1936 they immediately implemented their battleship building program which had been in the planning stage since 1930. It called for building seven *Yamato* class battleships of 69,500 tons, armed with nine 18.1in/45cal guns, and capable of 27 knots. Four were actually laid down. Two were completed as battleships. One was completed as an aircraft carrier and the fourth was cancelled and broken up on the ways. The *Yamato* is seen here running her speed trials off Sata Point on 30 October 1941.

approved the plans and managed the construction of the vessel.

The decision as to which design to press ahead with immediately was directly related to intelligence, or the lack of it. Good intelligence had been a problem as far back as the first Washington Treaty. The usual sources of information, diplomatic attachés, intelligence agents and the analysis of radio traffic, were inconclusive.

Japan guarded her naval construction program with extreme security measures, of which the physical measures were the most easily established and maintained. For example, in 1934 when the Japanese indicated their intention to withdraw from the second London Treaty, it was suspected that a new capital ship building program was already in the planning stage. This, of course, proved to be correct, the Imperial Navy's plan being implemented in March 1937. The first new battleship was laid down at the Kure Navy Yard on 4 November 1937 and almost immediately the shipway was shrouded with huge tarpaulins to prevent observation of the design characteristics and building progress. Intelligence reports indicated that the vessel was over 45,000 tons with a 16in main battery. Some reports speculated on an even larger vessel armed with 18in guns. The later speculations proved correct, for the ship was the 69,500 ton *Yamato* with its nine 18.1in guns.

Work on the 18in gun for the *Yamato* had actually begun in 1934 at the Kure Navy Yard and tests were conducted at the nearby Kamegakubi Proving Ground. The Japanese officially referred to the new gun as a 16in weapon and physical security was rather easily maintained in and around the navy yard and proving ground. Apparently the United States and other Treaty powers knew that

The US Navy's 18in/47cal Mark A gun photographed on display at the Naval Surface Weapons Center at Dahlgren, Virginia. It was originally developed after World War I and was considered for the main battery of the *Iowa* class. Its weight and size made it impractical for the 45,000 ton *Iowa*s. Had it been known that the Japanese were using an 18in/45cal gun on the *Yamato*s, it is likely that the *Iowa* design would have used the larger weapon also. For comparison, the 16in/50cal Mark 7 gun, which was used on the *Iowa* class, is shown towards the right of the photograph.

work on a new gun was in progress, but they believed it to be the 16in/50cal, or a derivative of the weapon planned for the battleship and battlecruiser programs cancelled in 1922 under the Washington Treaty.

In the case of the *Kongo*s, the US Navy did not seem to be aware of the extent of their first reconstruction, completed in the late-1920s, or that they were extensively modernized again in the mid-1930s and upgraded to battleships. During the second modernization, they were also reboilered and re-engined which increased their speed to 30.5 knots. No one knew of the remilitarization of the *Hiei*, fourth ship of the class, undertaken in November 1936. She was upgraded as the others, but in addition received new fire control systems which were the prototypes for the *Yamato* class.

The speed of the *Nagato* and *Mutsu* was also a very well kept secret, as was the extent of their reconstruction during the mid-1930s. Both ships had been commissioned just prior to the Washington Treaty conference where their speed was officially stated to be 23 knots. They were actually capable of 26.75 knots. An extensive modernization of both vessels was completed in 1936, which included the addition of blisters, new boilers and new engines, increasing their displacement by over 6,000 tons. With the new and more efficient machinery they were able to maintain their speed, even with the blistering and increase in tonnage.

Physical security measures worked very well indeed for the Japanese. They were also very skillful with regard to the manipulation of information, and the dissemination of misinformation. On the other hand, fleet operations and ship movements presented an entirely different situation. Once a Japanese vessel became operational any messages to and from her were always open to interception and became fair game for the US Navy's cryptographers. Records from pre-World War II naval communications histories regarding radio signal intelligence contain some interesting revelations. For instance, analysis of the *Nagato*'s radio traffic during trials after reconstruction in 1936, indicated that she had made over 26 knots. This is possibly the first indication the US Navy had that the *Nagato* class were capable of more than 23 knots. There may also be similar information on the 30 knot speed of the *Kongo*s, however, the fact that the *Hiei* was remilitarized probably did not become known until she was operational in January 1940.

Had the real tonnage and gun caliber of the *Yamato* been known in January 1938, it is difficult to speculate as to how the 'slow battleship' and 'fast battleship' designs of 1938 would have been influenced. Certainly the General Board would have at least sought parity with the *Yamato*.

DESIGN STUDIES

In the United States the 1938 'slow battleship' studies continued, featuring an increase in firepower and protection and retaining the 27 knots. Three schemes[1] added a fourth 3-gun 16in turret. One was an alternate arrangement with three 3-gun 18in turrets. In all the schemes, after accommodating the increase in weapons, what remained of the additional 10,000 tons was used for extending the armored citadel to accommodate an increase in power necessary to maintain the 27 knots. These studies eventually evolved into the *Montana* class design.

The records of the General Board do not indicate in every instance what information or specific intelligence was being used to initiate and evaluate designs. Their actions suggest that they did not believe the Japanese would undertake the construction of a vessel the size of the *Yamato*. They do seem to have been aware that a major portion of the Japanese battle fleet was capable of at least 26 knots. This could only have come from the analysis of radio traffic from operational units of the fleet. The *North Carolina* and *South Dakota* classes with their 27 knots appeared to be an adequate reply. Yet the General Board continued to ask for more speed. Certainly the new Japanese battleships would be capable of at least 26 knots also. There was still

The Battleship Design Advisory Board was organized in October 1937 for the express purpose of advising the Secretary of the Navy on matters of battleship design and construction. It was composed of prominent experts in the field of naval construction and armament. From left to right: (standing) John F. Metten, Joseph W. Powell and William Hovgaard; (seated) William F. Gibbs, Charles Edison and Joseph Strauss. The Board reviewed the early studies for a fast battleship and determined that a 33 knot *South Dakota* was feasible on 45,000 tons.

This preliminary design model is based on the characteristics approved by the Secretary of the Navy in June 1938. This full-length view shows the original configuration of the superstructure, with boat handling cranes and boat stowage amidships and four quadruple 1.1in/70 cal anti-aircraft mounts.

1 Detailed analysis and tables are not given since they are adequately covered in other publications, the most useful of which is, *US Battleships, An Illustrated Design History*, Norman Friedman, US Naval Institute.

As the *Iowa* class design progressed at the New York Navy Yard, full-sized mock-ups were made for many internal spaces. The fine exterior hull lines resulted in relatively little internal volume and the plywood models were of great value in perfecting details in the design. This wooden mock-up of the after secondary battery plotting room was photographed on 22 October 1940.

strong interest in a fast battleship.

The Bu C & R continued its parallel studies for the 1938 'fast battleship'. Departing from the enlarged *South Dakota* premise, very high speed and an endurance of 20,000nm at 15 knots was considered. The standard endurance was 15,000nm at 15 knots and the additional range would allow sustained operations among the 'mandated islands', striking at the Japanese communications network. The only requirement for size and weight was that they be able to pass through the Panama Canal. Two schemes carried twelve 16in guns and two were a scaled down version with nine 16in guns. One scheme with twelve 16in guns, capable of 35 knots and protected only against 8in fire, was clearly a cruiser-killer. Of the three other schemes studied all were protected against 16in fire. One, with nine 16in guns retained the 35 knot speed. The remaining two studies were for 32.5 knots with one carrying twelve and the other nine 16in guns. All of the studies were well over 900ft in length and exceeded 50,000 tons.

The Battleship Design Advisory Board reviewed the studies very carefully.[2] The sizes, weights and associated costs, of course, were more than the US Navy could convince the Congress to buy, especially with the scanty intelligence available on the Japanese naval building program. It was clear that the two 12-gun versions would be too heavy. If, however, the two 9-gun designs were prudently scaled down and the endurance cut back to the standard 15,000nm at 15 knots, a considerable saving in weight could be achieved. At least the 9-gun versions seemed possible on about 45,000 tons.

PRELIMINARY DESIGN

On 8 February 1938, the Advisory Board submitted its report on the studies to the Secretary of the Navy, who then referred the report to

2 In October 1937 the Secretary of the Navy organized the Battleship Design Advisory Board. It was composed of experts in the field of naval construction with the express purpose of advising the Secretary on matters of battleship design and construction. It was first convened on 8 October by the Assistant Secretary of the Navy, Charles Edison. Board members included Admiral Joseph Strauss, USN (Ret), former Chief of the Bu Ord, William F. Gibbs, Joseph W. Powell and Professor William Hovgaard, well-known naval achitects, and John F. Metten, president of the New York Shipbuilding Corporation.

the General Board for action. The unlimited studies had been a lesson in how much an ideal fast battleship would cost. Going back to the *South Dakota* as a starting point and scaling it up to accommodate the increased horsepower, it appeared that 33 knots was feasible on about 40,000 tons. This was encouraging for it allowed for the inevitable growth in the detail design phase.

On 10 February, the CNO met with the Secretary of the Navy and recommended that the General Board conduct studies on the main battery to determine the feasibility of using either the 16in/45cal, 16in/50cal or an 18in gun. The Secretary immediately approved and the General Board requested a comparative study from the Bu Ord.

After reviewing the findings of the Advisory Board and examining the scaled-up version of the *South Dakota*, on 10 March the General Board asked the Bu C & R for a new battleship design. On 31 March, the remaining Treaty powers indicated their intention to exercise the 'escalator clause' again, increasing capital ship displacement to 45,000 tons. The Bu C & R proceeded with work on the new requirements

and, on 2 June, the preliminary design for a 'fast battleship', now designated BB 61, was submitted to the General Board. This design became the *Iowa* class. On the same day, the United States, Great Britain and France formally signed the Treaty amendment authorizing the new tonnage.

On 6 April, the General Board met to consider the results of the armament study it had given the Bu Ord on 10 February. The study included the progress on a new series of overweight projectiles which the Bu Ord had been developing for several years. Testing was not complete but one 16in shell, a 2,700 pound armor piercing (AP) model, appeared very promising. The 16in/45cal gun had a range of 40,600 yards with the standard 2,240 pound AP shell, but with the new shell its range would be cut to 36,900 yards. The Board wanted to maintain at least a 40,000 yard range for the new vessels. The 16in/50cal gun, however, could fire the 2,700 pound projectile out to 42,500 yards. If the 2,700 pound projectile was adopted, the Board hoped that the 16in/50cal, or possibly the 18in gun with an even heavier shell, could be used. Both had the desired range capability and were considerably more destructive.

Although clearly a superior weapon, the 18in gun was just too heavy. It was not only the weight of the gun itself but a heavier structure would be required to carry the weapon. The turret and barbette consumed a larger volume and the ship would have to be

The keel for the *Iowa*, lead ship of the class, is 'truly and fairly laid', on 27 June 1940 at the New York Navy Yard. Shipyard superintendents, foremen and chargemen who will lead the yard workers on the project look on as Rear Admiral C. H. Woodward, Chief of the Bureau of Construction and Repair (Bu C & R), drives the first rivet.

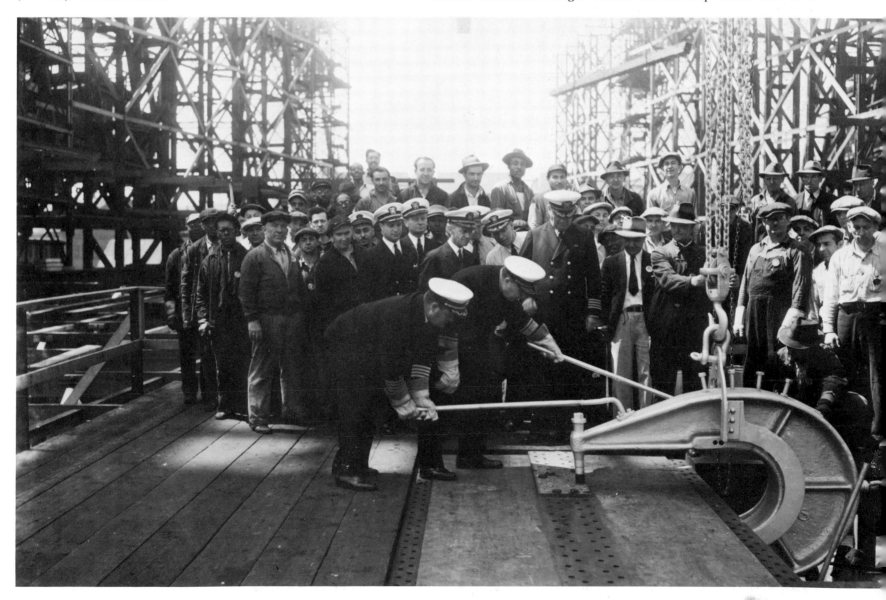

By mid-1942, the boilers and main engines of the *Missouri* were in place and the torpedo defense system was taking shape amidships. Segments of the lower main armor belt are visible. The keyway for fitting the upper belt and adjacent plates of the lower belt can be seen. Note the welded, scalloped butt straps vertically joining the lower belt plates.

Right: The *Missouri* is shown here, in November 1943, only two months before launching. Her hull is complete up to the main deck and much of the superstructure is in frame. Amid the maze of scaffolding, air hoses and welding leads, splinter protection for the light anti-aircraft battery is being installed and the teak decking is being laid.

In this photograph of the *Iowa*, taken on 30 September 1940, construction of the double and triple bottoms is clearly shown. The tunnel stern begins to take shape aft as the half siding for the keel rises on the plating supports. Note the prefabricated sections of the double and triple bottoms stacked aft ready to be dropped into place.

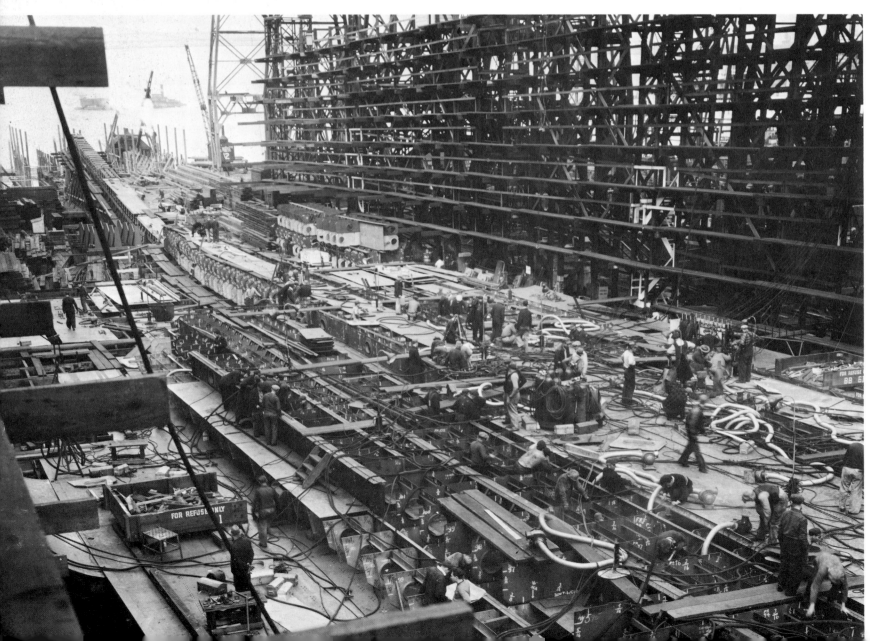

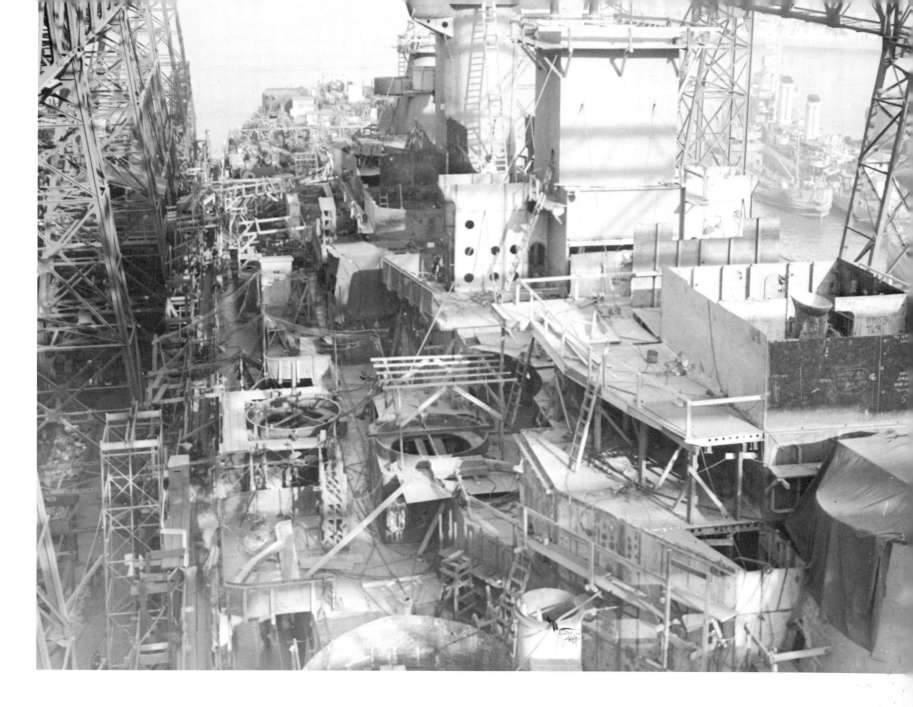

longer. The horsepower would have to increase to maintain the 33 knot speed, and so on. A battery of nine 18in guns was just not feasible on 45,000 tons unless the speed could be reduced to between 21 to 23 knots. A reduction in speed was unacceptable. There was every indication that the fast battleship was becoming universal among all of the major seapowers; however, it did not seem likely that any of them would develop an 18in gun. The US Navy did not want to be the one to further escalate the gun caliber but there remained the uncertainty about Japan. Japanese security notwithstanding, US Naval planners believed that early intelligence would certainly be obtained concerning the production of any quantity of such a large weapon. This, of course, was not the case for twenty-seven guns were actually produced. The feeling of the General Board was that the US Navy did have the 18in gun technology and could increase the gun caliber in the future if necessary. This was the last time the 18in gun was seriously considered.

The General Board recommended the 16in/50cal gun for the BB 61 class. The question was which one to use, the 16in/50 cal Mark II, or a new lightweight model developed along the lines of the 16in/45cal in the *North Carolina*.[3] The guns would be identical ballistically, but the effects of either gun on the design had to be carefully considered. The

Board asked the Bu Ord for design sketches for a 16in/50cal 3-gun turret to accommodate the Mark II gun as well as a new lightweight model. The sketches were submitted on 20 May with two using the Mark II gun having barbette diameters of 39ft 4in and 37ft 3in, and two for a new lightweight gun with a common barbette diameter of 37ft 3in. These diameters are to the inside of the barbette in all cases, and the turret roller path, with clearance, had to fit within these dimensions.

A number of 16in/50cal Mark II guns were available from inventory that were made for the battleship (BB 49 class) and battlecruiser (CC 1 class) programs cancelled in 1922. Many had been proof tested and some had been service tested by the US Army Coast Artillery. The Mark II was considered an excellent but heavy weapon. The new

3 The new lightweight guns were produced using advanced metallurgical technology. For example, the Mark II tube assembly used a nickel steel with a tensile strength of 90,000 pounds per square inch and an elastic limit of 55,000 pounds per square inch. The liner was of gun steel with a tensile strength of 86,000 pounds per square inch and an elastic limit of 46,000 pounds per square inch. In contrast, the Mark 7 tube assembly used an all-alloy steel with a tensile strength of 95,000 pounds per square inch and an elastic limit of 65,000 pounds per square inch; the liner was of the same material.

LAUNCHING OF BB·62.
VIEW OF BOW.
NAVY YARD. PHILA. DEC.7·1942.
1720·A2·A.

lightweight gun offered a 16 per cent saving in weight, but this advantage was lost because of the additional structure required to handle the higher trunion break pressures and to provide for a heavier recoil system. Finally, with the number of new 16in/45cal guns being produced, there was some doubt that adequate manufacturing capability existed to produce the new lightweight guns on schedule.

The General Board decided on the 16in/50cal Mark II gun with the turret design for a 37ft 3in barbette. The 16in/45cal 3-gun turret in the *South Dakotas* had used a 37ft 3in barbette and since the BB 61 was to be an enlarged *South Dakota* the smaller barbette design was chosen. In regard to the hull form, this made the scaling-up process easier for it saved as much volume and weight as possible, especially in the area of Turret No. I. The Board submitted its armament recommendations to the Secretary of the Navy on 21 April 1938 and approval was received on 29 April. The various bureaus immediately began work to finalize the preliminary design phase.

The *New Jersey* presents a massive and impressive appearance as her distinctive clipper bow overhangs the speaker's platform which is decorated with bunting. The shape of the underwater bulb and the extremely fine lines forward can be fully appreciated in this view. The large external hawse pipe castings are intended to stand off the anchors sufficiently so its flukes will clear the bulb when being raised and lowered.

The *New Jersey* glides into the Delaware River from the Philadelphia Navy Yard on 7 December 1942. Launching is a delicate operation. The weight of the vessel has to be transferred from the keel blocks, shoring timbers and other fixed supports to the sliding ways which carry the ship down the ground ways into the water. The ways are heavily greased to facilitate the ship's movement when the release mechanism, or trigger, releases the vessel.

The first two ships of the class were formally authorized in the Congress by the Act of 17 May 1938 and became the BB 61 (*Iowa*) and BB 62 (*New Jersey*). The preliminary design was completed and sent to the General Board on 2 June and, a week later, the following characteristics were presented to the Secretary of the Navy:

Displacement – 44,560 tons standard
                55,710 tons full load
Waterline length – 860ft waterline
Maximum beam – 108ft 3in
Maximum draft – 35ft 11.5in
Armament –   9 16in/50cal in three 3-gun turrets
            20 5in/38cal in ten twin mounts
            12 1.1in/70cal in four quadruple mounts
            12 0.50cal single machine guns
Protection – 16in/45cal
            18,000–30,000 yards (2,240 pound shell)
            20,500–26,500 yards (2,700 pound shell)
            16in/50cal
            21,800–32,000 yards (2,240 pound shell
            24,500–28,500 yards (2,700 pound shell)
torpedo resistance – 700 pounds of TNT
Shaft horsepower – 200,000 minimum
Maximum speed – 33 knots
Endurance – 15,000nm at 15 knots

The Secretary approved the preliminary design and the bureaus were directed to proceed with the contract design for the BB 61 class.

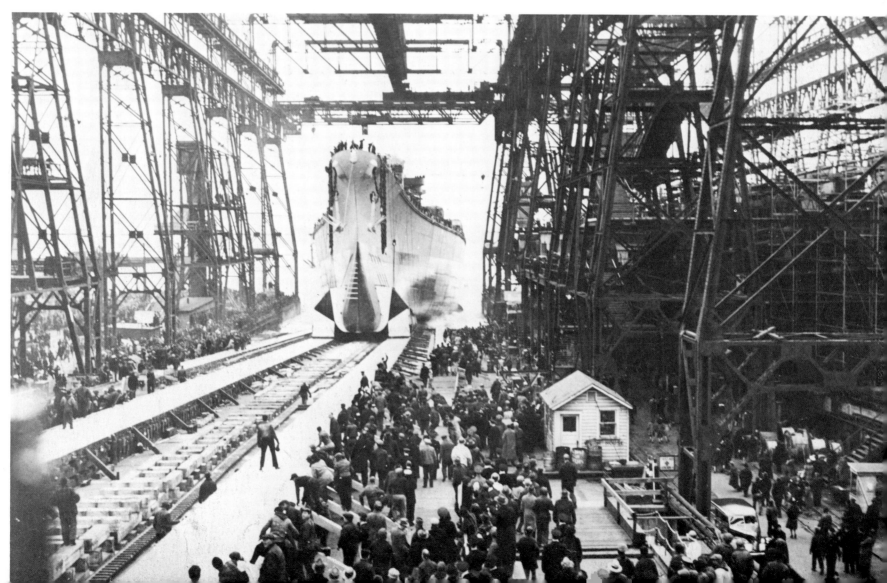

Waterborne in the Delaware River, the *New Jersey* awaits the tugs which will tow her to an outfitting pier where she will be completed. The launching weight of the *New Jersey* was 36,447 tons which was the heaviest vessel to be launched from a shipway in the United States at that time.

The specification for the light anti-aircraft battery for the *Iowa* class changed considerably from the time the design was approved in June 1938 until the first unit was completed. Originally, the battery consisted of four 1.1in/70cal quadruple mounts and twelve 0.50cal single machine guns. In June 1941, the battery was changed to four 40mm quadruple Bofors mounts and eight 20mm single Oerlikon mounts. By December 1941, this was increased to six 40mm and twelve 20mm mounts. These photographs are of a ⅛in = 1ft drawing room model at the New York Navy Yard showing the arrangement of the battery on 7 December 1942. It consisted of fifteen 40mm quadruple and sixty 20mm single mounts. The *Iowa* was completed to this configuration.

CONTRACT DESIGN

The Bu C & R worked to complete the hull design and general arrangement. In enlarging the *South Dakota*, the primary consideration was high speed, which externally meant fine hull lines and extreme length. There was considerable sheer forward worked into a clipper bow which rose from the waterline. The straight stem below the waterline featured a moderate-sized bulb which improved resistance at high speeds. There was a twin skeg arrangement aft which housed the inboard shafts and helped to support the cut-away stern during docking. This was a departure from the *South Dakota* design in which the skegs housed the outboard shafts. The fineness of the BB 61 lines did not have sufficient volume aft to allow alignment of the skegs with the outboard shafts. The skegs also helped to direct a clean flow of water to the propellers and twin rudders improving their efficiency. Finally, there was slight sheer aft which eased into the cut-away stern.

Internally, the same fine hull lines meant relatively little volume into which barbettes, ammunition, control stations, fuel, stores, the crew, and a minimum of 200,000 shaft horsepower could be fitted. The superstructure was compact so as not to unduly restrict the arcs of fire of the guns and the visibility of the fire control gear. A great deal of the superstructure proper was filled with gun mounts, ammunition hoists, dirctors, director tubes and control stations,

leaving a limited amount of space available for accommodation.

From the design of the hull form, the designers calculated the resistance and estimated that 212,000 horsepower would be required to make 33 knots at the full load condition. This was later confirmed by model basin tests. The design of the main and auxiliary machinery plants moved forward within the Bu Eng. The combination engine room, fire room arrangement of the *South Dakota* was retained which, with the increase in horsepower, created four large compartments amidships each 64ft in length. The valuable technical experience gained from the *South Dakota* enabled the designers to produce an even more compact lightweight plant for the BB 61 class.

While the hull, machinery and general arrangement designs were being completed, the Bu Ord was busy with the new turret design. The only experience with mounting a 16in/50cal gun in a 3-gun turret had been nearly twenty years earlier on the cancelled BB 49 class battleships. The old designs offered little help but they were a point of

The *New Jersey* lies outfitting in the shadow of the huge hammerhead crane of the Philadelphia Navy Yard. Seen here on 14 January 1943, the rotating structure of the turret has been set in place including the deck lugs and gun girders. The STS backing plates for the side armor are attached to the arches and wing girders. Note the former for aligning and holding the segments of the conning tower armor while they are welded together in place.

reference in that they served as a guide for the development of the new turret. Many detailed improvements were made and they could be directly compared with past technology. The new turret design featured improvements in performance with increased training and elevating rates and a maximum elevation of 45 degrees. Major changes were made in the ammunition hoists making them faster, safer and more reliable than in the older turrets. Finally, the turret machinery was larger and more powerful to handle the heavier loading and increased speed.

After five months work by the various bureaus, the contract plans were nearing completion. Early in November, the Bu Ord forwarded their completed turret drawings to the Bu C & R which, for the first time, found that the barbette diameter was 39ft! The Bu Ord had proceeded with the turret using a barbette diameter of 39ft 4in, which they had been able to reduce by 4in, and the Bu C & R had designed a ship with a barbette diameter of 37ft 3in. A special meeting of the General Board was convened to deal with the bizarre situation. The Board was shocked. It was inconceivable that the two bureaus had progressed so far before the incompatibility of their designs was discovered. Had there been no liaison whatever? Surviving records do not indicate specifically what had happened but it appears that the sketch using the Mark II gun on the 37ft 3in barbette, which was submitted on 20 May, was hypothetical and they were not able to incorporate the desired improvements. Apparently, not understanding how critical the size actually was, the Bu Ord designed the larger turret.

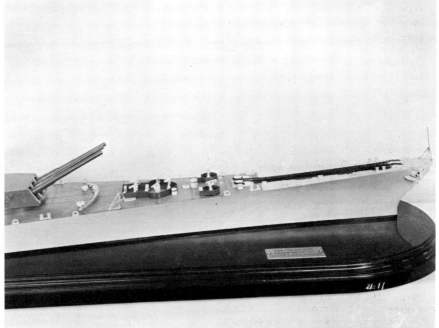

At this late date nothing could be done to change the hull form and retain the characteristics. To increase the size of the hull around Turret No. I to accommodate the larger barbette would reduce the speed. It would also tip the displacement over 45,000 tons. The 16in/45cal turret from the *South Dakota* would fit, but the 10,000 tons would have been spent for only 6 knots more speed. Either alternative was unacceptable. The Bu Ord was ordered to come up with an acceptable design, and work 'round the clock to do it', if necessary.

Improvements to the BB 49 design affecting performance, such as the faster ammunition hoists, had increased the bore separation of the

	Bore Separation	Outside diameter at breech
Mark II in BB 49	68in	56.5in
Mark II in BB 61	125in	56.5in
Mark 7 in BB 61	122in	49in

During the summer of 1938, the United States government contracted with some of the nation's largest steel producers to

guns considerably, which in turn enlarged the diameter of the roller path and the barbette. It became clear in less than a week that the Mark II gun could not be used if the improvements were to be maintained. Work was immediately begun on a turret for the new lightweight gun which would be designated the Mark 7. An acceptable turret design using the Mark 7 gun was completed by 1 December. It contained all the advantages of the larger design including faster and safer ammunition handling. The new turret was tight and access to functional assemblies and turret machinery was difficult, but in all respects it was comparable to the 16in/45cal turrets in the *South Dakota*. Ultimately, the smaller dimensions of the new gun did save weight for the designers were able to shave about 40 tons per turret from the larger design. The following comparison of some basic dimensions clearly show the advantages gained by using the Mark 7 gun:

reactivate several of their plants which had been closed in 1922 as a result of the Washington Treaty. The concerns of the General Board with regard to manufacturing and delivery schedules of the guns were, therefore, resolved.

The General Board forwarded its report to the Secretary of the Navy on 8 December 1938 recommending that the Mark 7 gun be used for BB 61 and BB 62 in lieu of the Mark II gun. The recommendations were approved by the Secretary on 10 December clearing the way for the completion of the contract plans and specifications.

This unfortunate and nearly disastrous situation is an example of how autonomous the various bureaus were and how little direct authority the General Board actually had in coordinating and dealing with them.

DETAIL DESIGN

The New York Navy Yard was selected to build the *Iowa* (BB 61), lead ship of the class, and the Philadelphia Navy Yard was assigned construction of the *New Jersey* (BB 62), the second ship. Except for the problems involved with the turret misunderstanding, the contract plans were fundamentally complete in January 1939. The customary practice of having the builder of the lead ship prepare the working plans for the class was followed. The New York Navy Yard assisted the Bu C & R in finalizing the contract plans and specifications. On 1

Armament – 9 16in/50cal in three 3-gun turrets
20 5in/38cal in ten twin mounts
12 1.1in/70cal in four quadruple mounts
12 0.50cal single machine guns
Protection – 16in/45cal
20,200-25,500 yards (2,700 pound shell)
16in/50cal
23,600–27,400 yards (2,700 pound shell)
torpedo resistance – 700 pounds of TNT
Shaft horsepower – 212,000 minimum

Opposite and above: The *Iowa* in drydock at the New York Navy Yard on 28 March 1943, during her inclining experiment. Her general topside configuration, and, in particular, the arrangement of the light anti-aircraft battery, is very nearly identical to the drawing room model.

July, contracts were signed and the New York Navy Yard formally began construction of the *Iowa* and the manufacturing drawings for the BB 61 class. The basic characteristics and specifications were as follows:

Displacement – 45,155 tons standard
56,088 tons full load
Waterline length – 860ft waterline
Maximum beam – 107ft 3in
Maximum draft – 35ft 7.8in

Maximum speed – 33 knots
Endurance – 15,000nm at 15 knots

It will be noted that these characteristics are very similar to those of the finished preliminary design. Displacement was up slightly, as expected. The beam had been reduced by 1ft and the protection reflected the effects of the new 2,700 pound AP projectile which was adopted in June 1939.

The size of the machinery spaces, which had been of some concern during the contract design phase, now had to be seriously addressed. In expanding the *South Dakota* design, the size of the machinery spaces had grown considerably to accommodate the increase in horsepower from 130,000 shaft horsepower to 212,000 shaft horsepower. The combination engine room, fire room arrangement had created four

Top left: The *Iowa* at anchor in the Hudson River off New York City on 4 April 1943, while operating off the East Coast. Note how closely she resembles the drawing room model; however, additional light anti-aircraft armament had been approved and would be installed before her first deployment.

Above center: As completed, the *New Jersey* was essentially identical to the *Iowa* except for the additional 40mm mount atop Turret No. II. In this photograph, taken on 8 July 1943, the *New Jersey* stands out in the Delaware River from the Philadelphia Navy Yard on her initial shakedown cruise.

Below center: By the time the last two ships of the class were completed the light anti-aircraft battery had again been increased to twenty 40mm quadruple and forty-nine 20mm single mounts. A number of modifications had also been made in the superstructure including the enclosing of the bridge and pilot house areas. The *Wisconsin* here leaves the Philadelphia Navy Yard for her shakedown cruise on 7 June 1944.

Bottom left and below: The *Missouri* was completed shortly after the *Wisconsin*. She also had the new enclosed bridge area and other late changes such as the late model SK-2 radar on the foretop. Here, the *Missouri* is anchored off Bayonne, New Jersey in August 1944 making ready for her shakedown cruise.

enormous compartments amidships. Each machinery space had been 40ft long in the *South Dakota* and they had now grown to 64ft in length. A single penetration at one of the main bulkheads would flood 128ft. The New York Navy Yard proposed an alternating fire room, engine room arrangement with two boilers in each fire room and one set of machinery in each engine room serving its propeller shaft. The four large machinery spaces would thus be broken up into eight spaces, each only 32ft long. Flooding from a single hit would be reduced by half. The new arrangement also simplified the trunking of the uptakes to the funnels and reduced the size of their penetrations through the armored decks, but it moved the beam back out to 108 ft 3in. At this point, a change as considerable as this would incur a delay in schedule and would increase costs. From a damage control and survivability point of view, the delay and expense were well worth the benefits which would be gained. The new machinery arrangement was approved by the Bu C & R and the contract plans were revised accordingly. This was the last major change to be made in the original *Iowa* class design.

The *Iowa* was laid down on 27 June 1940 and the *New Jersey* on 16

September 1940. By this time, their design displacement stood at 45,873 tons which was less than 2 per cent overweight. Tonnage really mattered little at this point for Great Britain and France, embroiled by now in World War II, had suspended all of the Treaty restrictions in September 1939 when the war in Europe began.

In June 1939, even before the contracts for BB 61 and BB 62 had been signed, the General Board and the War Plans Division met to consider the next battleship program. The US Navy expected to build two more battleships in Fiscal Year 1941. Originally, the Board had recommended only three 'fast battleships' to match the three Japanese *Kongos*, but War Plans made a strong case that both of the next two battleships should be fast. This again suggests that, with the available intelligence, there was reason to believe the new Japanese battleships under construction would be capable of at least 26 knots, not to mention the reconstructed *Nagatos*.

New strategic planning for joint operations with battleships, carriers and destroyers was also being developed by War Plans. The new 33 knot battleships would be as fast as the carriers and destroyers and they could work together as a powerful strike force. It was felt that such a force would have a considerable effect on Japanese strategy and tactics, because their 26 knot battleships would have to be detached from the faster carriers during flight operations leaving the carriers relatively unprotected. This early planning was perhaps the origin of the Fast Carrier Task Force. The Board finally agreed with War Plans and, on 12 June, the *Missouri* (BB 63) was ordered from the New York Navy Yard and the *Wisconsin* (BB 64) from the Philadelphia Navy Yard as 'fast battleships'.

Four units were considered sufficient to support the anticipated fast strike force and the General Board ordered studies to be resumed on the more conventional 'slow battleship', designated BB 65. After the fall of France, the Congress authorized a large emergency construction program. The 'Two Ocean Navy Act', passed on 19 July 1940, included 385,000 tons of capital ship construction. Two

The additions and changes to the light anti-aircraft battery were incorporated in the *Iowa* when she returned to the New York Navy Yard for her post-shakedown overhaul. The battery now consisted of nineteen 40mm quadruple and fifty-two 20mm single mounts which she carried throughout the war. These three photographs, taken on 9 July 1943, can be easily compared with the drawing room model. Note the 20mm gun tub on the bow.

battleships were to be included in the next fiscal year building program and the Board wanted these two units to be of the new design, but BB 65 was not far enough along and the Secretary of the Navy directed that the two new ships be duplicates of those already under construction. On 9 September 1940, the *Illinois* (BB 65) was ordered from the Philadelphia Navy Yard and the *Kentucky* (BB 66) was ordered from the Norfolk Navy Yard as units of the *Iowa* class. The 'slow battleship' design was redesignated BB 67 and named *Montana*.

GENERAL ARRANGEMENT

Within the hull proper there were three continuous decks: the main or weather deck, which also served as the bomb deck; the second deck, which was the main armored deck; and the third deck, which provided protection for and access to the machinery spaces and housed the 5in magazines. A splinter deck was fitted directly below the second, or armored deck, between barbettes No. 2 and No. 3. The splinter deck was not a full deck height and was placed so close beneath the second deck that the space was not really usable. The lower decks were 'platforms', interrupted amidships by the machinery spaces forming decks forward and aft. From the third deck down were the first, second and third platform decks. The hold was below the third platform and extended from forward of barbette No. 1 to aft of barbette No. 3. It formed a triple bottom below the vitals of the ship and, in the engineering spaces, it carried the foundations for the main machinery. The double bottom, directly below the hold, ran from the

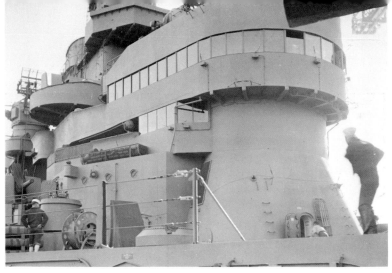

By November 1943 a number of changes were made to the bridge area of the *Iowa*. Windscreens have been installed on the open bridge and the walkway at the primary conning station has been enlarged to provide passage completely around the level. The pilot house level has not yet been permanently closed in.

The bridge area of the *New Jersey* was also altered. The work on her was somewhat more extensive than on the *Iowa* with the pilot house having a permanent enclosure installed. This photograph was taken after the completion of work on 11 October 1943. Note the different type of windscreen at the primary conning station.

stem to just aft of barbette No. 3.

The main deck provided the primary access to the ship and positions for two of the main battery turrets, many of the smaller anti-aircraft weapons, the anchor handling equipment forward and aircraft handling equipment aft. The superstructure rose above the main deck in two continuous decks, designated the 01 and 02 levels. A third main battery turret was located at the 01 level forward, and all of the ten 5in/38cal gun mounts of the secondary battery were concentrated on these two decks. A heavy armored conning tower, from which the ship was commanded in battle, was located near the forward end of the superstructure. The navigating bridge was at the 04 level around the conning tower with the pilot house directly aft. Accommodations for the captain and the flag were directly below the pilot house. The primary conning station was at the 08 level on the forward fire control tower, and the forward main battery director was located atop the tower.

There were two large stacks, indicating the ship's massive power plant. The leading edge of the forward stack was faired into the fire control tower with the flue gases venting from a flat just above the primary conning position. The after stack was free-standing and vented slightly lower than the forward one. Large caps were placed on each stack directing the gases aft. The centers of the uptakes were nearly 100ft apart and the main 40mm air defense battery was clustered between them.

The after fire control tower was located at the aft end of the superstructure with a second main battery director atop the tower. For weight and stability reasons, the after director could not be placed as high as the forward one, therefore, it was lowered enough to avoid most of the gases from the second stack.

The *New Jersey* underway, on 13 October 1943, off the Virginia Capes. The light anti-aircraft battery has been increased as in the *Iowa* except for the additional 40mm mount atop Turret No. II. There were three 20mm single mounts in this position on the *Iowa*. The battery consists of twenty 40mm quadruple and forty-nine 20mm single mounts.

Chapter 4

ACTIVATIONS AND MODERNIZATIONS

When the *Iowa* class ships were designed, their primary role was to reinforce the battle line. Their very high speed was justified by a number of additional tasks that could only be performed by a fast battleship. Among these additional duties was dealing with the Japanese *Kongo* class battlecruisers, chasing down commerce raiders, filling the role of commerce raiders themselves and serving as the primary unit of a special 'strike force'.

The special strike force was envisaged as a group of several *Iowa*s, escorted by carriers and destroyers, which would operate independently in advance areas, such as the 'mandated islands', and even probe for the main Japanese battle force. This strategy evolved into the 'Fast Carrier Task Force'. Originally, however, the carriers were in the subordinate role of supporting the fast battleships. The notion that the *Iowa*s were specifically designed to cover the fast carriers is entirely erroneous. In fact, before the Japanese attack on Pearl Harbor, the type of naval air war that developed in the Pacific was almost inconceivable.

A total of six *Iowa* class battleships were ordered; the *Iowa* (BB 61), *New Jersey* (BB 62), *Missouri* (BB 63), *Wisconsin* (BB 64), *Illinois* (BB 65) and *Kentucky* (BB 66). The first four were completed and became operational during World War II, but the last two were still under construction at the end of the war. The hulks of the last two were retained for over twelve years but neither was completed. Both were finally scrapped.

Their great speed, and thus an ability to operate with fast carriers, is undoubtedly the main reason that the *Iowa*s have survived, notwithstanding their tremendous firepower against surface and shore targets.

The *Iowa* had an extensive overhaul at the Hunters Point Shipyard in San Francisco lasting from 15 January until 19 March 1945. She is shown here in late-March off the Californian coast during post-overhaul trials and training exercises before returning to the war zone.

POST-WORLD WAR II REDUCTIONS

The four ships of the *Iowa* class remained in active service after World War II, longer than any other US Navy battleships. All older battleships were mothballed immediately after the war and the *South Dakota*s followed shortly thereafter. The *North Carolina*s served a little longer because they were not nearly as cramped. They were used to transport troops home from overseas during operation 'Magic Carpet' and for a few training cruises, but both were placed in reserve by mid-1947. By mid-1948, the *New Jersey* and *Wisconsin* fell victim to post-World War II austerity policies and were placed in reserve. The *Iowa* followed in less than a year. The *Missouri* was still active in June 1950 when communist North Korea crossed the 38th Parallel invading South Korea, and in less than two months she was on her way to the Far East. On 14 September 1950, she opened fire against hostile targets (for the first time since the end of World War II) in support of Republic of Korea forces at Samchok. The *Iowa*, *New Jersey* and *Wisconsin* were in mothballs only briefly, for they were recommissioned during 1950–1951. All four of the *Iowa*s deployed to the Far East during the Korean War and each had at least one tour in the combat zone before the war ended in 1953.

KOREAN WAR ACTIVATIONS

When the United Nations decision was made to oppose the invasion of South Korea by North Korea, it was uncertain as to just how much

In these two photographs, taken on 18 March 1945, the *Iowa* is leaving the Hunters Point Navy Yard after her first major overhaul since leaving the East Coast. A new enclosed bridge area, similar to that of the *Missouri* and *Wisconsin*, has been fitted as have new fire control and search radars. Her OS2U Kingfisher observation aircraft have been landed and the later SC-1 Seahawk has replaced them on the fantail.

force would be encountered and what its nature would be. There were obviously no large combatants to engage, but the extent and potential of the North Korean air arm was uncertain. The major change in air warfare was the introduction of jet aircraft and the attendant higher flight speeds. If the Soviet Union and China were willing to commit enough first line aircraft and pilots to the North Korean cause, the US Navy would have an air defense problem of major proportions. Fortunately, this did not happen during the Korean conflict and the US Navy encountered no significant naval or air opposition.

When operations against North Korea began, the *Iowa*s were very nearly identical to their final World War II configuration. The only noticeable change in their appearance was in the newer, more advanced radar and electronic equipment that had been installed after the war. There were no major structural changes in the superstructure except for the alterations and modifications in the masts necessary to support the new gear (see Chapter 7). The new radar equipment efficiently detected and identified both air and surface targets and assisted in directing air strikes to and from target areas. The electronics systems were effective in intercepting a wide range of

These two aerial quartering photographs show the *New Jersey* on speed trials in Puget Sound, on 30 June 1945, after her overhaul. Her cramped, round enclosed bridge has been replaced with a roomier square enclosure similar to those installed on her sisters. She has been fitted with new fire control and search radar and when joined by her air complement they will be the new SC-1 Seahawks.

Above: The *Wisconsin* screens carriers of Task Force 38 in August 1945, while conducting air strikes off the east coast of Japan only days before the Japanese capitulated. She operated continually from the time she left the Atlantic fleet until the summer of 1946 when she had her first major overhaul.

Below: The *Missouri* docked at the Pearl Harbor Navy Yard on 29 September 1945, on her way home after the Japanese surrender. Already some of her 20mm guns have been removed. Noticeable in this view are the three on either side of Turret No. II on the main deck.

transmissions and in jamming and masking a full range of hostile emissions.

There was virtually no change in armament, except for the 20mm battery. When reactivated, the single 20mm mounts were replaced with a smaller number of twins in an effort to obtain a denser pattern of fire against single targets. They were really unable to effectively track the faster jet aircraft and their shell was not heavy enough to disable a target unless a number of hits were scored. By October 1951, the 20mm battery had been eliminated from all four of the *Iowa* class (see Chapter 5).

The *Missouri* had landed her catapults and observation aircraft in 1948 but had retained the aircraft crane on the very stern. Helicopters replaced the observation aircraft, which had been used strictly for spotting. The helicopters were also used for spotting, but they were able to perform a variety of other functions as well. The same changes were made to the *Iowa*, *New Jersey* and *Wisconsin* when they were reactivated. With the removal of the catapults, the large, wide area of the fantail made an ideal landing platform for the helicopters.

it was expected that many changes would be necessary in radar, electronics and communications as well as to the anti-aircraft armament and fire control in order to bring the battleships up to an acceptable state of readiness.

Upgrading the anti-aircraft battery was a major priority. The 20mm gun had long been judged ineffective and by the end of the Korean War, the 20mm battery had been removed from all of the *Iowa* class ships. Even the 40mm gun was considered obsolete by the end of World War II because of its performance against the Kamikazes. A single hit would severely damage an attacker but, unless multiple hits were scored totally destroying the aircraft, it usually continued until it impacted with its target. A weapon with a shell heavy enough to destroy a target with a single hit was needed, but a high rate of fire was also necessary. The solution was a rapid firing 3in gun and, in 1944, the Bu Ord began work on a twin automatic version of the 3in/50cal gun.

Progress on the new gun and mounts slowed at the end of World War II, even though the program had a very high priority. The first

CLASS IMPROVEMENT PLANS

The experience gained during the Korean conflict had indicated a need for future mobilization planning, in order to quickly make improvements and changes to both active ships and those being reactivated in the event of future emergencies. In 1952 the Bu Ships[1] began generating class improvement plans (CIPs) for all battleships held in active reserve which included the two *North Carolinas* and four *South Dakotas*. The improvements would only be incorporated if the vessels were reactivated. Because of the rapidly changing technology,

Post-war activities of the *Iowa* included a number of training cruises off the West Coast. She is shown here at anchor off the Naval Air Station in Alameda on 22 May 1947 between cruises. She was taken out of service a year later in this configuration.

mounts did not become available until 1948. The new gun was used in all new construction, but installation in the fleet lagged because of post-war austerity measures. The new twin mount was planned as a one-for-one replacement for the quadruple 40mm mount. This was not possible in most cases, for although the physical requirements could be met, the mount turned out to be heavier than expected and the replacement was more on a two-for-three basis. A major armament conversion program was undertaken in 1950 when the Korean War began and the new automatic 3in/50cal gun became the standard medium range anti-aircraft weapon in the fleet.

---

1 In 1940 the Bu C & R, responsible for the general and structural design of ships and the Bu Eng, responsible for design of ships' machinery, were combined forming the Bureau of Ships (Bu Ships). In 1966 the Bu Ships became the Naval Ship Systems Command (NAVSHIPS).

In planning the *Iowa* class 3in conversion program, the Ship Characteristics Board (SCB)[2] determined that sixteen twin Mark 33 mounts would be fitted. Fire control for the new battery was to be provided by six Mark 56 and four Mark 63 Gun Fire Control System (GFCS). The Bu Ships prepared installation plans in 1955, but the project, designated SCB-74E, was never completely funded. Portions of the fire control systems were installed, but only in the *Iowa* and *New Jersey* (see Chapter 6). The twin 3in mounts were to be fitted in the same location as the 40mm mounts except for the turret tops and the high, center positions between the stacks; however, none of the guns were ever installed.

Improvements for the main battery were also planned. A 16in nuclear shell, the Mark 23 nicknamed 'Katie', was under development and prototype testing had been conducted at the Los Alamos range. Beginning with the *New Jersey* in late-1954, modifications were made to carry and assemble the projectile components. The *Iowa* and *Wisconsin* were also modified to carry the Mark 23, but the *Missouri* was being deactivated when the program began and was not so fitted. The

beginning with the *New Jersey* in August 1957, followed by the *Iowa* in February 1958 and the *Wisconsin* in March 1958. At this point, it seemed that the active duty life of the *Iowa*s might be over.

At the end of 1958, there were fifteen battleships remaining in the reserve fleet: the 'Big Five', two *California*s and three *Colorado*s; two *North Carolina*s; four *South Dakota*s and four *Iowa*s. Over the next several years, major cuts in the defense budget forced the reserve fleet to be substantially pared back. In regard to battleships, the 'Big Five' were the first to go being stricken in March 1959. In June 1960, the *North Carolina*s were placed on the sale list and finally, the *South Dakota*s were disposed of in June 1962. However, the *North Carolina*, *Alabama* and *Massachusetts* have survived as memorials, being preserved by their namesake states. The *Iowa*s were retained primarily for shore bombardment and in support of amphibious operations. Their massive firepower had been so effective during the Korean War that they were considered essential in this role. Their fire support value even increased as more of the 8in gunned cruisers were disposed of prior to the United States involvement in Vietnam.

standard allowance was ten Mark 23 nuclear and nine Mark 24 practice rounds. A drill projectile was also carried. All of the rounds were stored and assembled in Turret No. II; however, they could be moved to the other turrets by the monorail system on the third deck (see Chapter 5). Selected crew members were sent to special schools where they received training for handling and assembling the projectiles. Former crew members have indicated that ten Mark 23 and nine Mark 24 rounds were aboard the *Iowa* and the *Wisconsin* but that only a drill projectile was taken aboard the *New Jersey*. The *Wisconsin* is reported to have fired a number of Mark 24 practice rounds.

The *Missouri* was the first victim of the post-war cutbacks, being decommissioned in February 1955. Within the next three years, the remaining units of the class would be back in the reserve fleet

After the war the *Wisconsin* also operated off the East Coast and made deployments to Northern Europe and South America. She is shown here in late-1946 in the South Atlantic. Her post-war activities ended when she was mothballed in mid-1948.

HYBRID DESIGNS – THE MISSILE BATTLESHIP

At the end of World War II, the *Illinois* and *Kentucky* were still under construction. No serious consideration seems to have been given to utilizing the *Illinois*, except as a target, yet she was retained for over twelve years. The *Kentucky*, however, was the subject of two specific conversion plans. One would have converted her to an anti-aircraft battleship, BB (AA), and the other to a missile battleship (BBG). Although neither plan reached the contract design stage, both deserve some mention in this discussion, for they were the original attempts to apply state-of-the-art weaponry to the *Iowa* class.

The *Illinois*, laid down on 15 January 1945, was 22 per cent complete when construction was cancelled on 11 August, just three days after

2 The SCB was established in 1945 in the office of the CNO. Initially, it had cognizance over modifications to existing ships, but by 1946 it was involved with characteristics for existing ships and conversions. Eventually, the General Board was phased out in 1951. The SCB was not a complete successor to the Board since it was not involved in policymaking as the Board had been.

the Japanese surrender. Consideration was given to using her as a nuclear target, but it proved too costly just to bring her to the point where she could be launched. Eventually, she was broken up on the ways with demolition work beginning in September 1958.

The Kentucky did not die easily. Although her keel laying is officially listed as 6 December 1944, she was actually first laid down on a shipway at Norfolk on 7 March 1942. Her first launching was on 10 June 1942. Most of her bottom structure under the machinery spaces was complete up to the triple bottom. The shipway then was cleared for Landing Ship Tank (LST) construction which had a higher priority at that time; the bottom section remained tied up at a service pier until her official keel laying. However, work on her did not stop. A considerable amount of her material, including armor and machinery, was assembled. When her keel was again laid, this time in the yard's large graving dock, many hull sub-assemblies had been fabricated and work progressed very rapidly. She was not cancelled at the end of the war, but construction was suspended in August 1946 in order to consider major design changes.

Modification of the Kentucky's armament was being considered by the SCB to include special anti-aircraft guns. She was to become an

The *New Jersey* spent the years immediately following the war operating along the East Coast and in the Caribbean. She made a number of summer training cruises for midshipmen from the US Naval Academy. The *New Jersey* is shown here in early-1948 just before being placed in the reserve fleet. Note the folded wings of the SC-1 Seahawk spotting aircraft on the port catapult.

anti-aircraft battleship and the project was designated SCB 19. Surviving documents provide little detail on this conversion and no sketches have been found, but the study seems to have developed in parallel with the Gun Launched Guided Projectile–Arrow Shell project. Arrow Shell, later designated Zeus, was a fin-stabilized 4in sabot shell which was fired from an 8in/55cal smoothbore gun. The shell was guided by a small rocket motor, firing at right angles to the shell axis. By 1948, an improved Zeus II shell was to be rocket propelled after firing. The new 8in gun was envisioned as a triple or quadruple mount and possibly even a turret. Post-war funding reductions forced the abandonment of the Zeus program in the early-1950s.

Work on the Kentucky did not resume until August 1948 and then only to bring her to a point where she could be launched in order to clear the building dock. On 17 January 1950, the *Missouri* ran aground on Thimble Shoals in the entrance of the Chesapeake Bay and the *Kentucky* was floated clear of the dock on 20 January so repairs to the *Missouri* could be made. When launched, *Kentucky* was 73 per cent complete, with machinery installed and the second deck plated over. Basically, the hull was structurally finished to the third deck, but from construction progress photographs, it does not appear that the upper, Class A armor belt was fitted.

*Iowa*s. Although seventeen years and many Fast Carrier Task Forces later, the role of the *Iowa*s had gone full circle.

The original BBG studies retained 16in Turrets I and III for surface fire and shore bombardment, although the center gun could be removed if weight became critical. At least eight Regulus II missiles would be carried to give the BBG a long-range strike capability, which, as will be seen, was a major consideration in the 1980s modernization. New anti-aircraft armament would include six single

She remained tied up to a service pier at the Norfolk Navy Yard while the SCB decided her final configuration. On 6 May 1956, the *Wisconsin* collided with the destroyer *Eaton* (DDE 510) in heavy fog off the Virginia Capes, badly damaging the battleship's bow. To expedite repairs, a 68ft section of the *Kentucky's* bow, weighing 120 tons, was grafted on to the *Wisconsin* at Norfolk.

As a result of studies by the new Long-Range Objectives Group (LRO)[3] in 1955, the SCB proposed that the *Kentucky* be redesigned and completed as a missile battleship (BBG). The LRO group viewed a BBG as the central figure of a task force composed of attack and support carriers, missile cruisers and destroyers and radar picket submarines. The BBG had the capacity to carry long-range missiles and, therefore, would be the primary combatant in the task force. The carriers were to provide tactical air support and anti-submarine warfare (ASW) cover in conjunction with the escorts. It was planned to create five such strike forces, one around each of the remaining

3 The LRO Group was established in 1954 in the office of the CNO. It was responsible for developing future designs and concepts using evolving and state-of-the-art technologies.

The *Missouri* was still active when the Korean War broke out in June 1950. After two months of preparation, she was sent to the Far East and, on 14 September 1950, she fired on hostile targets for the first time since the end of World War II. The *Missouri* was the first of the *Iowa*s to be decommissioned after Korea, going to the reserve fleet as Bremerton, Washington in February 1955.

5in/54cal and ten twin 3in/50cal guns and two twin batteries of a combination of Terrier, Talos or Tartar missiles.

In mid-1956, the studies reached a point at which the Bu Ships was ready to proceed with the contract design phase for the Fiscal Year 1958 program. The main and anti-aircraft guns were as in the original studies. The anti-aircraft missile battery consisted of two twin Talos and four twin Tartar launchers. The long-range strike capability was now provided by the Polaris Intermediate Range Ballistic Missile (IRBM). Up to sixteen Polaris would be carried and two special ballistic missile launchers were to be fitted. By late-1956, however, the shipbuilding budget for new construction was strained by large cost overruns and the BBG program was set aside indefinitely.

Declared surplus, the *Kentucky* was finally struck from the Navy List on 9 June 1958. She was sold to the Boston Metals Company on 31

November and towed to Baltimore, Maryland where she was scrapped.

Other studies were conducted with hybrid uses for the *Iowas*. One was for a combination fleet oiler and anti-aircraft ship. Another was for a combination replenishment, commando ship with shore bombardment capabilities. There was even a study for a full service, fast replenishment ship. The latter concept developed into the Fast Combat Support Ship (AOE). These large, fast 'supermarkets'

support became a major concern and the forces ashore required fire support and air cover.

Air support was readily available, but fire support was limited to the 8in and 5in batteries of those heavy cruisers which were active and the smaller destroyers. Shore bombardment became a dangerous business, especially for the destroyers which had to stand in rather close in order to have any effective range. Many were hit by mobile communist shore batteries. As early as November 1964, the Bu Weps[4]

dispense everything from fuel oil to tooth paste during Underway Replenishment (UNREP) operations. Ironically, the *Kentucky* lives on, at least in part, for her main machinery was carefully removed and saved when she was cut up and now powers the *Sacramento* (AOE 1) and *Camden* (AOE 2).

Due to the escalating level of hostilities in Korea, life in the reserve fleet was short lived for the *Iowas*. The *New Jersey* off Norfolk, Virginia in December 1950 a month after her recommissioning. By May 1951, she was with the 7th Fleet off the coast of Korea.

VIETNAM REVIVAL

As the political and military struggle between North and South Vietnam intensified in the late-1950s, the United States increased its financial and military aid to the South in their struggle against the communist North. The two Vietnams were divided at the 17th Parallel, where the country was narrowest, by a neutral area designated as the demilitarized zone (DMZ). A large force of communist insurgents, the Vietcong, operated in the South and were supplied by the North Vietnamese freely using the DMZ. The Army of the Republic of Vietnam (ARVN) was unable to deal with the insurgents and, by 1965, the United States had committed substantial ground forces to South Vietnam in an effort to stabilize the military situation. The US Navy's role significantly increased. Logistical

conducted a tactical survey of fire support requirements for the entire Vietnam coastal area. It concluded that at least 80 per cent of all naval targets were within 16in range and recommended that two *Iowas* and two 8in gunned heavy cruisers be activated to adequately provide for fire support.

The Marine Corps vigorously supported the proposal, but the Naval Aviation community was totally opposed to the idea. Oppostion came from the very top of the Navy command structure, the CNO, who was an aviator himself. The notion that aircraft could furnish

4 In 1959, the Bu Ord, responsible for the development of weapons and the Bu Aer (Bureau of Aeronautics), responsible for the development of aircraft, were combined forming the Bureau of Naval Weapons (Bu Weps). In 1966 the Bu Weps was reorganized into the NAVORD (Naval Ordnance Systems Command) and the NAVAIR (Naval Air Systems Command).

close support or execute a surgical strike as well as 16in gunfire, when within range, is simply not so (see Chapter 10). This rivalry between the air and surface communities of the Navy undoubtedly cost many aircraft and the lives or imprisonment of most of their air crews over the next few years. For example, between 1965 and the 1968 bombing halt north of the 19th Parallel, nearly 700 attack sorties were flown against the Thanh Hoa railroad and highway bridge. More than 1,500 tons of heavy ordnance were used in the assaults and 50 aircraft were lost trying to destroy the bridge. The *New Jersey* could have handily destroyed the bridge in about an hour. For this type of surgical strike, the battleship is without peer.

By 1967, there was strong support in the Department of Defense (DOD), as well as in the Congress, for activating at least one battleship. Aside from the squabbling within the Navy, it seemed more cost effective. Aircraft losses were at that time averaging one a day at a cost of $2 million per plane and $1 million for pilot training. One of the *Iowa*s, with an austere refit, could be commissioned for about $25 million, or less that ten days of aircraft losses. (The actual cost was $21.5 million.) Putting a battleship on the firing line could not, of course, save all of the aircraft losses, but it could save more than enough to be worthwhile. On 1 August 1967, the day following the CNO's retirement, it was announced that the *New Jersey* would be reactivated for service in Vietnam.

Of the four *Iowa*s in mothballs, none had been active for much over ten years and all were in good material condition. The *New Jersey* was selected mainly because she had been regunned not long before being decommissioned and because it was determined that she would require the least amount of work to meet operational standards. The reactivation was described as austere, mainly to placate any opposition, but it included everything necessary to effectively perform its intended combat mission in Vietnam.

The main and secondary batteries were completely activated, but the refit was austere in regard to light/medium air defense capabilities. All of the 40mm guns were removed and were not replaced by the 3in/50cal automatics as called for in the CIPs. Some of the 40mm gun tubs were removed but most were retained, and the two forward on the 01 level were used as swimming pools.

The two Mark 38 GFCS for the main battery and the four Mark 37 GFCS for the secondary battery were activated. The aft Mark 38 system was upgraded by the addition of a Mark 48 shore bombardment computer to bring it up to the standard of the forward system (see Chapter 6). The Mark 56 directors, installed for the 40mm/3in batteries, were retained, but only the two high pair between the stacks were activated. The other four were kept covered. The Mark 56 GFCS was a dual-ballistic system and also controlled the 5in battery giving it an additional computing capability against air targets.

Spotting was performed in a variety of ways. Several different helicopters could be operated from the *New Jersey* and provide gun fire spotting information. The most popular model was the H-1 series, the 'Hueys'. There were also provisions for operating a modified Drone Anti-Submarine Helicopter (DASH) called 'Snoopy'. This remotely-controlled helicopter was equipped with a sensor package utilizing a television camera for line of sight spotting. Spotting was also performed by Marine Corps A-4 Skyhawks.

Several changes in the radar suite were necessary to accommodate the new communications and electronics gear which was to be

The success of the North Korean invasion brought fears that similar armed conflicts might break out in other areas of the world. To be ready for any contingency, the *Iowa* was brought back on line and recommissioned in August 1951. She is shown here off the Californian coast in early-March 1952.

As military operations increased in Korea, the *Wisconsin* was also reactivated and commissioned in March 1951. She is shown here off the coast of Korea operating with Task Force 77 on 21 March 1952. Only five days earlier she was hit by a shell from a North Korean 155mm shore battery.

installed. The foremast and mainmast were retained with only minor modifications being required. On the foremast, the SPS–6 air search set was retained, but the SG–6 surface/zenith search radar was replaced with the new SPS–10 surface search set. Finally, the SPS–8 height-finder radar was removed from the mainmast leaving it clear for a new array of communications antennas. Since the *New Jersey* was not intended to perform any command functions, no Tactical Air Navigation (TACAN) equipment was installed.

The installation of new communications and electronics suites received the most attention. The Soviets were known to have supplied the North Vietnamese forces with a number of SS–N–2 Styx missiles. The new equipment was necessary to bring the *New Jersey* up

to fleet standards in regard to tactical data and electronic counter-measures (ECM).

The new communications and electronics installations were also the most visible. Many new antennas were installed. The most prominent were the large discone/cage at the bow, which allowed the ship to receive integrated tactical data, and the antenna array on the mainmast, certain elements of which controlled the 'Snoopy'.

The most noticeable electronics additions were the ULQ–6 antennas located on each side of the forward fire control tower at the air defense level. The ULQ–6 was a passive ECM system used to detect missiles, such as the Styx, and initiate jamming signals to confuse their active radar guidance. The ULQ–6 worked in conjunction with four Zuni rocket launchers located in the four 40mm gun tubs between the stacks. Modified Zuni missiles loaded with chaff could be fired in the direction of an incoming missile to further confuse its guidance.

The interior as well as the exterior of the ship was completely refurbished; however, little was required in the way of repairs and changes in the general arrangement. Since there were no light/medium anti-aircraft batteries and their associated fire control equipment, personnel requirements were considerably less than during Korean operations. This is turn reduced the number of spaces which had to be rehabilitated for accommodation. The table below shows how the complement varied during the different periods of active service:

Design Complement: 1,921 – 117 officer/1,804 enlisted
New Jersey, 1945: 2,753 – 161 officer/2,592 enlisted
New Jersey, 1949: 2,688 – 234 officer/2,554 enlisted
New Jersey, 1968: 1,626 – 70 officer/1,556 enlisted
New Jersey, 1982: 1,518 – 65 officer/1,453 enlisted

As a result, living compartments were not overcrowded, the galley operated more efficiently and there was more flexibility with consumable stores. Flag accommodations were purposely not refurbished to avoid critics' assertions that the battleship was being reactivated as a comfortable command ship.

In retrospect, a clearcut policy as to how the *New Jersey* was to be employed in Vietnam seemed to be lacking. From the beginning, the reactivation had been subjected to political battles within the Department of the Navy and the DOD. With all of the air power that had been amassed by 1967, by both the US Navy and the US Air Force, effective close support of ground forces had not been achieved. Nor had the flow of men and supplies to the communist forces operating in the South, via the Ho Chi Minh Trail, been dampened. Within the Navy, the air community viewed the battleship as a threat

to their prowess and a competitor for funding while the Marine Corps considered it absolutely vital to maintain its position on the ground. With Soviet–supplied missiles exacting a heavy toll in aircraft, especially in the North and along the Ho Chi Minh Trail, the DOD had yet another view. Aircraft could only be used in good weather when they were most vulnerable, but Naval Gunfire Support (NGFS) could be used anytime. The battleship, therefore, was viewed by the DOD as a means of reducing aircraft losses and interdicting the supply lines to the Vietcong.

National political policies also had their effect on the deployment of the battleship. Only days before the *New Jersey* was recommissioned on 6 April 1968, President Johnson ended offensive operations above the 19th Parallel in an effort to de-escalate the war. This automatically eliminated many of the battleship's prime targets. Arriving off the

DMZ on 29 September, the *New Jersey* formally joined the war. She operated up to the 19th Parallel until 1 November when the President ordered all offensive operations against the North to cease, restricting operations to below the DMZ at the 17th Parallel. It was hoped that this further effort to de-escalate the war would bring all parties to the negotiating table.

The *New Jersey's* deployment to Vietnam ended in April 1969 and she docked at Long Beach Naval Shipyard on 5 May for a much needed availability period. Equipment was serviced and refurbished, most of the crew was rotated and the ship was drydocked for underwater hull maintenance. She was scheduled to leave on her second deployment to the Far East on 5 September. While final preparations for the deployment were being completed, on 21 August, less than three weeks before her scheduled departure, the DOD announced that the

Above: An aerial photograph of Battleship Division 2, taken on 7 June 1954 off Norfolk, Virginia. The nearest vessel is the *Iowa*, then *Wisconsin*, *Missouri* and *New Jersey*. The four battleships operated together for only a few hours when this family portrait was taken. This is the only time that the entire class was together.

Opposite page: The last battleship to be placed in reserve after the Korean War was the *Wisconsin*. Mothballed in March 1958 at the Philadelphia Navy Yard, she is shown here in late-1957 off Hampton Roads. She was laid up in this rig, which is similar to that of the *Iowa*.

Left: From left to right: the *Wisconsin*, *New Jersey* and *Iowa*. They lie moored to a pier in the south end of the Philadelphia Navy Yard, in about 1967. Vital equipment was covered and preservative coatings were applied to machinery where possible. Ventilation was provided and temperature and humidity were controlled. The *Missouri* was in the reserve fleet at the Puget Sound Naval Shipyard in Bremerton, Washington.

The *Kentucky* was still under construction when World War II ended in 1945. Her keel was first laid down on a shipway at the Norfolk Navy Yard on 7 March 1942. The deep keel section, which is the combined depth of the double and triple bottoms, and the lapping of the bottom strakes is clearly shown.

The *Kentucky* was first launched on 10 June 1942 when a section of her bottom under the machinery spaces was floated to clear the shipway for higher priority construction. The section was towed to a nearby dock where it remained until work resumed over two years later.

New Jersey would be deactivated along with about 100 other naval vessels. The crew immediately began preparing their ship for her long stay in the reserve fleet and on 17 December the New Jersey was placed out of commission at Bremerton, Washington.

Fiscal restrictions by the Congress were given as the reason, but again the decision was purely political. The New Jersey's performance in Vietnam had been outstanding.[5] In fact, she had performed so well that her presence in the war zone was considered extremely intimidating and destabilizing. She was able to move at will all along the coastline, stand in close to shore with complete immunity and devastate targets that were nearly unaffected by all the massive air power which had been brought to bear in the area. The enemy was forced to move inland, beyond the range of the 16in guns, and Vietcong pressure on the ground forces within twenty miles of the coast was thereafter almost non-existent. This capability was seen as counterproductive to peace negotiations by the new Nixon Administration. The, then, Under Secretary of the Navy, John Warner, protested the deactivation to the Secretary of Defense, but the order came down directly from the White House that 'the ship should be deactivated because it was impeding the peace negotiations'. (These facts did not become public knowledge until 7 April 1981 during the Senate debate on reactivating the Iowas for their present tour of active duty.)

5 Detailed accounts are not given since they are adequately covered in other publications, the most useful of which is *The Iowa Class Battleships*, Malcolm Muir, Blandford Press.

The Kentucky was considered for a number of conversions including an anti-aircraft battleship and guided missile battleship. She was finally declared surplus and struck from the Navy List on 9 June 1958. She is docking here at Norfolk on 16 July for the removal of her engines prior to scrapping. The upper portion of her original bow is forward of No. 1 barbette and the undamaged lower part of the Wisconsin's bow is just aft. Note the gun houses for her entire secondary battery on deck.

Work resumed on the Kentucky in early-1945 when the triple bottom section was moved into the large graving dock at Norfolk. A considerable amount of material had been assembled including armor and machinery. Work progressed very rapidly, as shown here on 11 June. Note the fabrication of the turret foundation bulkheads. The carrier outfitting in the background is the Lake Champlain (CV 39).

The North Vietnamese launched an offensive in the Spring of 1972 stalling the peace talks and prompting the President to resume offensive operations against the North. Consideration was given to taking the *New Jersey* out of mothballs again but reactivation would have taken too much time. The 8in gunned cruiser *Newport News* was rushed to the war zone but this action was described as 'too little, too late'. Ironically, the firepower of the *New Jersey* could have been put to good use conducting surgical strikes against the port city of Haiphong and other choice targets in the North. A final alternative to sealing off Haiphong was mining the harbor.

MODERNIZATION

During the 1970s, the *Iowas* survived several attempts to dispose of them. The earliest attempt was in 1972 when it was proposed to retain only the *New Jersey*. The Marine Corps opposed this proposal as they had backed the plan to activate the two *Iowas* for Vietnam. At least two were necessary if one was always to be on station during amphibious operations, or if they were expected to maintain coastal positions such as in Vietnam. If two assaults were to be made, all four *Iowas* would be needed. Once again, John Warner, who was now Secretary of the Navy, came to the rescue of the battleships and successfully resisted the pressure to declare them surplus. The next attempt came in Spring 1974, from the NAVSEA[6] command at about the time Secretary Warner was leaving office. They felt money spent

6 In 1974, the NAVSHIPS and NAVORD were combined forming the Naval Sea Systems Command (NAVSEA).

on battleship maintenance was wasted since there seemed to be little or no possibility that they would ever be used. Again the Marine Corps strongly objected to their removal. It appears that support for their retention came this time from Admiral Zumwalt, the CNO, who felt they were still important assets. Their 16in guns were certainly vital to any amphibious operations. They were also capable of carrying new strike weapons and they could be reactivated reasonably quickly.

While some factions in the Navy were trying to purge the battleships, a number of studies clearly showed their potential and adaptability to carry the latest in weaponry. (One such study was conducted by the respected naval architectural firm of Gibbs & Cox to determine the feasibility of carrying such systems as Harpoon, Sea Sparrow, Close In Weapons System (CIWS) and others. Their conclusions were most favorable.) A 1977 inspection survey found them fit and in excellent material condition. Their hulls, ordnance and machinery were sound, but they were not up to standard in regard to command and control facilities and general habitability. The survey report, however, recommended that the battleships be stricken. The Marines fought hard to save them again and this time seemed to be gathering more support in their effort to keep what firepower still existed in the fleet. The remaining handful of 8in gunned cruisers

The Fast Combat Support Ship *Sacramento* (AOE 1) is flanked by the destroyer *Walke* (DD 723) and the Combat Stores Ship *Mars* (AFS 1) for refueling on 24 November 1964. The *Sacramento* and *Camden* (AOE 2) are powered by the machinery from the battleship *Kentucky* which was removed when she was scrapped.

The *Illinois* was also still under construction when World War II ended. There were no plans for using her, except as a target, yet she was retained for over twelve years. Laid down on 15 January 1945, she was 22 per cent complete when cancelled on 11 August. These photographs show her construction progress as of 7 July. She was broken up on the ways at the Philadelphia Navy Yard beginning in September 1958.

The *Iowa* and *Wisconsin*, photographed in about 1972, remained in the reserve fleet at Philadelphia. During the 1970s all four of the *Iowa*s survived several attempts to dispose of them. With the ever increasing strength of the Soviet Navy, including the construction of large surface combatants such as the *Kirov* class battlecruisers and *Kiev* class carriers, by mid-1979 there was strong interest in modernizing and recommissioning the *Iowa*s once again.

were all in reserve and the few 6in gunned cruisers that were left were about to be retired. The new lightweight 8in gun program was also faltering. Within a year it was cancelled. The Pacific Fleet commander supported the Marines and recommended the battleships be retained. Admiral Holloway, the CNO and a former captain of the *Iowa*, agreed and the *Iowa*s remained.

The Carter Administration witnessed a very serious erosion of United States naval power. The outlook in 1979 was, in general, discouraging. As the US Navy was declining, the Soviet Navy was increasing significantly in size, technology and in overall capabilities. Two *Kiev* class aircraft carriers were in commission, two more were under construction and intelligence indicated that a nuclear carrier almost the size of the *Nimitz* class was soon to be laid down. Another alarming situation was that the Soviets would soon have a nuclear battlecruiser operational—another was on the ways and two more were about to be laid down. Except for carriers, they were the largest surface vessels to be built by any country since World War II. They were heavily armed with a variety of ballistic, anti-air and cruise type missiles and could make at least 32 knots. They, indeed, had a long-range strike capability. The Soviet Navy already had a very formidable submarine fleet and, for the first time, it appeared that they would now soon be capable of offensive operations in the air and on the surface as well.

Since the *Iowa*s seemed to always survive attempts at disposal, it could be reasoned that the four *Kirov*s were conceived and built to counter the known potential of the four *Iowa*s. The *Kirov*s appear to be comparable to the *Iowa*s except for the latter's 16in gun capabilities and the protection afforded by the heavy armor. Certainly the *Kirov*s

The first of the *Iowa*s selected to be modernized was the *New Jersey*. She was in the best material condition because of her 1968 reconditioning. The *New Jersey*, photographed in July 1981, being towed to the Long Beach Naval Shipyard where she was modernized and recommissioned.

As military operations in Vietnam escalated, the need for heavy gunfire support increased proportionally. Since at least 80 per cent of all naval targets were within 16in range, it was decided that the *New Jersey* should be activated. These two photographs of the *New Jersey*, taken in Delaware Bay during trials on 26 March 1968, show the full extent of modifications incorporated for her Vietnam deployment. The addition of new electronics and communications equipment are the most noticeable differences in her appearance.

gave the Soviet Navy a major projection of power in forward areas.

By mid-1979, there was strong interest in the Navy and the Congress to modernize and recommission all four of the *Iowas*. The matter first received public attention through the efforts of Charles E. Myers, Jr., a defense consultant/analyst and former pilot. President Carter was totally opposed to the idea. As support for the battleship gathered momentum, he ordered all naval personnel to cease lobbying for it. Next, the Congress was put on notice that the President would become personally involved in defeating any legislation in favor of reactivating the battleships. In fairness to the President, however, he may have been concerned that the battleships, employing current technologies, would have a negative impact with the Soviets on various arms control issues. In any case, the battleship remained an important asset which could have a destabilizing effect on the balance of power if modernized using 1980s technologies.

Fortune had turned against the Carter Administration by late-

The *New Jersey*'s activation for Vietnam service was surrounded by internal rivalry in the US Navy between the air and surface communities as well as political controversy at national level. In an effort to de-escalate the war the Administration ordered the *New Jersey* de-activated after only one deployment in the war zone. In December 1969, she was decommissioned and placed in the reserve fleet at Bremerton, Washington. She is shown here in July 1981 moored across the pier from the *Missouri*.

With about half of the topside work completed, the *New Jersey* is in drydock in March 1982 for reconditioning and painting her hull, shafting and rudders. Note the two *Spruance* class destroyers in the background.

1979. The Soviets invaded Afghanistan and Iranian revolutionaries siezed the US Embassy in Tehran. The US Navy had by this time declined to the point where it was gradually losing its fighting superiority to the Soviet fleet. Finally, the CNO broke ranks with the Administration and briefed members of the Congress on a proposal to reactivate a battleship and a carrier for an interim fix. There was also strong concern within the Congress and legislation was introduced to fund the modernization of one battleship. Still opposed to the battleship initiative, the Administration was able to block legislation for their revival until the Reagan Administration took over.

The new Administration viewed the reactivation and modernization of the battleships as a quick and inexpensive way to reverse the imbalance between the United States and Soviet navies. There was still, however, a tough battle within the Congress to fund the modernization of the *Iowa*s. The cause this time was championed by the new Secretary of the Navy, John F. Lehman, Jr., a Naval Reserve aviator. Aside from the practical, and sometimes emotional, debates[7] in the Congress, the arguments for modernizing the battleships were compelling. The cost to modernize the *New Jersey* was $326 million— about that for a new frigate. While she would cost more to operate than a frigate, there would be no comparison in terms of offensive capabilities and survivability (see Chapter 10).

7 Again, detailed accounts are not given since they are adequately covered in footnote 5 (above) and an excellent synopsis is also given in the article, 'The Iowa Class: Needed Once Again', Howard W. Serig, Jr., Proceedings/Naval Review 1982, *US Naval Institute Proceedings.*

Nearing the end of her modernization, the *Iowa* in January 1984. Changes in the superstructure area to accommodate the Tomahawk and Harpoon weapons systems are clearly visible. Note the ramps and landing platform on the fantail.

On 25 September 1982 the *New Jersey* is eased out into the channel from her berth at the Long Beach Naval Shipyard. She is about to get underway for sea trials. This was the first time she had moved under her own power in twelve years.

Opposite: The *Iowa* was the next one of the class to be modernized. In January 1983, work on the *Iowa* was progressing well. She is moored to the large outfitting pier at Ingalls Shipbuilding. On the next pier over, the destroyer *Hayler* (DD 997) is nearing completion. Note the plywood covering on the decks to protect the teak decking from damage during renovation.

Because of their experience with modernizing the *New Jersey*, and the excellent quality of their work, the Long Beach Naval Shipyard was selected to modernize the *Missouri*. Work on the forward fire control tower was extensive, as shown here in January 1985, because of the installation of electronic warfare equipment.

The last to be modernized was the *Wisconsin*. She is being docked here, at the large outfitting pier at Ingalls Shipbuilding, on 5 January 1987. The destroyer at the opposite side of the pier is the *Spruance* (DD 963) being refitted with the Mark 41 VLS (Vertical Launch System).

This was all part of a new naval strategy. The Administration saw the battleship battle group as a means of reinforcing carrier battle groups in high-threat areas. They would be able to engage the Soviets in their home waters and attack inland targets with long-range cruise missiles, risking fewer manned aircraft assets. In areas of lesser threat they could operate independently replacing a carrier battle group which could be employed more effectively elsewhere. As outlined by Secretary Lehman and reported in *US News and World Report*: 'Our naval strategy is to go back into the high-threat areas, the Persian Gulf, Eastern Mediterranean, North Atlantic, and defeat the best the Soviets can throw at us. The battleship can increase our firepower and bolster our ability to keep fighting. That's what high-threat warfare is all about.' Clearly, the US Navy intended 'to go in harm's way'.

Appropriations to begin work on the *New Jersey* were included in the Fiscal Year 1981 supplemental budget and work on the vessel began in Spring 1982. Funds to complete the *New Jersey*, along with long-lead money for the *Iowa*, was provided in Fiscal Year 1982. The balance of the *Iowa* funds came in Fiscal Year 1983. Modernization of the *Missouri* and *Wisconsin* was similarly funded in Fiscal Years 1984–87.

The *New Jersey* was in the best material state of the four battleships

By 17 September 1987, work was well along on the *Wisconsin*. Beneath the labyrinth of electrical lines, welding leads, air hoses, ventilation ducts and scaffolding, a new look begins to take shape. Note the protective covering over the teak deck.

The *Missouri* was the next of the *Iowa*s to be brought back on line. She is eased from her berth at Puget Sound in May 1984, where she had been for nearly thirty years, to begin the tow to Long Beach where she was modernized.

Below: All hands are manning the rail as the *New Jersey* enters Pearl Harbor on 24 May 1986. Ford Island and the quays for 'battleship row' are to the left and she is preparing to render honors to the battleship *Arizona* (BB 39) which was sunk 7 December 1941. The white memorial straddles the remains of the *Arizona*, but portions of the wreckage are visible below as are the side plates for Turret No. II. The flag is actually flying from the wreckage.

Above: The *Iowa* presents a sleek new appearance after the completion of her modernization. Shown here on 9 March 1984, in the Gulf of Mexico during builder's trials, she was recommissioned on 28 April 1984 after being in the reserve fleet for over twenty-five years.

The launching of the *Iowa* at the New York Navy Yard on 27 August 1942.

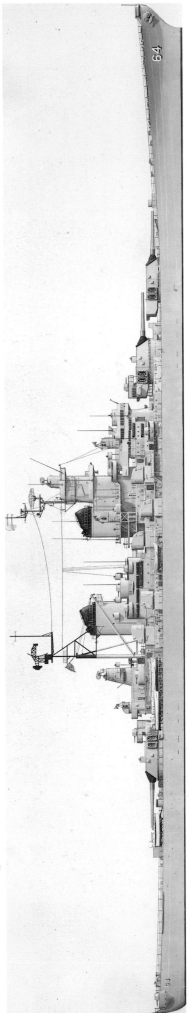

USS *Wisconsin* (BB 64) – as outfitted early-1952 and painted in standard haze gray. (Rendering by Paul Bender.)

USS *New Jersey* (BB 62) – as outfitted mid-1968 and painted in standard haze gray. (Rendering by Paul Bender.)

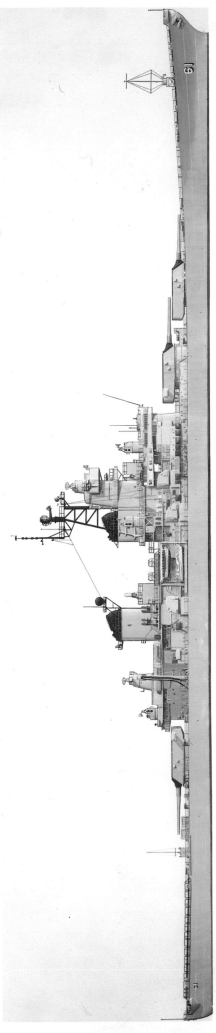

USS *Iowa* (BB 61) – as outfitted mid-1987 and painted in standard haze gray. (Rendering by Paul Bender.)

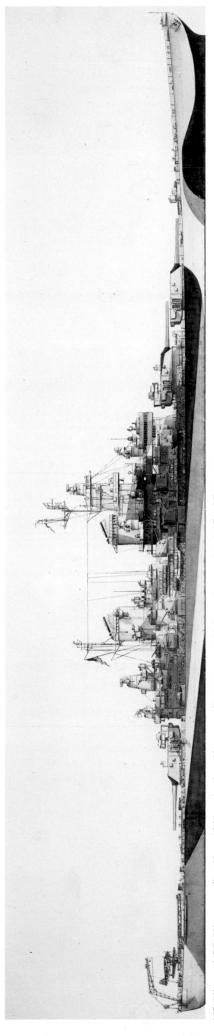

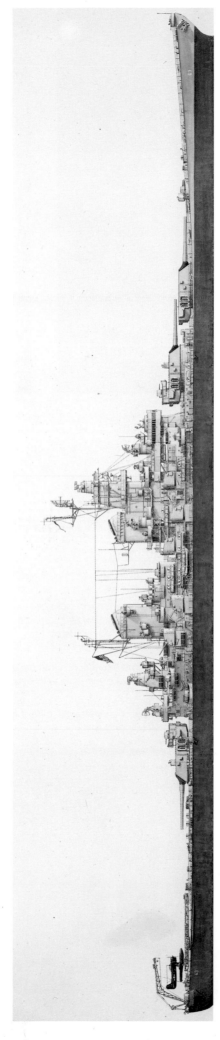

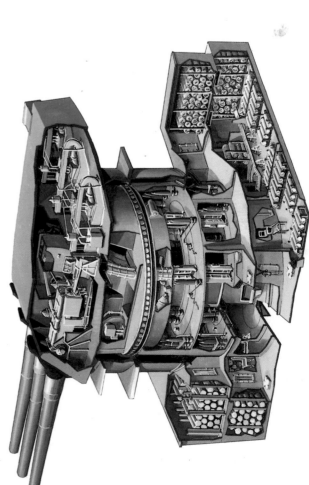

US *Missouri* (BB 63) – as outfitted late-1944 and painted in camouflage measure 32-D 22. (Rendering by Paul Bender.)

USS *Missouri* (BB 63) – as outfitted mid-1945 and painted in camouflage measure 22. (Rendering by Paul Bender.)

A cut-away of a 16in 3-gun turret showing the shell handling flats and powder magazines. (Rendering by Paul Bender.)

A cut-away of the Mark 28, 5in twin gun mount as installed in the *Iowa* class. (Rendering by Paul Bender.)

The *Iowa* outfitting at the New York Navy Yard in about October 1942.

The *Iowa* blows soot from the uptakes of her after stack during her shakedown cruise in May 1943.

The *Missouri* displays the distinctive bow of the *Iowa* class during her shakedown cruise in August 1944. Note the disruptive effect of the Measure 32, Design 22 D camouflage.

Tugs ease the *Missouri* into the East River at the New York Navy Yard to depart on her shakedown cruise in August 1944.

The *Missouri* fires a salvo from her forward turrets during her shakedown cruise in August 1944.

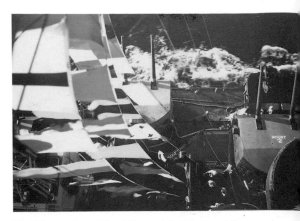

Signalmen aboard the *Missouri* air the signal flags and pennants while underway in August 1944.

The *New Jersey* with the frigate *Meyerkord* (FF 1058), one of the ships in her battle group, during maneuvers off the coast of California.

An OS2U-3 Kingfisher observation aircraft is readied for launching from the starboard catapult of the *Missouri* in August 1944.

The *Wisconsin* is being refueled from the tanker *Cahaba* (AO 82) in early-1945. The photograph was taken from an *Essex* class carrier which is also being refueled.

The battleship *New Jersey* fires a 16in broadside at a target near Beirut, Lebanon, on 9 January 1984.

A conventional Tomahawk land attack cruise missile is launched from the *New Jersey* off the coast of Southern California on 10 May 1983. The missile will travel nearly 500nm to a target in the Nevada Desert.

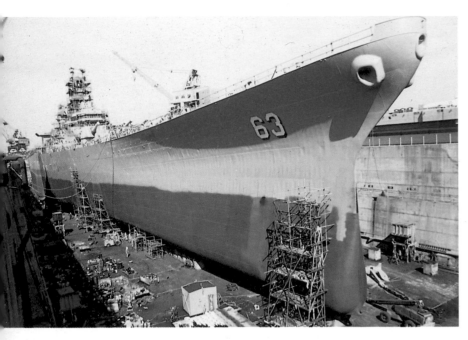

The *Missouri* in drydock at the Long Beach Naval Shipyard in 1985 during the final stages of her modernization.

The modernization of the *Iowa* well underway at Ingalls Shipyard in October 1983.

The *New Jersey* was reactivated in 1968 and is photographed here steaming off the coast of Vietnam during her deployment to the war zone.

The *Missouri* passes under the Golden Gate Bridge on 10 May 1986 *en route* to her recommissioning at San Francisco. This was a proud day for the ship on which the Japanese surrender was signed and she approached the city with her call letters flying and the crew manning the rail. Note the color guard on top of Turret No. II.

because of her 1968 reconditioning and, therefore, was selected for the first modernization. The *Iowa, Missouri* and *Wisconsin* were to follow in that order. Many items that could be repaired and refurbished on the *New Jersey* would have to be included in the modernization of the other three. The modernization would feature updating the weapons, sensors, countermeasures and supporting systems to bring the battleships up to fleet standards.

Design feasibility studies for installation of the modernization features began in February 1981 and, by July, the *New Jersey* was being surveyed compartment by compartment, component by component. This design ship check was to verify the actual ship against the information and assumptions used in the feasibility study. The survey was made by specialists and experts from the Navy and private industry. This effort was coordinated by the Surface Combatant Design Directorate (Nav Sea 03D) to facilitate the completion of contract drawings and specifications. The primary modernization features are outlined below.

Surface warfare capabilities were to be significantly increased. New weapon systems would include thirty-two long-range Tomahawk cruise missiles in armored box launchers, sixteen medium-range Harpoon cruise missiles in armored canister launchers and four CIWS gatling guns for defense against airborne attack (see Chapter 5). Sensor capabilities were updated to include the 2-D, SPS-49 long-range air search radar, the SPS-10 or SPS-67 surface search radar, a cruiser size communications suite with NTDS LINK 11 receiver for Tomahawk control and LINK 14 for receipt of tactical data (see Chapter 7). New ECM equipment consisted of the SLQ-32 (V) 3 ECM system, eight Mark 137 SRBOC chaff launchers and the SLQ NIXIE torpedo defense system. Supporting systems updated included converting the boilers to burn Diesel Fuel Marine (DFM), the installation of a sewage collection, holding and transfer (CHT) system and the provision for 400 Hz power.

The design feasibility studies included a number of options such as installation of fleet flag facilities, a NATO Sea Sparrow missile system, digital fire control, full NTDS LINK 11 capabilities, a ship signature exploitation system, fragment path barriers and upgrading the propulsion system. None of these features were planned for the original modernization but any of them could very well be incorporated in the vessels during future major refits.

Chapter 5

ARMAMENT

A warship serves as a platform to carry its armament into combat. It exists for no other reason. As a type, the battleship was intended for offensive operations against other battleships and was designed to carry the heaviest of guns. Secondary and anti-aircraft guns were also provided as a defense against attacking destroyers and aircraft. The armament of the *Iowa* class is arguably the finest ever conceived and produced. The guns, their mountings and operating machinery were fashioned into a complex and sophisticated weapons system which, after nearly half a century, is still the finest of its type afloat.

MAIN BATTERY

The main armament of the *Iowa* class is the 16in/50cal Mark 7 gun. The *Iowas* are the only battleships to mount this new weapon which is a considerable improvement over the 16in/45cal guns mounted in the

North Carolina and *South Dakota* classes.

During the early-1938 studies which led to the *Iowa* class, the General Board seriously considered using the 18in/47cal gun developed by the Bu Ord during the 1920s.[1] Although it did present some advantages, especially the penetration of plunging fire at extended ranges, the 16in/50cal was considered an all-round better weapon. Also, the design would have had to grow considerably, and the new 45,000 ton weight limit was taken seriously in the *Iowa* design.

The 16in/50cal gun

The Mark 7 gun fires two basic rounds; a 2,700 pound AP (Armor Piercing) and a 1,900 pound HC (High Capacity) shore bombardment projectile. Nine of these weapons are mounted in three 3-gun turrets. They are designated 3-gun turrets, as opposed to triple turrets, because each gun is mounted on an individual slide with its own elevation drive. A triple turret has a single slide providing bearing surfaces for all three guns and uses a common elevation drive. Two turrets are located forward and one aft of the superstructure.

The gun is a lightweight, built-up type consisting of a liner, tube, jacket, hoops, locking rings, a liner locking ring and a yoke ring. Assembly is accomplished by heating and expanding each piece before sliding it into position over the tube. When the components cool and shrink, a tight single unit is formed. The liner is inserted from the

1 If the 18in caliber had been selected, a new lightweight 48cal or 50cal gun would have been built. The 18in/47cal Mark A, formerly the 18in/48cal Mark 1, equates in time and technology to the 16in/50cal Mark II, predecessor to the 16in/50cal Mark 7. A new 18in gun would have mirrored the 16in/50cal Mark 7 design techniques with a 2,500ft/sec initial velocity for the 3,850 pound AP projectile rather than the 2,400ft/sec initial velocity as in the 18in/47cal Mark A.

The forward main battery guns of the *Iowa* at near full elevation on station off Central America, 27 February 1985. The 16in/50cal Mark 7 gun is arguably the finest heavy weapon ever used at sea.

Opposite page: A battleship is designed as a platform to carry its armament into combat. This is most graphically depicted by the *Iowa* firing a broadside to starboard during gunnery exercises on 15 August 1984. The main battery guns are timed to fire microseconds apart and some of the guns can be seen in various positions of recoil. Note the smoke rings from the 5in battery.

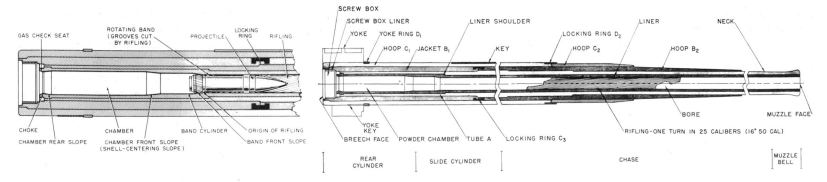

The cross-section (*above right*) shows the general arrangement, assembly and details of construction of a typical 16in/50cal Mark 7 gun. The cross-section (*above left*) shows the details of the breech and chamber of the 16in/50cal Mark 7 gun with a projectile seated.

Right: A 16in/50cal Mark 7 gun assembly, shown mounted in an individual Mark 6 slide assembly with the Mark 4 breech mechanism.

breech end, while in an electric shrink pit, and its locking ring prevents expansion aft when the gun is fired. The liner is rifled with ninety-six grooves, 0.15in deep, with a uniform right-hand twist of one turn in twenty-five calibers.

Each gun is mounted in an individual slide with its own elevating gear. The gun assembly includes a breech mechanism, firing lock, gas ejector and yoke. It is designed for removal from the slide and gun port without dismantling the turret. The breech mechanism is a rotating Welin interrupted screw plug and Smith–Asbury swinging carrier type. The screw box liner and breech plug are segmented with stepped screw threads arranged in fifteen sectors of 24 degrees each. The first sector is blank followed by four threaded sectors and this pattern is repeated three times for a total of twelve threaded and three blank sectors. The breech plug is locked with a 24 degree rotation after the plug threads are engaged. The firing lock receives a hand-inserted plug-like brass cartridge about the size of a 30cal

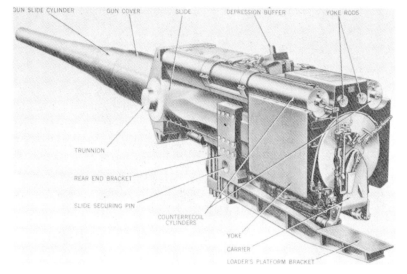

Opposite: The *Missouri* was regunned in January 1954 at the Norfolk Navy Yard. The right gun from Turret No. II has just been removed. The 16in/50cal Mark 7 gun is designed for removal from the slide and through the gun port, without dismantling the turret.

A 16in/50cal Mark 7 gun, with sleeve and yoke, is placed on a barge at the Philadelphia Navy Yard on 14 January 1944. The barge was to be towed to the *Wisconsin*, in a nearby outfitting basin, for installation. Lettering just forward of the trunion indicates it is the center gun for Turret No. III.

The 16in Mark 4 breech mechanism is shown in the open and closed position. The breech mechanism is a rotating Welin, interrupted screw plug and a Smith-Asbury, swinging carrier type. The screw box liner and breech plug are segmented with stepped screw threads arranged in fifteen sectors of 24 degrees each.

The nine gun assemblies are mounted in three turrets, all on the centerline with arcs of train providing fire concentration of nine guns on either beam, six guns forward and three guns aft. The three turret assemblies are very similar in design and construction, the main difference being in the depth of their structures. Each consists of a gun house with rotating structure, a fixed structure, a barbette, magazines and associated equipment.

The gun house is the armored portion of the rotating structure

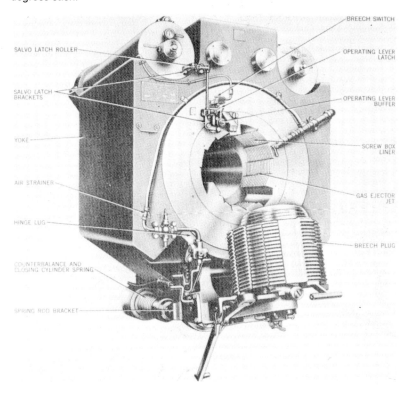

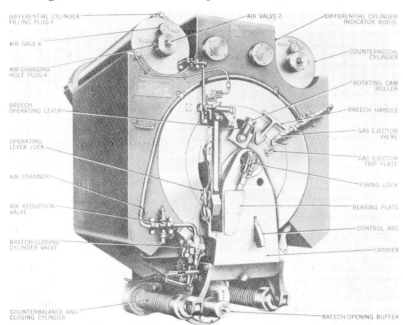

carbine shell loaded with FFG black powder. There is a provision for electric or percussion firing of the primer when the breech is closed. When the breech is opened after firing the bore is cleared automatically by 175 psi low-pressure air from the gas ejector system. The gun yoke is a large counterbalancing unit mounted on the gun shoulder providing seats for the recoil cylinder piston rod and counter recoil cylinder yoke rods.

extending above the barbette. The individual gun and slide assemblies, the two sight stations and the rangefinder's station are each located in separate flameproofed compartments in the gun house. The gun pit and the machinery flat extend below the shelf plate of the gun house and the upper roller track is attached to the underside of the gun pit pan plate.

A central column extends from the machinery flat down to the base

of the turret foundation and supports the rotating upper and lower projectile handling flats or shell decks. Each handling flat level has its own machinery for moving the projectiles. This machinery is located inside a circular bulkhead attached to the central column.

The fixed circular foundation bulkhead, or stool, supports the rotating elements of the gun house from the roller bearings on the lower roller track. Each gun house rests on seventy-two coned roller bearings of the following dimensions: 22.7in long across flanges, 17.58in length of path contact, 14.25in diameter at inner flange, 15.19in diameter at outer flange and 546 pounds weight apiece. The lower roller track is on the top surface of the training circle assembly which is an internally toothed annular rack. Twin pinions in the gun house machinery flat, located inside the training circle, engage the rack to train the turret. The fixed upper and lower handling flats, or shell decks, are supported from the stool sides.

Turret II is mounted one deck higher than Turrets I and III and is provided with another fixed handling flat below the upper and lower handling flats. Projectiles are carried stored on the fixed (outer) and rotating (inner) handling flats. The powder handling room for each turret is at the base of its stool adjacent to the magazines.

There is a weather seal between the gun house and the barbette, but the gun house is not supported by, nor does it rotate on the barbette.

Each turret can be trained at the rate of 4 degrees per second, and the guns can be elevated together or individually to 45 degrees at the rate of 12 degrees per second. The guns can be depressed 5 degrees.

The gun captain of a 16in/50cal Mark 7 gun is shown opening the breech. Segments of the interrupted, stepped screw threads of the screw box liner and breech plug are clearly visible. The powder hoist door is on the bulkhead at the left. Photographed aboard the *Wisconsin* in about 1952.

A longitudinal section at the centreline looking to the left side of Turret No. I showing the general arrangement of the fixed and rotating parts of the structure.

A transverse section forward of the transverse bulkhead looking to the face in Turret No. I showing the general arrangement of the fixed and rotating parts of the structure.

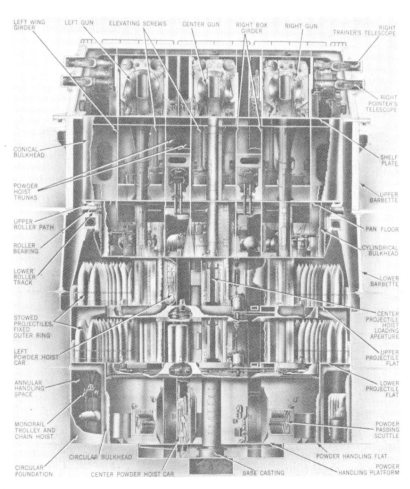

Above: The upper rotating assembly for Turret No. II of the *New Jersey* is lowered onto a barge from the turret shop of the Philadelphia Navy Yard on 12 January 1942. The barge will take the assembly to the pier where the ship is outfitting. The two openings in the front of the machinery flat bulkhead are for the training pinions which engage the training rack. Note the deck lugs for the trunions of the gun slides on the gun house shelf plate.

Above right: The upper rotating assembly, consisting of the gun house, gun pit and machinery flat, for the *New Jersey*'s Turret No. II is lowered into the barbette.

Below: Looking down on the upper handling flat, or shell deck, on the *New Jersey* just prior to the installation of the gun house. Some of the seventy-two coned rollers on the lower roller track can be seen beneath the canvas cover. The annular, internal teeth are the training rack portion of the training circle assembly. The two cone-shaped pieces forward are the stops for the training buffers. Note the central column and power hoist trunks in the center compartment. The round segments leaning against the foundation bulkhead, or stool, are holding-down clips which will be bolted to the bottom of the machinery flat after the upper rotating assembly is in place. They act against the lower surface of the training circle assembly preventing the turret from upsetting.

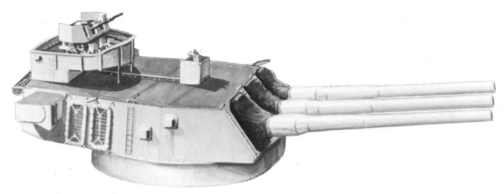

The 16in 3-gun Turret No. III of the *Iowa* class as it appeared during World War II with a quadruple 40mm mount and Mark 51 director mounted on the roof. (Rendering by Paul Bender.)

Left: The upper rotating assembly for Turret No. II of the *New Jersey* is nearly in place on the roller track. The gun house transverse bulkhead is in place and is supporting the 0.75in STS side armor backing plates. Note the gun girders in the center and on the outboard sides of the gun house. The mounting brackets for the rangefinder will be carried by the supports angled from the center gun girders to the top of the outboard gun girders.

These are transverse sections at the turret officer's booth. The top view is looking forward to the transverse bulkhead and the bottom view is looking aft to the rangefinder.

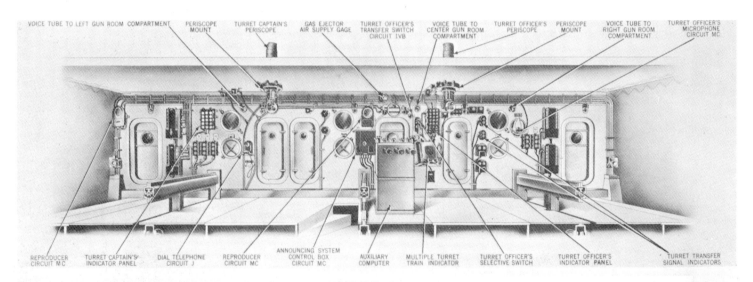

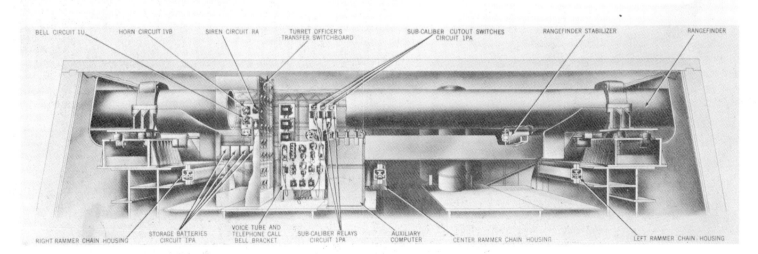

Loading is at a fixed angle of 5 degrees elevation. The guns are capable of firing at a rate of two rounds per minute, with a firing cycle of 1.3 seconds for the gun to recoil and return to battery.

The 16in projectiles

The 16in/50cal Mark 7 gun uses two basic rounds, the 2,700 pound AP and the 1,900 pound HC projectiles. The gun was originally designed to use the 2,240 pound AP projectile and when the 2,700 pound AP shell was adopted in mid-1939, some range (4,500 yards) was sacrificed. The new shell, however, has considerably more striking power and also operates at a lower muzzle velocity, which reduces liner erosion prolonging the life of the gun. The 1,900 pound HC projectile (originally the EX–1) was introduced in late-1942.

The 2,700 pound Mark 8 AP projectile uses the Mark 21 Base Detonating Fuze (BDF) 0.033sec delay and has a 1.5 per cent bursting charge. Fuze activation requires a resistance equal to 1.5in of armor at 0 degrees obliquity or 0.375in at 65 degrees obliquity. A full charge of powder (660 pounds) gives the projectile a muzzle velocity of 2,500ft/sec. A special charge giving a muzzle velocity of 2,300ft/sec and a reduced charge giving a muzzle velocity of 1,800ft/sec can also be used. The special charge has a steeper angle of fall with a trajectory similar to the 16in/45cal gun. The effects of the smaller charges used against an armored surface target would be to shrink the target's immune zone at the outer end and to enhance defilade (reverse slope) capabilities against land targets. The smaller charges are also substantially less erosive to the rifled bore and can be used for very low dispersion shooting at reduced ranges.

The standard 1,900 pound Mark 13 HC projectile can be fuzed with either the Mark 29 Point Detonating Fuze (PDF) or the Mark 48 BDF

This photograph was taken inside Turret No. I of the *Iowa* in May 1943, looking to the right-hand side of the gun house. The transverse bulkhead is at the left, and the Mark 53 coincidence type rangefinder is to the right. The turret officer is sitting on the enclosed rammer for the center gun. The right-hand turret periscope, in the overhead beyond the turret officer is manned, the left-hand periscope is not. Note the J-type rotary switches on the turret fire control switchboard behind the phone talker.

The face plates of the forward turrets of the *Iowa* photographed in 1951 after she was activated for Korean service. The face plates are 17in Class B armor over 2.5in STS backing plates which have the resistance equivalent to a single plate 18.75in thick. The gun bucklers have been removed to clean the gun ports. The gun shield plates are clearly visible and the bucklers, extension tubes and clamping bands can be seen on the gun house roof.

Below right: Battleships were originally intended to fire armor-piercing projectiles at other battleships and surface ships. In this photograph, in about 1985, projectiles have just been stacked on the *Iowa*'s deck and are waiting to be uncrated and struck down. In the foreground is a 2,700 pound Mark 9 target projectile with its rotating band exposed. Behind it is a 2,700 pound Mark 8 AP round. The projectile at the far right with the diamond coding on the ogive is a 1,880 pound Mark 144 ICM round. (Courtesy FCCM (SW) Stephen Skelley, USNR.)

The rear of Turret No. III of the *Iowa* photographed in July 1943 after her post-shakedown overhaul. Note the cast armor enclosure for the rangefinder and the ventilation ducts and access hatch underneath the gun house. The back plates of the gun house are 12in Class A armor and the roof plates are 7.25in Class B armor.

Above center: The 16in Mark 23 atomic shell was developed in the early-1950s for use with the 16in/50cal Mark 7 gun. The shell weight was 1,900 pounds and the body appears to be similar to the Mark 13. The warhead was designated W 23 and had a yield in the kiloton range. The shell was stockpiled between 1956 and 1961. This is one of the shells which is now at the National Atomic Museum. (Courtesy the Department of Energy.)

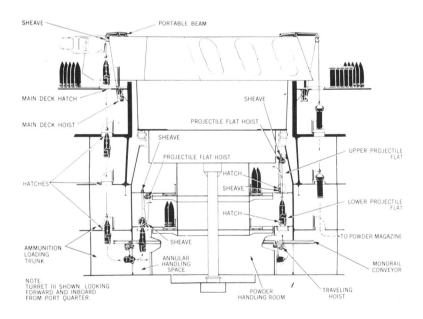

A diagrammatic drawing of the ammunition handling, transfer and stowage system in the turret.

(0.15sec delay) and has a 8.1 per cent bursting charge. A full charge of powder gives the shell a muzzle velocity of 2,690ft/sec. There are two special Mark 13 HC service rounds, both using steel nose plugs. The first round is the HC/PD minus the Mark 29 PDF with a Mark 55 Auxiliary Detonation Fuze (ADF) remaining and a Mark 48 BDF. The second uses a Mark 21 BDF. Another service round is the Mark 13 HE

(High Explosive) which is fuzed with a M564 Mechanical Time Fuze (MTF) which has a 100sec capability. This shell was a Vietnam War replacement for the Mark 13 projectile with a Mark 62 45sec time fuze (Navy). Few, if any M564 fuzed projectiles still exist, having been replaced by the Mark 143 HE/CVT and Mark 145 HE/ET projectiles.

There are four new special purpose 1,900 pound projectiles now in service which use the Mark 13 body. The Mark 143 HE uses the Army M732 Controlled Variable Time (CVT, or proximity fuze). The Mark 144 Improved Conventional Munition (ICM) is fuzed by the M724 Electronic Time Fuze (ETF) and dispenses 400 M43A1 wedge grenades. The Mark 145 HE uses the M724 ETF, and the MK 146 ICM uses the M724 ETF to dispense 666 shaped charge bomblets.

A new extended range projectile is in the developmental stage. It is a 13in (approximate) spin-stabilized round with a sabot adapting it to the 16in bore. After the shell exits the muzzle, the sabot is discarded. The flight weight of the shell is 1,000 pounds and when fired with a full charge of powder has a muzzle velocity of over 3,600ft/sec and has an anticipated range in excess of 70,000 yards.

During the early-1950s a 16in nuclear projectile was developed and tested at the Los Alamos range. The projectile was designated Mark 23 and the warhead W23. It weighed 1,900 pounds and measured 5ft 4in in length. The body appears to have been similar to, or possibly was, a modified Mark 13. The W23 warhead had a yield in the kiloton range and was designed as a low air-burst munition. A practice round, the Mark 24, and a drill projectile were also produced. The stockpile entry was in 1956 and the retirement was in 1961.

Most of the projectiles are stored on the fixed and rotating rings of

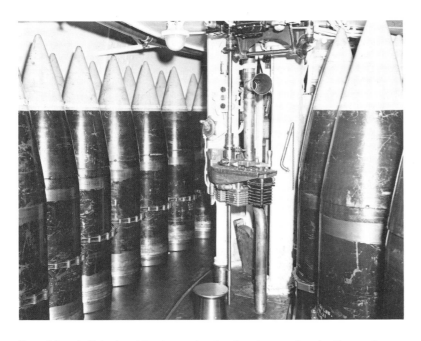

One of the shell decks of the *Iowa*, showing the storage of projectiles on the outer (fixed) and inner (rotating) shell flats. The projectiles are moved by a parbuckling system of power driven capstans, one of which can be seen on the deck. The projectiles are the 1,900 pound Mark 13 HC which were new when this photograph was taken in May 1943.

A drill dummy of the new sub-caliber extended range projectile is being struck down to one of the Turret No. III shell decks on the *Iowa* in the fall of 1986. This practice dummy is used to determine clearances and compatibility with the projectile handling and transfer system. The projectile is still in the developmental stage and is expected to have a range well in excess of 70,000 yards. (Courtesy FCCM (SW) Stephen Skelley, USNR.)

the upper and lower shell flats in the turrets. Each storage flat is sub-divided into three concentric rings. The outer, or fixed, ring is attached to the stool. The center ring, or shell-handling platform, is part of the rotating structure and contains the three projectile hoists in its after portion. It also mounts the parbuckling gear for moving the projectiles and no projectiles are stored on this ring. The inner, or rotating, ring is a power-driven platform resting on rollers which can be rotated in either direction. It is also supported by the rotating structure. The machinery for operating the shell flats and parbuckling gear, as previously mentioned, is located within the circular bulkhead around the central column.

All projectiles are stowed erect on their base and each is separately lashed to the adjacent fixed or rotating bulkhead. The projectiles are moved from the fixed and rotating rings onto the handling platform by a parbuckling system of power-driven capstans. In this arrangement, all three projectile hoists can be served simultaneously. Nominal storage per turret is: Turret I, 390 rounds; Turret II, 460 rounds; Turret III, 370 rounds. Allowance is made for nine drill projectiles per turret.

There are presently twenty 16in powder magazines serving the three turrets: six for Turret I; eight for Turret II; and six for Turret III. There are powder scuttles in the magazines for feeding the powder flats. Turret I has four scuttles and Turrets II and III each have six scuttles. Each turret has three dumbwaiter powder hoists which

Cross-section showing the general arrangment and details of the Mark 8 16in projectile hoist.

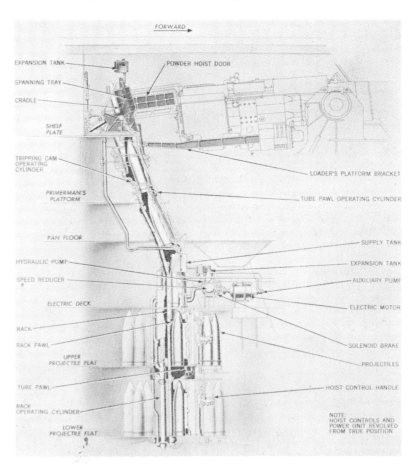

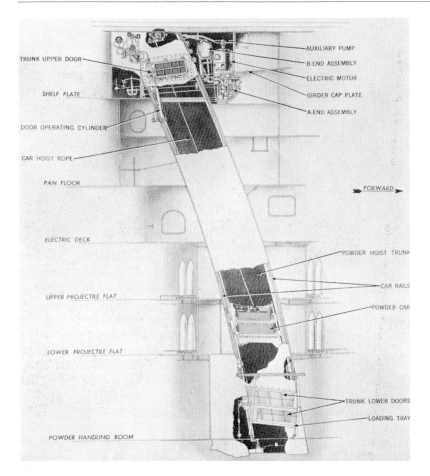

Above: A bag of SPD power is placed on the loading tray of the powder hoist in the powder handling room of Turret No. II aboard the *Iowa* in May 1943. The ignition pad is on the opposite end of the bag from the handling strap. The weight of the bag is 110 pounds and six bags make up a full charge of 660 pounds.

Cross-section showing the general arrangement and details of the Mark 9 16in powder hoist.

Cross-section showing the general arrangement and details of the Mark 5 16in rammer.

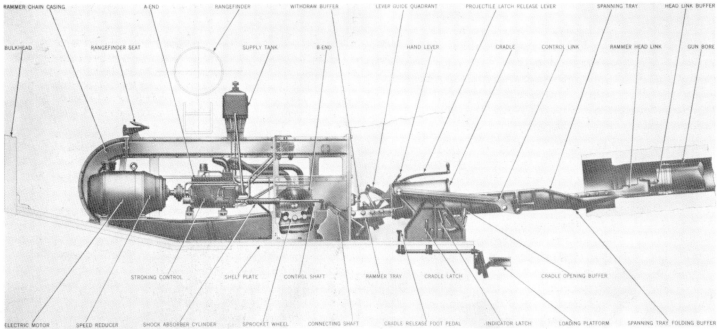

move the powder bags from the first platform to the second platform magazines.

Projectiles may be transferred between turrets via 'Broadway', the main fore-and-aft passageway on the third deck. The shells are moved on an overhead monorail from Turret I to Turret II, around the starboard side of Turret II to 'Broadway', and then aft to Turret III. The rail is attached to the underside of the splinter deck and is entirely within the armor citadel. Removable portions of the rail allow transverse watertight closures to be made when projectiles are not being moved.

The 16in propellant

The 16in guns are termed 'bag guns', meaning that the propellant charge is contained in bags which are loaded separately from the projectiles. The guns require a large amount of powder for the projectile to attain its required initial velocity. If the powder was placed in a single container, the size and weight would make loading difficult and slow and would greatly complicate the powder-handling machinery. By breaking up the charge into sections and packing the powder grains in fabric bags, the sections can be easily handled by the

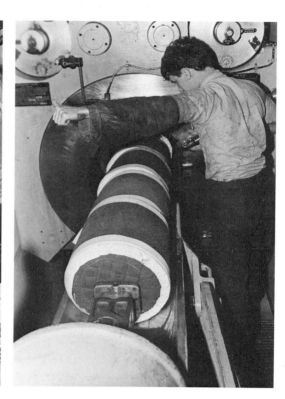

turret crew.

The powder bag is usually made of silk so that it will completely burn away leaving no smoldering embers when the charge is ignited. Rayon will shortly be introduced for use with reduced charges and later with full charges. As mentioned above, the gas ejection system automatically clears the bore after firing as a safety precaution. The powder can be loaded by either stacking or dumping the grains into the bag. In a stacked charge the powder grains are arranged in layers with their axis parallel to that of the bag. In an unstacked charge the powder grains are dumped into the bag randomly without regard for positioning of the individual grains. The bags are cylindrical and are provided with handling straps and lacings to take up any slack in the bag. An ignition pad containing black powder is fitted to the back of the bag. The pad is quilted to the bag to spread the black powder evenly insuring instant ignition between bags, and is usually painted red to ensure proper alignment of the charge.

Smokeless powder is the propellant used in propelling charges for the 16in guns. Designated SP, smokeless powder is a uniform ether-alcohol colloid of purified nitrocellulose. A quantity of diphenylamine or eithyl centralite is added for stability. Other additives are used to obtain suitable form, burning character and stability.

An understanding of the basic methods used to manufacture smokeless powder is useful at this point. While no means complete, this is intended to give the reader a rudimentary background in the production of smokeless powder for the US Navy.

Nitrated cotton is the primary ingredient in SP. Short-fibered cotton is bleached and purified to a point where it is 90 per cent pure cellulose. A mixture of ether and alcohol is used as a solvent for the cellulose and it is combined with one part nitric and three parts sulphuric acids for the nitrating process that converts the mixture into nitrocellulose, or 'pyro'. The spent acids are removed and the pyro is water purified after which it is pulped and dehydrated. Excess water is forced out with alcohol under hydraulic pressure. Enough alcohol is left in the resulting pyro cake to mix the desired colloid. The

These three photographs show the full sequence of loading the 16in/50cal Mark 7 gun. First, a projectile is brought up in the hoist to the spanning tray of the center gun of Turret No. II on the *Iowa*, 12 December 1986. The projectile is a 1,900 pound HC round. Note the folding action of the tray to bring the shell into alignment with the bore. When the tray reaches the fixed loading angle of 5 degrees the projectile is rammed and seated in the bore. This projectile is a 2,700 AP round being loaded into the right gun of Turret No. III on the *Iowa*, 23 November 1987. Last, the powder is placed in the tray and rammed into the chamber cavity. These six bags are being loaded into the center gun of Turret No. III behind a 1,900 pound HC round, on the *Iowa*, 23 November 1987. The powder bags are dressed in wear reducing, polyurethane foam jackets. Note the quilted ignition pad on the back of the last bag. (Courtesy FCCM (SW) Stephen Skelley, USNR.)

The protective coating deposited on the liner surface from the wear reducing jackets, as the powder burns, protects against erosion caused by hot gases. The effects of friction from the rotating band of the projectile, however, causes the liner to stretch and it distends from the end of the muzzle as shown here on the *Iowa* in 1987. (Courtesy FCCM (SW) Stephen Skelley, USNR.)

pyro cake is then broken up into a coarse, fluffy mass and ether and diphenylamine are added and thoroughly mixed. The resulting uniform colloid is then forced through the dies of the graining press, emerging as a continuous circular cord which is immediately cut to length by the grain cutters. The green powder is then dried and

original 16in/50cal powder and the ▓▓▓▓ powder. Both propellants are from ▓▓▓▓ inventory and have recently been remix▓▓▓ propellant is authorized for use with th▓ pound shells, but the D846 propellant is cur▓

MISSOURI

blended with other lots for proof firing, acceptance and indexing. The entire process can take as long as six months depending upon grain size. A grain of 16in powder is 2in long, 1in in diameter and has seven perforations 0.060in in diameter with a web thickness range of 0.193in to 0.197in (quickest to slowest) between perforations and the grain diameter.

There are two types of SP propellants in general use with full charges utilizing the 16in granulation. They are referred to by their Naval Ammunition Logistics Code/Department of Defense Inventory Code (NALC/DODIC)—D839 and D846. The D839 propellant is the

The secondary battery of the *Iowa* class uses the 5in/38cal Mark 12 gun in twin Mark 28 mountings. This dual purpose weapon can be used against surface, shore and anti-aircraft targets. The original anti-aircraft battery consisted of the 40mm gun in the Mark 2 quadruple mountings and the 20mm gun in the single Mark 4 mountings. All of the secondary battery and most of the anti-aircraft battery were concentrated amidships as shown in this photograph of the *Missouri*, taken in the Hudson River on 27 October 1945.

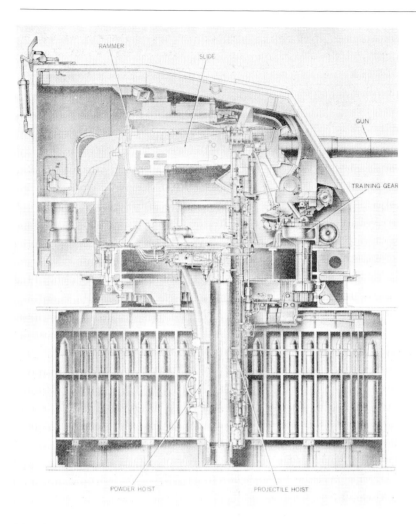

A longitudinal section at the centerline looking to the left side of a typical twin 5in/38cal Mark 28 gun mount showing the general arrangement and details of the mount.

The twin 5in/38cal gun mounts of the *Iowa* are being rehabilitated at the Philadelphia Navy Yard prior to the ship being towed to Ingalls Shipbuilding for modernization. The *Iowa* class was originally fitted with ten mounts but for the current modernization only six were retained: mounts No. 3, 4, 5, 6, 7 and 8. Note the mount numbers sprayed on the gun shield and the outboard bulkheads of the handling rooms directly below.

with the 1,900 pound shell only.

There are also two types of SP propellants in use with reduced charges utilizing an 8in granulation: D840 (reduced) and D845 (reduced flashless), both of which can be used with either the AP or HC rounds.

Smokeless powder is basically unstable because it contains nitrocellulose and three volatiles, ether, alcohol and water (water is considered a volatile because it promotes the deterioration of the propellant). Even though it is stored under special conditions it deteriorates in time and some of the volatiles are lost. This is especially true of the grains stored near the top of the storage tanks or stacked near the outside surfaces of the bags. The deterioration affects the muzzle velocity of the projectile producing erratic range and dispersion of the shot. For example, when the D839 propellant was first produced in the 1940s, the original acceptance standards were +/– 10 ft/sec deviation in initial velocity. The actual variation was less than +/– 5ft/sec with the 2,700 pound projectile. During the Korean War it was about +/– 14ft/sec with the 1,900 pound projectile. The *New Jersey*'s Vietnam deployment recorded about +/– 23ft/sec with the 1,900 pound shell and on station off of Lebanon during 1984 it was about +/– 32ft/sec using the 1,900 pound shell.

The condition of the powder was the main reason for the lacklustre gunnery performance of the *New Jersey* off of Lebanon in 1984. A comprehensive gunnery improvement program was undertaken by the Naval Surface Weapons Center, Dahlgren, Virginia, using the *Iowa*

for testing and evaluation. The program included reworking of the powder and installation of specialized monitoring equipment (see Chapter 6).

In order to reduce the variation in muzzle velocity, the 16in/45cal propellant, of 0.158 to 0.169in web thickness, is thoroughly remixed to distribute the varying grains evenly. Bulk propellant is remixed in sections of about 100,000 pounds. Then the sections are blended together, forming a lot of approximately 600,000 pounds. It is then bagged to a tolerance of 1/10 of a pound per bag, which amounts to two grains of propellant, and is fired in at least two guns for charge weight assessment. The resulting round-to-round muzzle velocity variation is very low. In regard to the D839 propellant, most lots still perform within the original acceptance standards of +/– 10ft/sec when used with the 2,700 pound projectile.[2]

---

2 The following are notes on pattern accuracy from a firing on 23 November 1987 by USS *Iowa* (BB 61) off Augonisil Island, Crete. A total of fifteen rounds were fired, five rounds from the right gun of each target. Measurement represents a mean for three gun salvos using photo analysis.

  Projectile – Mark 8 AP, 2,700 pound
  Propellant – D839 (SPD 10625)
  Range – 34,000 yards
  Pattern size – 219 yards (0.64 per cent of range)
  Round to round dispersion (standard deviation) – +/– 123 yards
  (0.36 per cent of range)

Overall, fourteen of the fifteen rounds plotted within +/– 250 yards of the target center and eight of the fifteen rounds plotted within +/– 150 yards of the target center. This is considered superb performance and the combination of the Mark 7 gun, Mark 8 projectile and D839 propellant has probably never been equalled.

The life of the gun is expressed in the number of Equivalent Service Rounds (ESR) that can be fired before the gun must be relined. Relining is necessary because of the erosion caused each time the gun is fired. Erosion is caused by the hot, high velocity gases ravaging the bore surface embrittling the liner and washing it away. The liner is also subject to the effects of friction from the rotating band of the projectile as it travels the length of the bore, causing it to distend. The distension must eventually be trimmed from the muzzle.

As designed, the life of the 16in/50cal Mark 7 gun was determined to be 290 ESR, based on the 2,700 pound projectile fired with a full charge producing a muzzle velocity of 2,500 ft/sec. When firing a lighter projectile and/or using lighter charges, the wear on the liner is reduced considerably.

Efforts to reduce liner erosion have resulted in the development of wear-reducing jackets. Two types are now in service: titanium dioxide and wax and polyurethane foam. Data on the titanium dioxide jacket indicate that wear from the 2,700 pound shell at a muzzle velocity of 2,500ft/sec would be 0.26 ESR. The polyurethane jacket is now in service. No hard data are available, but early indications are that it will reduce wear significantly more than the titanium dioxide jacket.

One wear-reducing jacket is used with each bag of the charge. The pocketed titanium dioxide and wax jacket is laced in place on the bag. The polyurethane foam jacket is simply a sheet of foam with a fabric border around the ends that is tied to the bag. When the round is fired, a protective layer is formed over the surface of the bore which significantly reduces gaseous erosion.

The wear reduction program has been so successful that the Fatigue Equivalent Rounds (FER) (fatigue life expressed in the number of mechanical cycles) is now the more important criteria rather than the ESR. The 16in/50cal Mark 7 gun is now considered to have a liner life of 1,500 FER.

SECONDARY BATTERY

The armament of the secondary battery is the double purpose 5in/38cal Mark 12 gun which can be used against surface, shore and aircraft targets. The guns are mounted in a twin arrangement completely enclosed in an armored shield which was first introduced with the *North Carolina* class. This mount became the standard secondary battery for all subsequent US Navy battleships. Many of the older battleships which were rebuilt during World War II were also fitted with this mount.

The 5in/38cal gun

The Mark 12 gun fires two basic rounds; an anti-aircraft Common (AAC) and an HE/HC surface and shore bombardment projectile. The round is semifixed with a 54 pound projectile and a 28 pound shell case, which includes a 15 pound powder charge. (Nominal weights are given—weights vary depending on the round combination.) The mounting is the Mark 28 twin gun mount, so designated because both guns use a common elevating gear and power drive.

The original battery consisted of twenty 5in guns in ten twin mounts. Two mounts were located on each side at the 01 Level and three were mounted on each side at the 02 Level. Because of the large superstructure, their arcs of fire were somewhat restricted and they were most effective against targets approaching abeam. The already crowded superstructure did not allow placing any 5in mounts on the centerline. During the current modernization, the battery was reduced by eight guns. The two aftermost mounts on the 02 level

This photograph, taken in 1985, shows 5in gun mount No. 8 aboard the *Iowa* after rehabilitation. The Mark 28 gun mount used a barbette, which is clearly visible, protecting the fixed stand for the mount. There is a weather seal at the top of the barbette but the gun house is not supported by, nor does it rotate on the barbette. Directly above the mount are the port side pair of quadruple Mark 141 ceramic armored Harpoon launchers. Above and to the left is one of the four Mark 15, 20mm Phalanx CIWS mounts. (Courtesy FCCM (SW) Stephen Skelley, USNR.)

were removed to make room for the addition of missile batteries.

In the Mark 28 twin gun mount, the right and left gun assemblies are identical except for the opposite-hand arrangement of the gun housings. The gun barrel is a radially expanded monoblock cone-piece of alloy steel. It is rifled with forty-five grooves and has a uniform right-hand twist of one turn in thirty calibers. The bore is chromium-plated for the entire length. The barrel is secured to the gun housing by a bayonet-type joint using interrupted threads. It is locked in place with a key and key-bolt seated in a keyway in the barrel. This arrangement allows regunning without dismantling the breech mechanism or other parts. The housing supports the gun in the slide and includes a wedge type sliding breechblock assembly, recoil cylinders and pistons, counter recoil mechanism and gas ejector. The loading tray-type slide is designed for hand loading, power ramming and automatic case ejection. The breechblock assembly consists of a firing pin, case extractors, cocking lever and salvo latch. The recoil and counter recoil systems limit the recoil movement and buffer the guns as they return to battery position. When the breech is opened after

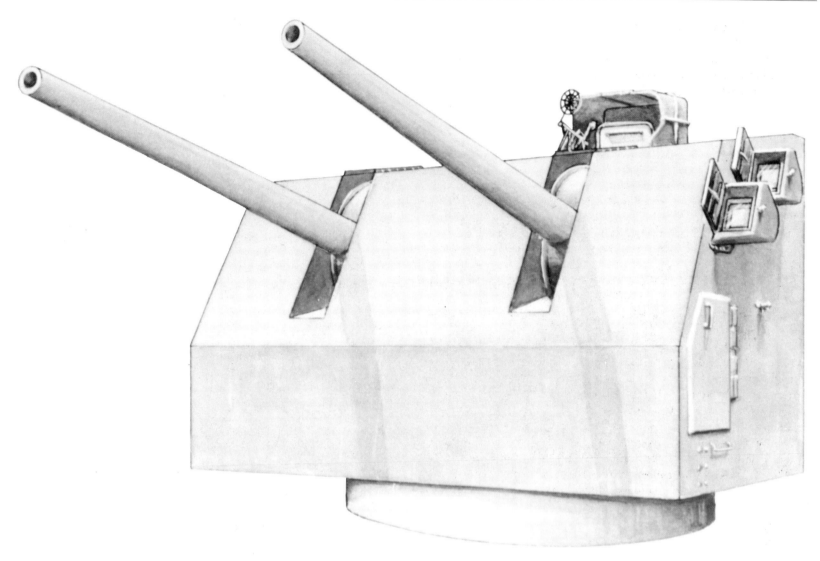

A typical Mark 28, 5in twin gun mount. The secondary battery originally had ten of these mounts and six are still in use. (Rendering by Paul Bender.)

firing the bore is cleared with 175psi air from the gas ejector system preventing powder gases from entering the gun house.

The Mark 28 gun mount assemblies are of the base ring-type and consist of a gun house and carriage with rotating structure, a fixed stand for mounting the base ring and the foundation bulkheads to support the fixed stand.

The gun house is the armored portion of the rotating structure that contains the gun and slide assemblies, gun laying equipment and fire control equipment. It rests on the carriage which is a heavy framework supported by the base ring assembly. The base ring rotates on roller bearings within the fixed stand and a central column extends down to the deck of the handling room below and seats and rotates in the base casting. The projectile and powder hoists are suspended from the underside of the base ring and are steadied by the central column.

The fixed stand is a heavy steel casting that is bolted to the ship's structure and houses the roller bearings which support the base ring and carriage and training circle. The mount rotates on horizontal, coned steel roller bearings and lateral movement is contained by smaller vertical, or radial steel roller bearings. The training circle is an internally toothed annular rack which is bolted to the inside of the stand just below the horizontal rollers. The pinion of the training gear extends down from the gun house inside the training circle and engages the rack to train the mount. The stand is bolted to a machined steel ring on the deck and enclosed by a barbette with a water seal on top.

The foundation bulkheads are strengthening members built into the ship's structure to distribute the loads from firing the guns. They form a rectangular compartment which is covered over with a deck of equal strength. The compartment, which is directly below the mount, serves as a ready service ammunition handling room. A machined steel ring is welded to the deck for seating the fixed stand. The deck also supports a barbette around the stand providing it with ballistic protection.

Projectiles and powder, stored in adjacent magazines, are brought up to the handling rooms in separate dredger-type hoists from the third deck within the armored citadel. Originally, six pairs of magazines serviced the 5in battery, but only four pair are currently used as such.

Each gun mount is equipped with two independently-operated endless-chain projectile hoists, one for each gun, to raise the projectiles from the handling room to the gun house. The projectile fuzes are set automatically during hoisting. Two independently-operated endless-chain powder hoists, one for each gun, are also located in the gun mount to deliver powder from the handling room. Both projectile and powder hoists can reverse their cycles for striking down after a ceasefire.

The mounts can be rapidly trained, elevated to 85 degrees, and loaded at any angle. The gun is capable of a higher rate of fire than the gun crews can handle. An experienced crew can maintain a rate of 15 rounds per minute and as many as 22 rounds per minute at ideal loading angles. Originally, all US Navy combat vessels that mounted any model of the 5in/38cal gun carried a 5in practice loading machine on which the gun crews drilled constantly to maintain their proficiency. During the current modernization, the loading machines were removed and their space was allotted to other weapons. The crews now drill directly on the guns. The normal magazine allowance is 500 rounds per gun, plus 40 special types, with 55 rounds per gun stored in the ready service compartment directly below each mount.

The 5in/38cal ammunition

Ammunition for the 5in/38cal gun is in the separated ammunition category where the projectile and the propelling charge are not attached but are loaded and rammed in a single operation. The projectiles and the propelling charges are packed, shipped, stored and issued separately.

There are a number of projectile and fuzing combinations available

Above: The Mark 2, 40mm quadruple gun mount was the standard intermediate range anti-aircraft weapon carried from World War II until the late-1950s. (Rendering by Paul Bender.)

Below: These two photographs show the front and back sides of a 40mm Mark 2 quadruple gun mount aboard the *Iowa* on 9 July 1943. The battleship version of this mount was provided with a STS splinter shield and the gun tub also was a STS splinter shield. The slotted racks on the inside of the gun tub hold clips of four shells. Note the protective covers over the breech mechanisms.

which makes the 5in/38cal weapon one of the most versatile in use today. The basic projectile configurations are as follows:

HE–CVT, high explosive, controlled variable time
HE–MTF, high explosive, mechanical time
HE–MT/PD, high explosive, mechanical time/point detonating
HE–PD, high explosive, point detonating
HE–IR, high explosive, infrared
HE–VT, high explosive, variable time
HC, high capacity, dummy nose plug/point detonating
AAC, high explosive, mechanical time
RAP, Rocket assist, high explosive, controlled variable time
COM, common, base detonating, spotting dye
ILLUM, illuminating, mechanical time
ILLUM, illuminating, mechanical time/point detonating
WP–MTF, white phosphorus (smoke), mechanical time
WP–PD, white phosphorus (smoke), point detonating

TP PUFF–PDF, target (puff), point detonating
TP PUFF–MTF, target (puff), mechanical time
VT–NONFRAG, target, nonfragmenting, variable time
CHAFF, chaff dispensing, mechanical time
BL–PT, blind loaded and plugged tracer
Dummy, drill projectile

Most of the HE, HC and AAC projectiles differ mainly in their fragmentation capabilities and their selection is determined by the type of target damage which is desired. Not all of these combinations are carried aboard the *Iowa*s as part of their regular onboard allowance. Special purpose rounds can be interchanged, however, to meet the changing mission requirements of the vessel. The projectiles are painted different colors or combinations of colors for quick indentification while loading.

One of the significant fuzes developed during World War II was the variable time (VT, or proximity) fuze. Originally developed for use

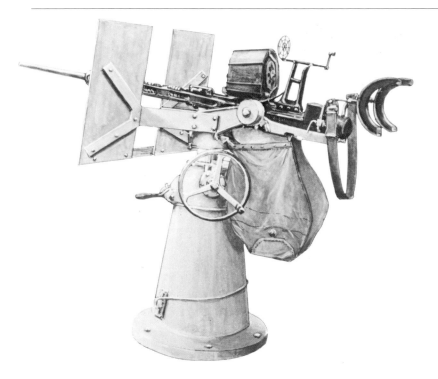

The Mark 4, 20mm single gun mount was the standard close-in anti-aircraft weapon used during World War II until the early-1950s. (Rendering by Paul Bender.)

The Mark 10, 20mm twin gun mount replaced many of the 20mm single mounts in the late-1940s. They were also removed by the early-1950s. (Rendering by Paul Bender.)

against aircraft, it is used with several different projectiles, as shown in the table above. The VT fuze carries a self-contained radio transmitter-receiver. When the projectile comes within effective fragmentation range of the target an echo of the transmission is reflected back to the receiver causing detonation.

ANTI-AIRCRAFT BATTERY

The 5in/38cal guns, as described above, are double purpose weapons in that they can be used against aircraft as well as surface targets and are also considered as part of the anti-aircraft battery. In addition to this longer range gun the US Navy also developed new intermediate and close-range weapons in an effort to literally throw up an in-depth 'blanket defense' against enemy aircraft. By the end of World War II, these later weapons had become obsolescent with the great increase in the speed of aircraft. More recently, rapid firing close-in weapons have again become important as a 'last ditch' defense against cruise missiles and certain other targets.

The 40mm Bofors gun

The intermediate range weapon was the 40mm gun, an adaptation of the Swedish Bofors which was originally developed by Krupp near the end of World War I. The gun could be mounted with single, twin and quadruple barrel arrangements. The standard for the *Iowa*s was the quadruple mount. As originally outfitted, the *Iowa* carried nineteen— and the *New Jersey*, *Missouri* and *Wisconsin* each carried twenty— quadruple 40mm gun mounts. The mounts were distributed along the main deck and in the superstructure so as to obtain the greatest arcs of fire possible. Each gun was capable of firing a 2 pound shell at the rate of 160 rounds per minute. This was one of the more potent anti-aircraft weapons of World War II.

The 20mm Mark 4 single mount was also provided with an individual STS splinter shield. The mounts were fitted in groups where possible, sharing ready service lockers and enclosed with an additional STS shield. The bracket on the shield in the foreground is for holding the magazine while tensioning the magazine spring prior to loading it on the mount. This photograph was taken on the *Iowa* in the New York Navy Yard, 9 July 1943.

The 20mm Oerlikon gun

The original close-range weapon was the single 20mm gun, an adaptation of the Swiss Oerlikon. It was a free-swinging mount requiring no external power source that could literally be bolted anywhere. The *Iowa* and *New Jersey* carried sixty of these mounts and the *Missouri* and *Wisconsin* carried forty-nine. They were located in every area of the main deck from the very bow to the stern and were spotted throughout almost every level of the superstructure. The gun

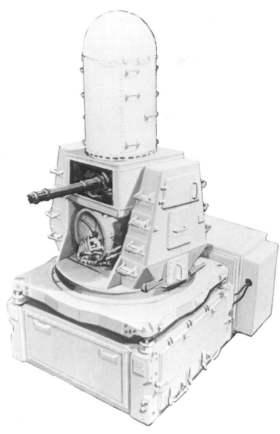

The new 20mm Mark 15 Phalanx CIWS is shown aboard the *Iowa* in 1986. The CIWS is intended as a final defense against anti-ship missiles. The Mark 15 Phalanx is a self-contained unit that can be bolted almost anywhere aboard ship. The *Iowa* class has four systems which provide a full 360 degree target coverage. (Courtesy FCCM (SW) Stephen Skelley, USNR.)

The Mark 15, 20mm Phalanx CIWS as installed aboard the *Iowa* class today. (Rendering by Paul Bender.)

could fire a shell slightly over a quarter of a pound at the rate of 450 rounds per minute.

As the speed of aircraft increased, and suicide tactics such as the Kamikazes became more commonplace, the 20mm became less and less effective. Either a heavier shell was required or the density of fire needed to be increased. A heavier weapon would take time to develop, so the Bu Ord designed twin and triple versions of the 20mm in order to further saturate the anti-aircraft pattern. The Armament Summaries of the Bu Ord indicate that the *Iowa*s were each fitted with eight twin 20mm mounts in 1945 for evaluation purposes. It is uncertain if this installation was carried out in any of the class.

The 20mm Phalanx CIWS

In the mid-1960s, the Bu Ord recognized the threat posed by the growing number of anti-ship missiles and sponsored the development of a close-in defense system capable of defending against such weapons. The new 20mm Mark 15 Phalanx CIWS is a final defense against anti-ship missiles. Much like its predecessor, the 20mm Oerlikon, Phalanx is a self-contained unit that can be bolted almost anywhere aboard ship.

In their current configuration, the *Iowa*s have four systems providing full 360-degree target coverage. It is a six-barrel Gatling-type gun[3] capable of firing 3,000 rounds per minute (six barrels at 500 rounds per minute each). The Mark 15 uses an adaptation of the M61 Vulcan gun used by the US Air Force. It fires a Mark 149 round,

which consists of a 12.75mm sub-caliber penetrator, a sabot adapting the penetrator to the 20mm bore, a pusher which imparts spin to the penetrator and a 20mm shell casing. The sabot and pusher are discarded after the round exits the muzzle. The penetrator is a heavy metal bullet made of depleted-uranium and its maximum effective range is 2,000 yards. Magazines hold approximately 1,000 rounds and each mount has two ready service lockers with a capacity of 1,000 rounds. The total shipboard allowance is 8,000 rounds per system.

The 0.50cal MS machine gun

The 0.50cal Browning Machine Gun (BMG) used aboard the *Iowa* class is the heavy barrel version of the M2 also used by the US Army. It has a range of 7,400 yards and a cyclic rate of fire of 500 to 600 rounds per minute. The 0.50cal BMGs are for use against hostile small surface craft and commando-type attacks which might occur in restricted waters.

The *Iowa*s have four 0.50cal machine mounts all located on the edge of the main deck. Two mounts are on each side of Turret II and two are on each side of Turret III. The barrels are mounted on a light tripod at the lifelines. Ready service ammunition lockers are located as close as possible at the deckhouse. When not in use the barrels are stowed by the ready service lockers.

---

3 The 20mm Phalanx CIWS is styled after the machine gun invented by Richard J. Gatling and introduced in the mid-1800s. The original 'Gatling gun' was an early machine gun with a crank-operated revolving cluster of barrels fired once per each revolution.

The starboard pair of quadruple Mark 141 ceramic armored Harpoon launchers are shown aboard the *Iowa* in 1986. The *Iowa* class carries sixteen RGM-84 Harpoon missiles which give her an over-the-horizon strike capability. The Harpoon has a range of up to 85nm depending on the firing mode. (Courtesy FCCM (SW) Stephen Skelley, USNR.)

The *Iowa* class carries sixteen RGM-84 Harpoon cruise missiles in four Mark 141 quadruple ceramic armored canisters. (Rendering by Paul Bender.)

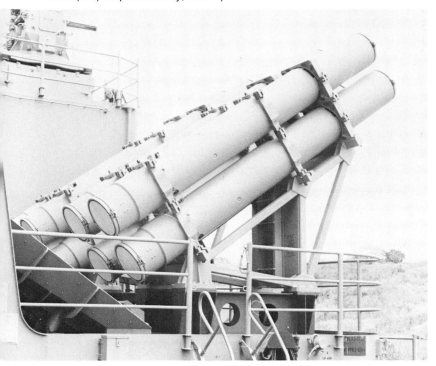

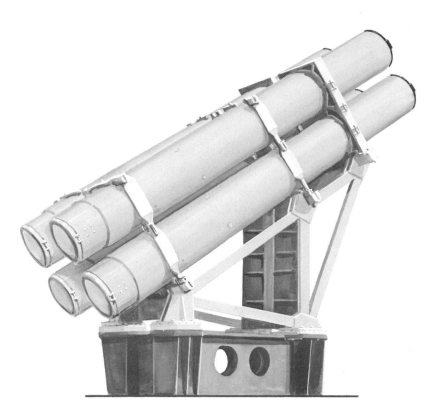

MISSILE BATTERY

During the current reactivation of the *Iowa* class, two cruise missile systems were installed giving the ships a long-range strike capability against both surface and land targets. This new armament, together with the original ordnance, places the *Iowa*s among the most heavily armed ships at sea today.

The RGM–84 Harpoon cruise missile

The Harpoon Weapons System is an anti-ship missile system which gives the *Iowa* class an over-the-horizon strike capability against surface targets. There are two complete Harpoon systems which consist of four Mark 141 launchers and sixteen RGM-84 missiles. Each Mark 141 launcher holds a cluster of four All-Up-Round (AURs) in ceramic armored canisters. The missiles are stored and fired from the canisters at a fixed angle.

The surface launched RGM-84 uses the same airframe body as the air launched version plus a booster. There are five component sections in all:

Guidance Section – uses active guidance (see Chapter 6)
Warhead Section – is composed of 510 pounds including 215 pounds Destex HE
Propulsion Section – is composed of a liquid fueled turbojet engine for cruise and attack flights
Bobtail Section – houses actuator fins which control the flight after booster separation
Booster Section – solid propellant propels missile away from ship

When fired, the booster propels the missile away from the ship approximately 5 miles and is discarded. The dropoff zone for the discarded booster section is about $1\frac{1}{2}$ miles. The turbojet engine propels the missile from booster separation to the target. The stabilizing and actuator fins are stored folded in the canister and spring out into position after launching. During the flight the actuator fins receive inputs from the guidance system directing the missile to the target (see Chapter 6 for details of launch modes).

The firing weight of the RGM-84 Harpoon is 1,530 pounds, which includes a booster weight of about 362 pounds. It has a cruising speed of 0.87 Mach. The maximum range is 64.5nm in Range and Bearing Launch (RBL) mode and 85.5nm in Bearing Only Launch (BOL) mode.

The BGM–109 Tomahawk cruise missile

The Tomahawk Weapons System is an offensive missile system which gives the *Iowa* class a long-range strike capability against both surface and land targets. In their current configuration, the *Iowa*s carry thirty-two BGM-109 series missiles in eight Armored Box Launchers (ABLs). Each Mark 143 ABL holds a cluster of four AURs consisting of a canister and the missile. The ABL is mounted horizontally with front-end access to the canisters. The canister cluster is attached to the top of the ABL which is hydraulically raised to the firing position.

The Tomahawk BGM-109 series has three basic configurations: the Tomahawk Anti-Ship Missile (TASM); the Tomahawk Land-Attack Missile–Conventional (TLAM-C); and the Tomahawk Land-Attack Missile–Nuclear (TLAM-N). All use the same airframe body as the air launched version plus a booster. There are five component sections in all:

Guidance Section –
TASM, uses active guidance/modified Harpoon system

The firing end of two of the *Iowa*'s Mark 143 ABL Tomahawk launchers. Four BGM-109 series Tomahawk missiles are stored in individual canisters in each box. For firing, the doors are opened and the top half of the box is raised to a fixed firing position. (Photograph, in about 1986, by the author.)

The blast end of a Mark 143 ABL on the *Iowa*. The trunion for elevating the launcher can be seen in the lower corner of this end. The round doors are opened for blast exhaust when firing. The *Iowa* class has a long-range strike capability against surface and land targets with the BGM-109 series Tomahawk cruise missile. Each strip carries thirty-two missiles in eight Mark 143 ABLs. The Tomahawk also has a nuclear capability against land targets. (Photograph, 1986, by the author.)

The *Iowa* class carries thirty-two BGM-109 series Tomahawk cruise missiles in eight Mark 143 quadruple armored box launchers. (Rendering by Paul Bender.)

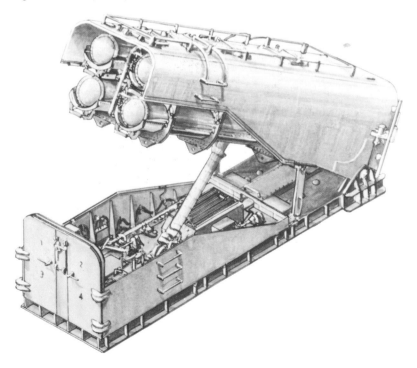

TLSM, uses inertial navigation system/TERCOM (Terrain Contour Matching) (see Chapter 6)

Warhead Section –

TSAM, 1,000 pounds conventional

TLAM–C, 980 pounds conventional

TLAM–N, 293 pounds nuclear

Propulsion Section – is composed of a liquid fueled air-breathing turbofan engine for cruise and attack flights

Control Section – Actuator fins control the flight after booster separation

Booster Section – solid propellant propels missile away from ship

When fired, the booster propels the missile away from the ship approximately 11 miles and is discarded. The dropoff zone is about 1 mile. The turbofan engine propels the missile from booster separation to the target. The wings and actuator fins are stored folded in the canister and spring out into position after launching. During the flight the actuator fins receive inputs from the guidance system directing the missile to the target.

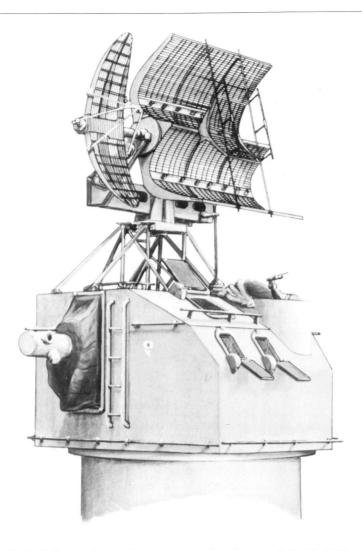

The Mark 37 director for the 5in secondary battery is shown in its World War II configuration with the Mark 12/22 radar antennas. (Rendering by Paul Bender.)

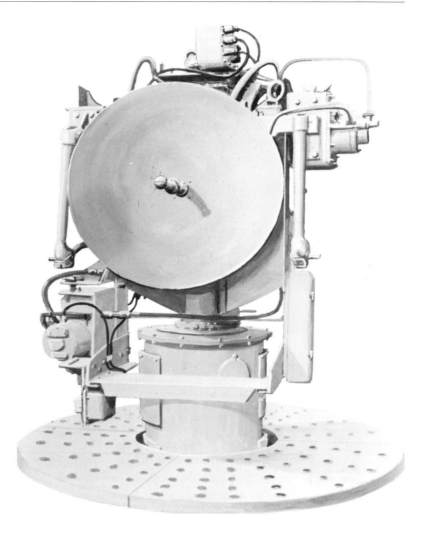

The Mark 57 director for the 40mm anti-aircraft battery was a late-World War II development which could be used for blind fire. (Rendering by Paul Bender.)

The Mark 38 director for the 16in main battery is shown in its original configuration with the Mark 8 radar antenna atop. A long-based Mark 48 stereoscopic rangefinder is enclosed in the armored extensions. (Rendering by Paul Bender.)

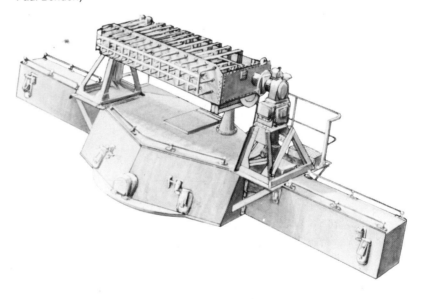

The firing weight of the BGM–109 series Tomahawk is 2,650 pounds plus a 550 pound booster. It has a cruising speed of 0.5 Mach and an attack speed of 0.75 Mach. The TASM has an operating range of 250nm and a maximum range of 470nm, TLAM–C has a maximum range of 675nm and TLAM–N a maximum range of 1,500nm.

The FIM–92 Stinger surface-to-air-missile

The Stinger is a short-range anti-aircraft missile which is fired from the shoulder. The missile is tube-launched and stabilized by four forward and four after fins. The fins are stored folded in the tube and spring out into position after launching. The missile is 5ft long with a diameter of 2.75in and uses infrared homing guidance. It has a high explosive warhead and uses solid-propellant rocket fuel. The maximum range is about 3nm and it is used as a final defense against incoming aircraft.

The *Iowa*s have five Stinger positions at which the weapons and ready service rounds are stored. Four positions are on the 05 level with two on each side of the armored conning tower and two just aft of the barbettes for the Mark 37 directors on each side of the forward stack. The fifth position is on the 02 level aft, port side at the platform where the boat boom is secured.

Chapter 6

FIRE CONTROL

The importance of fire control cannot be overstated. The finest weapons are of little real value if they cannot hit the target quickly and consistently. Fire control comprises the entire system of directing the operation of the offensive and defensive weapons of a vessel. The fire control systems of the *Iowa* class are the finest, most sophisticated of their type ever produced.

The fire control problem is handled by three distinct systems: surface, dual-purpose and relative-rate. The solution of the problem is determined by the primary use of the system. For example, a single purpose surface system operates on the assumption that all targets are on the surface and can disregard the effects of small angles of elevation or depression in the line of sight. The system can fire at elevated targets in shore bombardment, or even at aircraft, but arbitrary corrections or interconnection with the dual-purpose computer is necessary. A dual-purpose system is similar to a surface system but must also consider the changing elevation of the target. Relative-rate systems deal with incoming targets at close range and are not concerned with the point of fall and other units which are essential to the surface and dual-purpose systems.

The various fire control systems all have their own specialized radar equipment which is included in this discussion. If necessary, certain fire control radar can be, and is, used as a backup for navigational purposes. In a similar manner, search radar can furnish advanced information to the various fire control systems and the electronics can help the fire control systems to function without interference. (Although these areas are all closely related, the search radar and electronics are covered in the following chapter.)

MAIN BATTERY

When the *Iowa* class battleships were built, their main battery fire control system was without peer among all of the world's navies. It incorporated high-grade optical instruments, state-of-the-art radar, excellent stabilization, precise and accurate computation, electrical data transmission and remote control. When the *Iowas* were designed, radar was only in the developmental stage. Its addition greatly enhanced the system, providing target acquisition and spotting of shot at night, in fog, through smoke and all blind firing conditions. Improvements have been made which make it the finest system afloat for anti-surface warfare and NGFS. The system is designated the Mark 38 GFCS.

The *Iowa* has two complete Mark 38 GFCS aboard. Components of the system, both new and old are listed below:

> Turret optics/DR–810 radar
> Mark 38 director/Mark 8/Mark 13 radar
> Mark 40 director/Mark 3/Mark 27 radar
> Mark 8 rangekeeper

This view of Spot 2 on the *Iowa* shows the details of the back side of the Mark 38 director. The directors on the *Iowa* and *New Jersey* had this 'V-back', six-sided shield, while those on the *Missouri* and *Wisconsin* had the 'square-back', seven-sided shield. The director is shown here with the Mark 13 radar antenna mounted atop. A long-based Mark 48 stereoscopic rangefinder is enclosed in the armored extensions. The Mark 13 gives the system a complete blind firing capability, but when there is clear visibility it is used with the Mark 48. For spotting, the rangefinder is used to plot deflection while the radar is used for plotting the range. (Photograph by the author.)

Opposite: Both Mark 38 gun directors for the two main battery Mark 38 GFCS are shown in this photograph of the *Iowa*, taken on 19 December 1986 at Pier 12, Norfolk Naval Station. The director on the foward fire control tower is designated Spot 1 and the director atop the after fire control tower is Spot 2. Two of the Mark 37 gun directors for the four Mark 37 GFCS of the secondary battery are also visible. Note the OE-82 satellite antenna on the aft side of the second stack and the radome for the RPV control and communications antenna on the forward side. (Photograph by the author.)

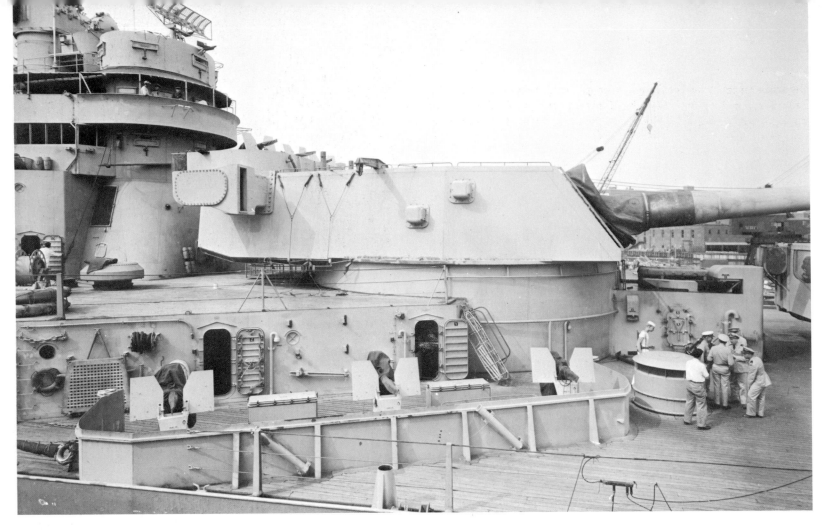

Mark 41 stable vertical
Mark 48 shore bombardment computer
HP–85 initial ballistic computer
Fire control switchboard
Spotting aircraft/RPV

This equipment is located in various places throughout the ship. Optical instruments such as rangefinders, telescopes, periscopes and spotting glasses, together with the antennas for the radar sets, are located with the directors and turrets. The directors are placed atop the fire control towers in the superstructure so their optics can see as far as possible. The turrets are located just above the main deck to allow the widest possible arcs of fire. System components not physically part of the turrets and directors are housed in two plotting rooms located within the armored citadel of the ship. One room is forward on the first platform deck and the second room is aft on the third deck. Each plotting room contains a Mark 8 rangekeeper, Mark 41 stable vertical, Mark 48 bombardment computer, Mark 13 radar console and power supply and fire control switchboard.

Ranging and spotting

The Mark 38 GFCS optical and radar equipment perform the functions of ranging and spotting. Ranging is the process of determining the distance to the target from the ship and spotting is the assessment of where shells fall in relation to the target.

These important functions are performed by more than one component and on multiple targets. The input from each component is identified at the fire control switchboard and given a specific designation as follows:

Turret No. II of the *Iowa* is shown here on 9 July 1943 at the New York Navy Yard. Note the cast, armored enclosure for the Mark 53 rangefinder and those for the Mark 66 telescopes. There were two Mark 66 on each side of the turret for sight pointers and sight trainers. There were three 20mm guns mounted on the turret top instead of the quadruple 40mm mount as on the other units. This arrangement was only used on the *Iowa* which had a lower level in the conning tower to accommodate a flag control station. As evident here, a 40mm mount would have obstructed the flag's view from the armored viewing ports.

Rangefinding – Range 1, Turret I/Mark 53 Coincidence rangefinder
　　　　　　　　Range 2, Turret II/Mark 52 Stereoscopic rangefinder
　　　　　　　　Range 3, Turret III/Mark 52 Stereoscopic rangefinder
　　　　　　　　Range 4, Director 1/Mark 48 Stereoscopic rangefinder
　　　　　　　　Range 5, Director 2/Mark 48 Stereoscopic rangefinder

Spotting – Spot 1, Director 1/Mark 38
　　　　　　Spot 2, Director 2/Mark 38
　　　　　　Spot 3, Director 3/Mark 40
　　　　　　　　Director 4/Mark 41, forward. Stable vertical
　　　　　　　　Director 5/Mark 41, aft. Stable vertical

Spotting references are given in two ordinates, which are range and deflection. Range being the distance over or under the target along the line of sight, and deflection being the distance to either side of the target normal to the line of sight. Spotting preference, assuming clear visibility and all equipment in operating condition, is as follows:

Deflection – 1, Optical　　2, Radar　　3, Air

Range –　　1, Radar　　2, Air　　3, Optical

Splash colors are assigned in order to identify shell splashes, by individual ship, when more than one vessel is concentrating fire on the same target. This is accomplished by filling the void between the ballistic cap and windshield with color dye in AP and APT projectiles. Spotters correct for the color assigned to their vessel. Splash colors assigned to the *Iowa* class are as follows:

Iowa – Orange	*Missouri* – Red
New Jersey – Blue	*Wisconsin* – Green

Turret, rangefinders, optics and radar

The primary rangefinders are placed in the main battery turrets under the protection of their heavy armor. Long-base (46ft) rangefinders are incorporated in the after end of each turret. The rangefinder in Turret I was removed from all of the *Iowa*s after World War II. The rangefinder in Turret I was a Mark 53 coincidence-type which had an astigmatizing lens for ranging on points of light while those in Turrets II and III are Mark 52 stereoscopic-type. (All are 25× power.) They are stabilized by the Mark 4 rangefinder stabilizer which greatly facilitates staying on target in a rolling, pitching ship.

Each turret has four Mark 66 telescopes (12× power) mounted in director-type carriage sights which protrude from the turret sides. They are manned by two sight pointers and two sight trainers. There are two sight setters, each manning an indicator for a pair of telescopes. Each turret also has two Mark 28 or Mark 29 periscopes (12× power) mounted on the turret roof. They are manned by the turret officer and turret captain.

There is a Mark 3 mechanical–analog computer located in each turret which allows the turret to be fired locally from its own inputs or from inputs supplied from another turret. Any turret can act as a director and control the other turrets in indicating or automatic modes.

Currently, all four *Iowa*s carry DR–810 radar velocimeters. One is installed over the center gun of each turret just behind the face plate. An elevation drive is provided which follows the gun elevation order signals to the center gun. The antenna 'sees' and tracks each round fired from all three guns. This information provides a quick and accurate assessment of mean muzzle velocity of the gun or guns. The information is displayed in the turret and can be recorded on a printer in each plotting room. This greatly enhances the accuracy of subsequent fire.

The Mark 38 director, rangefinders and radar

There are two Mark 38 directors located aloft, atop the forward and after fire control towers. In this position, they are best able to establish the line of sight to a target and can supply the target's relative bearing to the other elements of the fire control system.

A long-base (26ft 6in) Mark 48 stereoscopic rangefinder (25× power) is mounted in each director. The height of these rangefinders (116ft forward and 68ft aft) provides initial ranges at a much greater distance than those in the turrets. They could not be nearly as well protected that high in the ship, however, and could be brought down more easily as the battle range closed. The Mark 48 is used for spotting the fall of shot in both range and deflection. It is excellent for deflection spotting.

Other optics housed in the directors are two Mark 69 telescopes, a Mark 56 telescope and a Mark 29 periscope. The Mark 69 scopes (12× power) are manned by the pointer and trainer. The Mark 56 scope (4× power) is operated by the crossleveler. The pointer, trainer and crossleveler keep the director on target. The Mark 29 scope (12× power) is used by the spotter to continuously scan for other targets.

The armored enclosure for the Mark 53 long-base rangefinder of Turret No. III is in the foreground. Directly above is a Mark 37 director. Above and to the right is the Mark 38 director of Spot 2 with its Mark 13 radar. The photograph was taken from the main deck of the *Iowa* on 19 December 1986. (Photograph by the author.)

The crew of Turret No. I mans the rangefinder aboard the *Iowa* during her shakedown cruise on 13 May 1943. This rangefinder is a Mark 53 coincidence type which had an astigmatizing lens for ranging on points of light while those in Turrets No. II and No. III are the Mark 52 stereoscopic type. The Mark 53 was removed from all units between 1948 and 1952. The rangefinders are stabilized, which greatly facilitates staying on target in a rolling, pitching ship.

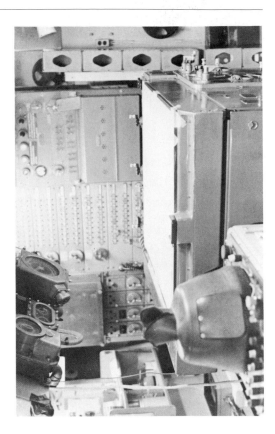

A Mark 8 rangekeeper in the after main battery plotting room of the *Iowa*. An identical unit was located in the forward main battery plotting room. This mechanical-analog computing device is commonly referred to as a ballistic computer because it computes quantities such as the projectile time of flight, how far the target will move while the projectile is in flight and how much the guns must be offset from the line of sight to hit the target. Gun and turret train orders are generated from this information. (Courtesty FCCM (SW) Stephen Skelley, USNR.)

Above center: The Mark 41 stable vertical is a gimballed gyroscope that measures the roll and pitch of the ship to produce level and crosslevel corrections to the various elements of the fire control system. There is a Mark 41 in both main battery plotting rooms. The one in the aft room is shown here. The Mark 41 is also the firing station for the plotting room. Note the pistol-grip firing keys. The television set mounted on the bulkhead is a monitor for signals from a Remotely Piloted Vehicle (RPV). (Courtesy FCCM (SW) Stephen Skelley, USNR.)

Above right: The white top is the plotting surface of the Mark 48 shore bombardment computer in the after main battery plotting room of the *Iowa*. All of the *Iowa*s now have a Mark 48 in each main battery plotting room. It is used for indirect fire where shore targets are obscured by terrain features. A known reference point is plotted and the ship's position is established. The target is then plotted and its position is computed. The information is then sent to the Mark 8 rangekeeper to generate gun and turret train orders. (Courtesy FCCM (SW) Stephen Skelley, USNR.)

Left: The HP-85 initial ballistic computer for Turret No. I on the *Iowa* with its radar transparent dome removed. An HP-85 is located above the center gun of each turret. The computer furnishes the initial velocity and a range and deflection spot for each round. The data is used to make corrections in gun and turret train orders. (Courtesy FCCM (SW) Stephen Skelley, USNR.)

Two different director shields are used. The *Iowa* and *New Jersey* have the V-back shields (Mark 38, Mods. 1–5) and the *Missouri* and *Wisconsin* have the square-back shields (Mark 38, Mods. 6–7). All are protected with 1.5in STS armor plate.

By the time the *Iowa*s were completed, fire control radar had advanced considerably and a Mark 8 unit was installed atop each Mark 38 director. An improved unit, the Mark 13, was later installed and is still in service today.

The new Mark 13 sets were phased in as they became available. Where it was not possible to install both units at the same time, the forward set was replaced first. The *Iowa* received her forward set in 1945 and her after set in 1946. Both Mark 13s were installed aboard the *Missouri* in 1946. The *New Jersey* and *Wisconsin* had their forward

The armored conning tower is shown at the right in this photograph, taken in November 1943 at the Boston Navy Yard. The Mark 40 director, consisting of two Mark 30 and one Mark 32 periscopes mechanically linked together, is mounted in the top level. This position is designated Spot 3. The Mark 30s are used for level and crosslevel and the Mark 32 is for spotting. A Mark 3 radar antenna is installed over the Mark 32 scope. A Mark 27 replaced the Mark 32 and was mounted behind the scope. Note the Mark 4 radar antenna atop the Mark 37 director and a Mark 51 40mm director in the tub in the foreground.

Fire control switchboards are located in both main battery plotting rooms controlling the various functions of the Mark 38 Gun Fire Control System. Shown here is the after Mark 21 main fire control switchboard on the *Iowa*. It features 130 J-type rotary switches which allow various elements of the fire control system to be selectively interchanged.

antennas fitted in 1945 but their after sets were not provided until 1952.

The original Mark 8 used an antenna composed of numerous 'polyrods' with the elements sending out timed pulses. This was the first phase–scanning set in the US Navy and produced a fairly narrow beam. It was rather complex mechanically which led to the Mark 13 development. The Mark 13 antenna is a horn-fed paraboloid which sends out a series of pulses while the antenna is rocked horizontally. Each pulse is very narrow and rocking the antenna allows the target area to be scanned.

Both the Mark 8 and Mark 13 antennas are aligned with the director optics so that full radar or optical or a combination of both can be used for tracking. In blind firing, the director trainer uses a radar indicator and turns his handwheels to track the target. These units provide range and bearing information for surface targets and

are capable of spotting shell splashes in both range and deflection. The Mark 13 is excellent for range spotting.

The Mark 40 director, optics and radar

The Mark 40 director is mounted in the top level of the armored conning tower. It consists of two Mark 30 and one Mark 32 periscopes mechanically linked together. (All are 12× power.) One Mark 30 scope is used for level and the other for crosslevel. They can interchange function by being rotated 90 degrees in their mountings. The Mark 32 scope is used for spotting and is superior in deflection spotting to any of the radars. The Mark 9 spotting glass, normally part of the Mark 40 director, was not installed on the *Iowas*.

A Mark 3 radar was installed atop the director in the *Iowa* and *New Jersey* after their shakedown. It was intended as a functional substitution for the Mark 9 spotting glass. The Mark 3 used a long 3ft × 12ft cylindrical antenna to generate two identical signals, one from each side of the antenna. Each side, or half, produced a separate beam at a slightly different angle. When the returning signals were equal in strength, the target lay on a line directly between the signals bisecting their angle of separation. The *Missouri* and *Wisconsin* were completed with Mark 27 radars, the replacement for the Mark 3. The Mark 27 had an antenna in the shape of a paraboloid which produced a narrower beam, or lobe, reducing the side effects of the returning signal. In 1945, the *Iowa* and *New Jersey* were retrofitted with Mark 27s and all units carried them into the mid-1950s. In spotting the fall of shot, range error determination is one of radar's strong points, as is blind fire.

The Mark 8 rangekeeper

The Mark 8 rangekeeper is a mechanical–analog computing device. The *Iowa* class is outfitted with two Mark 8 rangekeepers, one in each main battery plotting room. The target's course and speed are plotted to predict its position when the shells will hit. It is commonly referred to as a 'ballistic computer' because it computes the ballistic quantities necessary for the guns to hit the target such as how long will the projectile be in flight, how far will the target move while the projectile is in the air and how much the guns must be offset from the line of sight to hit the target. Among the mechanical devices used to compute the ballistics are various gears, cams and multipliers.

The computation process requires a number of informational inputs such as target motion, ship's motion, individual gun ballistic data, type of ammunition, meteorological data and stabilization data. Target motion data is received from the directors and radars. Ship's motion data is received from the ship's gyro and pitometer log. Stabilization data is received from the Mark 41 stable vertical. Some of the input quantities are set into the rangekeeper by hand, such as the ship's course and speed which is determined from plots. Other data is put in automatically by mechanical shafting or synchro receivers. From this data, the rangekeeper computes values for gun elevation and turret train orders, which are sent to the turrets automatically.

Cams are available for making ballistic computations for the following initial velocities:

2,700 pound Mark 8 AP shell – Full Charge, 2,500ft/sec
Special Charge, 2,300ft/sec
Reduced Charge, 1,800ft/sec

Left: One of the *Iowa*'s Kingfishers is fired from the starboard catapult, while another is warming up for launching from the port catapult. The catapults are Type P, Mark VI, which use a 5in Mark III smokeless powder cartridge to launch the plane. The smoke issuing from the catapult is from the black powder ignition charge. When recovering aircraft, the ship would turn, forming a wide slick wake for landing. A steel net was dropped overboard and the plane taxied onto it. There was an arrestor hook in the bottom of the main float and when the hook made fast in the net, the crane lifted the plane onto the catapult. This photograph was taken in mid-1944.

An SC-1 Seahawk is shown on the starboard catapult of the *Iowa* on 22 June 1947 while anchored off the Naval Air Station at Alameda in San Francisco Bay. The Seahawk replaced the Kingfishers in the *Iowa*s, beginning in 1945. The US Navy used spotting aircraft well after World War II with the last flight being made from the *Missouri* in early-1948.

1,900 pound Mark 13 HC shell – Full Charge, 2,690ft/sec
Special Charge, 2,525ft/sec
Reduced Charge, 2,075ft/sec

The Mark 13 HC shell (originally the EX–1) was introduced in late-1942 and the Mark 8 rangekeepers and Mark 3 turret computers were not modified to fully compute for the round until late World War II or early post-war.

Computations can be made for target speeds of up to 45 knots and ranges of approximately 50,000 yards.

The Mark 41 stable vertical

The *Iowa* class has two Mark 41 units, one located in each of the plotting rooms. The Mark 41 stable vertical is a gimballed gyro, or gyroscope, that measures the roll and pitch of the ship in reference to the line of sight established by the director and the ship's course and speed. Outputs from the Mark 41 are called level and crosslevel corrections and are sent to various elements of the fire control system for stabilization. Level and crosslevel corrections stabilize the gun orders sent to the turrets.

The heart of the stable vertical is a gyroscope that spins at 8,500rpm. When spinning, the gyro stays erect in the vertical and measures the movement of the ship around the erect gyro.

The Mark 41 is also the firing station for the plotting room and is equipped with firing keys to control the fire of the turrets.

The Mark 48 shore bombardment computer

The Mark 48 computer is a post-World War II improvement to the main battery fire control system. It operates in conjunction with other elements of the system to provide an accurate solution for NGFS by indirect fire. It can also be used with the secondary battery Mark 37 GFCS for the same purpose. Currently, each *Iowa* class vessel has two Mark 48 computers. They were installed at various times as indicated below:

BB 61–1 Mark 48, mid-1950s/forward plotting room
1 Mark 48, 1984/after plotting room
BB 62–1 Mark 48, mid-1950s/forward plotting room
1 Mark 48, 1967/after plotting room
BB 63–2 Mark 48, 1986/forward and after plotting rooms
BB 64–1 Mark 48, mid-1950s/forward plotting room
1 Mark 48, 1988/after plotting room

Indirect fire is used where shore targets are obscured, usually by terrain features. In this method of fire, the radar and director track a known reference point such as a lighthouse. The reference point is plotted on the NGFS grid reference, or bombardment, chart. The range and bearing of the reference point establish the ship's position on the chart. The target is then plotted on the chart and the information is entered into the Mark 48 computer. The range and bearing from the ship and the fixed target height is electronically and mechanically computed. This information is sent to the Mark 8 rangekeeper for computation of gun and turret train orders. When used with the Mark 37 GFCS, the information is sent to the Mark 1A computers in the seconday battery plotting rooms.

Another method of indirect fire is using the NGFS grid reference chart for blind fire or when a known reference is not available. The ship's position is determined by navigational methods and plotted on

This close-up shows the details of the *New Jersey*'s catapults and recovery crane. The Mark VI catapult could handle a combined launching car and plane weight of 8,150 pounds at an end speed of 65 miles per hour. The crane was hinged at the top and pinned at the bottom of the boom at the center angle. Removing the bottom pins would allow the boom to be straightened out and stored flat on the deck in heavy weather. This photograph was taken during an inclining experiment on 24 June 1945. Note the inclining weights being moved into position on the tracks.

A Pioneer RPV is assisted on take-off by a rocket-booster, which is discarded after it is expended. The RPV system consists of one stationary and two portable control stations, a fueling station and portable hangars for storing the vehicles when not in use. Up to eight Pioneers can be stored in the hangars which protect against the blast effects of the 16in guns. The Pioneer is a fixed wing, gasoline-driven aircraft used for basic gunfire support. It carries a stabilized television camera and a laser designator which provides an over-the-horizon targeting and reconnaissance capability. Extensive use of fiberglass in the structure of the craft results in a low radar cross-section. The system is currently operational only aboard the *Iowa*, but installations are planned for all of the class.

Opposite: The *Iowa*, on 19 December 1986, showing the radome enclosed communications antenna for the Pioneer RPVs, as mounted to the mast platform on the forward side of the second stack. This antenna transmits control signals to the RPVs and receives their transmissions which are replayed at the shipboard control stations. (Photograph by the author.)

Crewmen disengage a Pioneer RPV from the recovery net erected on the stern of the *Iowa*. The fueling station for the RPVs is in the former 40mm gun tub at the left and below the metal grating. This series of photographs shows the launching and recovery operations on 12 December 1986.

the chart. Knowing the ship's course and speed, a future position is chosen and plotted on the chart together with the target's bearing, distance and fixed height from the future point. These values are sent to the Mark 48 computer and are processed in the same manner as stated above.

Using the Mark 48 shore bombardment computer, the *Iowa*s are unmatched in NGFS using indirect fire.

The HP-85 initial ballistic computer

A recent improvement for the main battery fire control system is the addition of an initial ballistic computation system using two HP-85 digital computers.

Computer IBC 1 provides quick computation of initial velocity expected from each gun based on erosion, powder temperature and velocity history statistical weighting. Erosion corrector settings are then made for each gun based on expected initial velocities.

Computer IBC 2 provides corrections for trunion height, target height, earth's curvature and rotation, ballistic density and temperature. A range and deflection spot for all projectile selections is furnished including an elevation spot and fuze time setting for the Mark 144, 145 and 146 projectiles.

The system also computes cam-error corrections for the Mark 8 rangekeeper at long ranges.

The fire control switchboard

A fire control switchboard is located in each plotting room and controls the various inputs and outputs of the fire control system. They are used to route data circuits as needed in the event of damage or to use the best data available. These switchboards allow either of the plotting rooms and various elements of the fire control system to be selectively interchanged and control the different configurations that can be attained with the Mark 38 GFCS.

Both switchboards can be interconnected with the two secondary battery switchboards which allows interchanging of functions between the Mark 38 and Mark 37 GFCS. In this manner, either the main battery or secondary battery can be controlled from any of six directors through any of the four switchboards.

The spotting aircraft

The ship's aircraft are an important element of the fire control system. In addition to locating the enemy much in advance of when they could be seen from the fire control towers, they can spot the fall of shot. As originally outfitted, the *Iowa*s carried manned observation aircraft which were discontinued in the late-1940s. During their current reactivation, it is planned to equip all units with unmanned remotely piloted aircraft, but currently only the *Iowa* carries the craft.

With the original manned aircraft, the purpose of the observation of the fall of shot was to report by radio an estimate of the correction necessary to place the mean point of impact of the densest part of the pattern on target. The new unmanned aircraft, with their daylight or infrared video camera, replay similar information to a video display at the shipboard control stations in Spot 1, the forward and after plottings rooms and the Strike Warfare Center (SWC) for viewing the fall of shot. Correction estimates are then made for the next salvo.

The original aircraft complement for the *Iowa* class was three float planes. Two catapults for launching the aircraft were located aft, one on each side of the fantail. There was no hangar to house the aircraft

so they were stored on the catapults in their launching cradle or on deck between the catapults. All four *Iowas* originally carried three OS2U Kingfishers which were later replaced by the newer SC-1 Seahawk. The US Navy continued to use spotting aircraft well after World War II. The last Seahawk flight was made from the *Missouri* in 1948 after which her catapults were landed. Catapults were removed from all other units by the time they were reactivated for Korean service.

Late in 1986, the *Iowa* received the first aircraft carried by the class since 1948. It is the Pioneer RPV system and consists of a ground control station, two portable control stations and eight Pioneers. The system missions are reconnaissance, surveillance, search and rescue, weapons targeting and battle damage assessment. The first successful RPV flight and recovery was on board the *Iowa* 12 December 1986.

SECONDARY BATTERY

When the *Iowa* class battleships were completed, their secondary battery fire control system was unmatched by any foreign competitor. It provided the following primary functions:

A UH-1 Iroquois helicopter is parked on the port flight deck ramp of the *Iowa* on 13 February, off Costa Rica. As presently configured, the *Iowa* class can land six types of helicopters: the UH-1 Iroquois, H-2 Seasprite, CH-46 Sea Knight, CH-53 Sea Stallion, CH-53E Sea Stallion and the LAMPS III SH-60B Seahawk.

Continuous automatic gun positioning
Continuous sight-angle and sight-deflection indication at the guns
Continuous selected-level and crosslevel fire
Automatic fuze setting
Star shell fire control
Searchlight control

In surface fire, anti-aircraft fire and shore bombardment no other system performed as well or provided as many functions. It incorporated quality optical instruments, advanced radar, excellent stabilization, exact computation, electrical data transmission and remote control. Improvements have been made which make it comparable to systems more recently developed and currently in use. This linear-rate system is designated the Mark 37 GFCS and controls the twin 5in/38cal double purpose gun mounts.

The *Iowas* have four complete Mark 37 GFCS aboard. System

components, both new and old, are listed below:

Gun mount control equipment
Mark 37 director with Mark 4; Mark 12/22; Mark 25 radar
Mark 1/Mark 1A computer
Mark 6 stable element
Mark 1 starshell computer
Fire control switchboard
Target designation
Illumination control

Equipment for the four Mark 37 systems is located in various places throughout the ship. Optical instruments such as rangefinders and telescopes together with the antennas for the radar sets, are located with the directors and gun mounts. The four directors are placed as high in the the superstructure as practical. The gun mounts are positioned on each beam in the first and second levels of the superstructure. Target designation transmitters were installed adjacent to the conning stations and in the air defense stations. Illumination control transmitters are located in the forward and aft air defense stations. All other system equipment is housed in two plotting rooms in the armored citadel of the ship. One room is forward on the first platform deck and the second room is aft on the third deck. Both rooms are adjacent to the main battery plotting rooms. Each plotting room contains two Mark 37 systems which include two Mark 1A computers, two Mark 6 stable elements, two Mark 1 starshell computers, one starshell spot transmitter and one fire control switchboard.

Target acquistion and spotting

The Mark 37 GFCS optical and radar equipment perform the function of determining target position by making initial estimates of range, target angle, horizontal speed and rate of climb. Service projectile fire is spotted (shell splashes or air bursts) and the information is transmitted to the computer for correction of subsequent fire. These important functions are often performed by more than one component and on more than one target. The input from each component is identified at the fire control switchboard and given a specific designation as follows:

Sky No. 1 – Forward Mark 37 director
Sky No. 2 – Port Mark 37 director
Sky No. 3 – Starboard Mark 37 director
Sky No. 4 – After Mark 37 director

Gun mount control equipment

The three basic methods of fire control for the twin 5in/38cal gun mounts are primary, secondary and local. Each method is designed to produce rapid, accurate and continuous fire.

In 'primary' control the director system provides for controlling gun movement by remote control or by dial–indicated gun orders. In remote control, director signals, via the computer, automatically train and elevate the guns. In the dial-indicated mode, director signals, via the computer, are transmitted to the mount indicator-regulators and gun orders are issued by the mount pointer and trainer matching pointers. Fuze setting is also controlled by either method. In both cases, director targets are designated by a coordinating station. The

director establishes a line of sight to the target and its movements are automatically transmitted to the computer and combined with other inputs which enable gun laying and fuze setting orders to be generated. These orders are continuously transmitted to the gun mount indicator-regulators.

The 'secondary' method is a stand-by system of director control. Gun laying can be performed as in 'primary' control, either automatically or by gun order to the indicator-regulators. In 'secondary' there is a loss of signal transmission between the director and computer, and all values are sent to the plotting room by telephone to enable the computer to issue gun orders.

In 'local' control, the mount is operated by the pointer, trainer, sight setter and fuze setter from gun orders issued by the mount captain. Target acquisition, sighting and spotting are accomplished using the

The fueling station for the Pioneer RPV is shown in the former starboard 40mm gun tub on the stern. Aviation gasoline is stored in a heavy rubber bladder carried on a wheeled cart. The cart, which has a quick release mechanism, is secured to a set of inclined tracks and can be jettisoned in an emergency. (Photograph by the author.)

turret's optics which are manned at all times. This enables mount personnel to take control if there is a failure in the director system. Each mount is equipped with two sets of sights, the Mark 36 and Mark 39, which constitute the local target-sighting, gun-laying controls.

The Mark 36 sight assembly is carriage-mounted consisting of the trainer's, pointer's, and checker's telescopes with a common sight-setting mechanism. They are interconnected by shafting and gearing to provide simultaneous, equal movement of the lines of sight at each position. The trainer's station is equipped with a Mark 68 telescope and the pointer's and checker's stations have Mark 68 scopes. (All are 6.3× power.) The checker's position and scope are not manned during combat, and are used only for drill fire and target practice to see where the shot would land. The Mark 39 sight assembly is located in the roof of the gun mount and manned by the mount captain. The

There are four Mark 37 GFCS on the *Iowa* class and they are controlled from two plotting rooms. Some of the equipment in the aft secondary battery plotting room is shown here. One system is in the foreground including a Mark 6 stable element and a Mark 1A computer with a Mark 1 starshell computer atop. Another system is in the background. (Courtesy FCCM (SW) Stephen Skelley, USNR.)

The Mark 11 switchboard in the aft secondary battery plotting room. There is one switchboard in each plotting room which serves two Mark 37 GFCS. There are 252 J-type rotary switches on each board allowing various elements of the fire control system to be selectively interchanged. Both switchboards were also interconnected to the boards in the main battery plotting rooms which allowed the interchanging of functions between the Mark 37 and Mark 38 GFCS. (Courtesy FCCM (SW) Stephen Skelley, USNR.)

sight is an eyepiece and ring assembly mechanically linked to the pointer's and trainer's telescopes. This permits the mount captain to observe and transmit target train, elevation, range, speed and spot correction information to the pointer and trainer.

The Mark 37 director, rangefinders and radar

The four Mark 37 directors are located aloft in the superstructure, one forward and one aft on the centreline and one on each beam. In this positioning, they can cover the widest possible range of target angles with overlapping fields of view.

The optical equipment of each director as currently outfitted consists of a stereoscopic rangefinder, two telescopes and a slewing sight. The rangefinder is a (15ft base) Mark 42 dual power (12× or 24× power) type. The telescopes, for pointing and training, are the Mark 60 (6× power) moveable–prism type. The slewing sight is used by the control officer to designate a target and rapidly bring it into the field of the optics.

When the *Iowa* and *New Jersey* were first commissioned they had an early modification of the director using three Mark 60 telescopes, the third scope being used by the director officer in addition to the slewing sight. The *New Jersey* received her present directors in 1952 and the *Iowa* in 1955.

Originally two different director shields were fitted. The *Iowa* and *New Jersey* had the taperback, and the *Missouri* and *Wisconsin* the squareback, type. Both types were protected with 1.5in STS plate. All directors were modified to the current squareback cockpit type but the *Iowa* and *Wisconsin* have lightweight shields protected with only 0.5in STS plate.

Three different types of radar, the Mark 4, Mark 12/22 and Mark 25 have been used with the Mark 37 directors since the *Iowas* first became operational. In each case, the antennas were aligned in train and elevation with the director optics so that full radar or optical or a combination of both could be used for tracking. As with the main battery director, optical pointing and training and radar ranging is the most accurate method of tracking.

As first outfitted, the *Iowa* and *New Jersey* had the Mark 4 antenna mounted atop each director. The Mark 4 radar was essentially two halves of a Mark 3 antenna (see Mark 40 director above) stacked vertically. Each antenna half produced a separate beam at a slightly different angle. When the returning signals were equal in strength, the target lay on a line directly between the signals bisecting their angle of separation.

The radiating beams, or lobes, produced a side effect which was duplicated in the returning signal and the Mark 12 was developed in an effort to reduce this effect. The Mark 4 and Mark 12 antennas were very similar in appearance and actual operation. Both sets had difficulty in tracking low-flying targets because of signal reflection from the surface of the water. The Mark 22 'orange peel' radar was developed to resolve this problem. An auxiliary of the Mark 12, the Mark 22 was mounted on its right side. They functioned together and the Mark 22 could not be operated separately.

The *Missouri* and *Wisconsin* completed with the newer Mark 12/22 sets. The Mark 4 was replaced on the *New Jersey* with the Mark 12/22 during an August 1944 availability period at Pearl Harbor and the *Iowa* was fitted with the new sets in March 1945 during a refit at San Francisco.

The Mark 25 radar, which is currently in use, introduced a dish antenna in which the feed was rotated slightly off-center. The radiating beams, or lobes, formed the trace of a cone producing a conical scanning pattern eliminating the need for a separate height-finding antenna. The *Missouri* was the first to be fitted with the new Mark 25 set during a 1948 overhaul, followed by the *Wisconsin* in 1953 and the *Iowa* in 1955. The *New Jersey* received Mark 25s for her centerline directors in early-1953 but did not have the new sets fitted to the side directors until 1954.

The Mark 1/1A computer

The *Iowa* class has four Mark 1A computers, two are installed in the forward and two in the after secondary battery plotting rooms. The Mark 1 computer, originally installed aboard the *Iowas*, was a mechanical–analog device which computed ballistic values to automatically and continuously aim the 5in/38cal guns. The Mark 1A computer currently in use has been updated by a series of ordnance alterations (Ord Alts) to enable tracking of faster moving airborne targets. The Mark 1 could track targets moving at rates between 400 and 450 knots while the Mark 1A is capable of 880 to 900 knot tracking.

A number of informational inputs are required for the computation of the fire control problem including the ship's speed and course, director elevation and train, target angle and speed, target rate of climb, and stabilization data. Target motion information is transmitted to the computer from the director and radar and the ship's motion data is received from the gyro and pitometer log. Stabilization information, including level and crosslevel data, are supplied by the Mark 6 stable element. Ballistic data such as initial velocity, windage, air-density and sight deflection are included. From all of this data the Mark 1A computes relative target motion in terms of range, relative bearing and elevation from which gun orders are continuously transmitted to the gun mount to automatically aim the guns.

The Mark 6 stable element

The four Mark 6 stable elements are installed in the plotting rooms adjacent to the computers which they serve. They provide stabilization for gun orders and the director in line of sight (level) and across the line of sight (crosslevel).

The Mark 6 uses a gyroscope to establish the horizontal reference plane for measuring level and crosslevel angles. Level and crosslevel data is sent to the computer for processing information to the various elements of the fire control system and it is also transmitted to the director to keep the optics and radar stabilized in crosslevel.

The Mark 6 is also the firing station for the plotting room and is equipped with firing keys to control the fire of the gun mounts.

The Mark 1 starshell computer

There are four Mark 1 starshell computers, one being mounted atop each Mark 1A computer forming an integral unit. The computer calculates and transmits data to the 5in/38cal guns for firing starshells and can also be used to control the firing of smoke projectiles.

Gun orders from the Mark 1A computer are modified to compute starshell gun train, gun elevation and fuze-setting orders. The starshell spot transmitter, located in the director, is used to send range, elevation and spot information to the computer for correction of shell placement. Gun orders are calculated to place the shell burst 1,000 yards beyond and 1,500ft above the target.

This arrangement allows simultaneous starshell and surface fire against a common target by the same Mark 37 GFCS.

The fire control switchboard

A fire control switchboard is located in each plotting room and controls the various inputs and outputs of the fire control system. These switchboards allow either of the plotting rooms and the various elements of the fire control system to be selectively interchanged and control the different configurations that can be attained with the Mark 37 GFCS.

Both switchboards can be interconnected with the two main battery switchboards which allow interchanging of functions between the Mark 37 and Mark 38 GFCS. In this manner, either the secondary battery or main battery can be controlled from any of the six directors through any of the four switchboards.

Target designation

The target designation system, which was originally installed, consists of instruments and signal equipment for detecting targets and quickly distributing accurate position information to the various fire control stations. The equipment includes the Mark 3 target designation transmitter and receiver and the Mark 5 and Mark 6 target designation transmitters. Target train and elevation information can be exchanged between the Mark 3s and sent to the Mark 37 directors. Target train data can be sent to the Mark 40 director by the Mark 3, Mark 5 and Mark 6 for use with the Mark 38 main battery directors.

The system installed in the *Iowa* class used eight Mark 3s, one Mark 5 and one Mark 6. The Mark 3s were installed, one to port and one to starboard, in the following locations: primary conning station walkway, navigating bridge, forward air defense station and after air defense station. The Mark 5 was fitted on the starboard side of the conning station and the Mark 6 to port. This system is no longer in use.

Illumination control

As originally outfitted, the *Iowa* class had five 36in searchlights mounted high in the superstructure. One was atop the bridge between the Mark 40 and Mark 37 director, two were fitted just aft of the base of the beam Mark 37 directors and two were mounted on the after stack.

Searchlights operate in a manner similar to the guns and could be controlled manually or remotely. For remote operation a searchlight control transmitter was installed in each Mark 37 director which used gun order data for training and elevating the lights. Shutter control was exercised by inputs from the illumination correctors at the forward and after air defense stations.

By interconnecting the secondary battery switchboards with the main battery switchboards the searchlights could also be controlled by the Mark 38 directors. This allowed them to be trained with the main battery and controlled from any of the four fire control boards.

When the *Iowas* were being built, great importance was placed on these large searchlights and their elaborate method of control. This was especially true in view of the success the Japanese had enjoyed during the early night actions in the Southwest Pacific. By 1945,

ANTENNAE

WIRING TRUNKS

STBD.

PORT

HUT BUILT FOR CONTROLS
ON FIXED STRUCTURE

CONFIDENTIAL
U.S.S. BB 62
MARK 49 DIRECTOR WITH
MARK 19 RADAR
LOOKING AFT
PHILA. NAVY YARD — OCT. 29, 1943.

1871·49

Both the Mark 49 and Mark 51 directors for the 40mm anti-aircraft are shown aboard the *New Jersey* on 29 October 1943. The *New Jersey* carried both systems until early-1945 but none of the other *Iowa*s carried the Mark 49 system. Note the pair of 36in searchlights. They could be manually or remotely controlled. Remotely, they were operated similarly to the secondary battery guns and controlled by the Mark 37 GFCS.

however, it appeared that they would never be used for their intended purpose.

Although all of the *Iowa*s were completed with five 36in searchlights, they did not retain their full complement for long. The *Iowa* lost her forward light in 1943, her after lights in 1946 and the forward pair about 1951. The *New Jersey*'s after lights were removed in 1945, her forward two were landed in 1951 and the forward light came off in 1953. The *Missouri* carried hers perhaps the longest, losing the two pairs about 1947 but retaining her forward light until about 1952. The *Wisconsin* seems to have lost her forward pair in 1945 and the forward single in 1946 but she retained the pair on the after stack until 1952.

ANTI-AIRCRAFT BATTERY

The fire control problem for the intermediate and short range weapons was different from the solutions of the Mark 37 system in that the solution time was greatly reduced. This resulted in the development of a family of lead-computing, or relative-rate, gun sight systems which measured the rate of change in bearing and elevation as angular quantities by tracking the target. Although the lead-computing gun sight was relatively simple, it was a fine fire control system.

The 20mm battery

The Mark 14 gun sight was the first lead-angle computing mechanism developed for use with the 20mm machine guns. It used two mechanically restrained rate-of-turn type gyros, one for train and one for elevation, to generate lead angles. When tracking, the gimbal frame turns at a rate equal to the angular velocity of the line of sight to the target. The sight computed the lead angle while the target was being tracked. The Mark 14 gun sight could be mounted on either the

single or twin 20mm mount.

Pointing and training was effected by the operator's body movement through a set of handle bars and shoulder rests. In the usual magazine load every fifth round was a tracer which assisted the operator in spotting his fire.

The free-swinging 20mm gun mounts could also be equipped with mechanical ring sights for aiming. This arrangement relied on the operator's judgement to lead the target and tracer fire was a major assist.

The 40mm battery

The *Iowa* class was originally equipped with the Mark 51 director which was developed for control of the 40mm power-driven gun

In this photograph of the *Iowa*, taken in January 1958, the two Mark 63 GFCS fitted to the stern 40mm guns are clearly visible. They were intended to control the twin 3in/50cal anti-aircraft guns which were planned as a class improvement but were never installed.

mount. It was a simple lightweight relative-rate system incorporating the Mark 14 gun sight. The directors were located near the gun mounts they controlled, usually just above the mount to be relatively free from the mount's vibration and smoke. The Mark 51 was trained and elevated with a set of handle bars. A range estimate was manually set on the side of the director and the lead angles computed by the Mark 14 sight were transmitted to the power drives of the mount. The director was also equipped with a ring sight for use when the Mark 14 sight was inoperative.

An improved gun sight, the Mark 15, was retrofitted to the Mark 51 directors in 1945. The sight was similar to the Mark 14 but incorporated a telescopic sighting system which resulted in more accurate tracking and shorter solution times.

The Mark 49 director was an early attempt to solve the fire control problem for heavy machine guns. A telescope was used to determine bearing and elevation while measured range was provided by the Mark 19 radar, which was also intended to give a blind firing capability.

Lead-angle tracking was so limited that fire could not be directed to attacks against other ships in close company and the small size of the Mark 19 antenna proved inadequate for ranging and blind fire. By mid-1943 some 343 Mark 49s had been delivered and many were

The 20mm Mark 15 Phalanx CIWS (Close-in Weapons System) is shown with its radome removed exposing the AN/VPS-2 pulsed doppler type radar antennas. The search and the track antennas operate off a common transmitter. The system can be operated in either manual or automatic modes. It has no IFF feature and any high-speed incoming target will be engaged. A Mark 37 director is to the left. (Courtesy FCCM (SW) Stephen Skelley, USNR.)

installed in fleet units. By this time adequate quantities of the more successful Mark 51 were available and the Mark 49 program was abandoned.

Although originally completed with all Mark 51s, the *New Jersey* had six Mark 49 directors installed in 1943. They first appear in photographs taken during an October availability period at the Philadelphia Navy Yard and seem to be aboard as late as February 1945. No specific installation records were found and it is not clear why this installation was made, which mounts they controlled and if control could be interchanged with the Mark 51s. None of the other *Iowas* appear to have been outfitted with Mark 49 directors. The Mark 57 was under development at the time and it is possible that this installation was used for testing and evaluation of system components, since many of the Mark 19 radars were converted for use with the Mark 57.

The installation of the Mark 57 GFCS, which began in 1945, gave

the *Iowas* their first true blind firing capability with the 40mm battery. The Mark 57 system was used to augment the individual Mark 51 directors associated with each mount and could control a group of 40mm mounts from a remote location. Two directors were mounted above the bridge and aft of the Mark 37 director, two were fitted amidships between the stacks and two were mounted on the aft Mark 38 director tower providing a wide range of target angles.

The director was manually operated with a set of handle bars and mounted a telescope, Mark 34 radar, radar scope and Mark 17 computer. The operator could track the target optically or on the radar scope in an undisturbed line of sight. The Mark 34 antenna was a parabolic reflector with a nutator feed line which deflected the beam slightly producing conical scanning. The computer, using two rate-of-turn gyros and a cross-roll gyro transmitted target data to components below decks for computing the problem.

The system power supply, amplifier, radar console and Mark 16 computer were located below decks. The mechanical and electrical devices in the Mark 16 combined the train and elevation lead angles with director train and elevation to compute and issue gun train and elevation orders to the mount or mounts under control

The Mark 56 GFCS was installed aboard the *New Jersey* in 1954 and on the *Iowa* in 1955. It was intended to control the twin 3in/50cal mounts which were planned as a replacement for the 40mm battery. A dual-ballistic system, the Mark 56 was capable of issuing simultaneous gun orders to two different-sized batteries. It was used to control the 40mm guns and gave them an enhanced blind firing capability. It could also be used to control the 5in/38cal battery. The 3in guns were never installed in any of the *Iowas* and the *Missouri* and *Wisconsin* did not receive the Mark 56 systems.

The system consists of a director with a radar mounted above decks and various computing units located in a computing room below decks. Targets were tracked either optically or by radar. Optical tracking was accomplished using a telescope, mounted in the Mark 56 director, which was controlled by a handgrip-type control unit. Automatic tracking was provided by the Mark 35 radar antenna. The Mark 56 measures target angular rates and the director line of sight is stabilized by vertical and rate gyros located in the director. Target data is transmitted below to the Mark 42 ballistic computer which converts the angular rates to linear rates, corrects ballistic quantities and transmits true lead-angle values to the Mark 30 gun order converter. The Mark 30 converts lead-angle information to gun orders which are then sent to the gun mounts. The system could cover lead angles up to 30 degress and target speeds of up to 630 knots.

Six systems were fitted to the *Iowa* and *New Jersey* and their six directors were located to port and starboard as follows: two at the base of the side Mark 37 directors, two replacing the high 40mm gun mounts between the stacks and two on the sides of the aft Mark 38 director tower.

Some Mark 63 GFCS installations were also made. The system is manually operated and designed for use with the 40mm and 3in/50cal guns against air targets at ranges between 800 and 7,000 yards. The director is pedestal mounted nearby the gun mount and the radar antenna is carried on the gun. Targets can be tracked either optically or by radar. The system uses a disturbed line of sight in which the sight housing and gun barrels are aimed at the future target position while the optical line of sight and the radar beam remain on the present target position. The director resembles the Mark 51 but uses a Mark 15 or Mark 29 sight and a cross-roll gyro. The Mark 34 radar antenna, with Target Acquisition Unit (TACU), was mounted in a gimbal above the gun trunion. The TACU equipment was mounted inside the ship directly below the director pedestal.

Four systems were planned for each ship to control the two 3in mounts forward near the bow and the two aft at the stern. Two Mark 63 systems were installed on the *Iowa* and were used to control the two quadruple, 40mm mounts on the stern. Some elements of the systems still remain aboard the *Iowa*. It does not appear that any of the other ships in the class were so fitted.

The 20mm Phalanx CIWS

The 20mm Mark 15 Phalanx CIWS is a stand-alone, automatic unit which searches for and automatically engages missiles which 'leak through' longer range defenses. The current configuration of the *Iowa* class carries four CIWS systems. They are located high in the superstructure, one on each side of the forward fire control tower and one on each side amidships just forward of the second stack.

Control is by the AN/VPS-2 pulsed doppler-type radar. The radome houses two antennas, a search antenna and a track antenna, operating off a common pulsed doppler transmitter. When the search radar picks up a return signal, target speed and angle of approach are compared with data stored in the computer. If the target parameters meet the criteria of the attacking missile, the target is turned over to the track radar.

The system is controlled by a remote control panel located in the SWC and can be operated in either automatic or manual. When in automatic, the system will search, track, fire, kill assess and return to search. In manual operation an operator is required to press a firing key to begin the operational sequence. The CIWS can also be assigned to search for and destroy normal air targets. The system has no Identification Friend or Foe (IFF) and any high-speed incoming target will be engaged.

Missile battery

The Harpoon and Tomahawk weapons control systems are similar and targeting data is provided by the various informational systems in the SWC where their launch controls are located (see Chapter 7 for details of the SWC.) All missiles are preprogramed with a range of target data. When target selection is made, the SWC transmits the data to the individual missiles for programming into their guidance system.

The Harpoon data processor is a digital computer which receives targeting and altitude data and computes the necessary missile and launch orders. After launch, guidance is provided by a mid-course guidance system consisting of an altitude reference assembly and a digital computer. No inputs from the launching platform are required after launching. Flight control is maintained by four fin surfaces, each driven by an electromechanical actuator and cruise altitude is monitored by a radar altimeter. An offset launch capability of up to +/– 90 degrees is provided for all launch modes.

The flight sequence of all types of launches is the same. After launching the missile moves to its low-level cruise altitude which is maintained until it reaches the target area. When the target comes within the search area of the active radar seeker, the high resolution system detects and 'locks-on' to the target. The lock-on is maintained until target impact. A terminal 'pop-up' maneuver counters close-in enemy defenses and maximizes warhead effectiveness.

The Tomahawk Land Attack Missile (TLAM) utilizes a modified Harpoon guidance system with a greatly increased range and payload capacity. The flight sequence is similar to that of the Harpoon but the

The Mark 37 director for the 5in/38cal secondary battery in its present configuration with the Mark 25 radar antenna. The Mark 42 rangefinder has dual power capability of 12x or 24x. The two doors on the face of the director are for the Mark 60 pointing and training telescopes. The slewing sight, in the vertical shield, is also mounted on the face and allows the control officer to quickly designate a target and quickly bring it into the field of the optics. Note the Mark 38 director of Spot 1 and the port SLQ-32(v)3 ECM antenna. (Courtesy FCCM (SW) Stephen Skelley, USNR.)

improved guidance system has a wider range of targeting capabilities including the ability to maneuver to confuse defenses in the target area.

An inertial navigation system is used by the TLAM for its flight over water. For guidance from landfall to the target a terrain contour matching (TERCOM) system takes over. Terrain elevation is measured by the missile guidance package and compared with the measured contour elevation maps stored in its memory. This allows the missile to evaluate its position and make course corrections to the target.

Chapter 7

RADAR AND ELECTRONICS

The development of radar and electronics systems by the US Navy during World War II provided a technical superiority which significantly affected the operational capabilities of the fleet. Although the principles of radar were known before World War II, technical advances made during that period and the post-war years have opened up entirely new fields in radar and electronics which are still expanding today.

The technical nature of radar makes the subject rather complex. The many related electronics systems are equally complex. Although not a complete technical explanation of the radar and electronics systems used aboard the *Iowa* class, this overview will provide the reader with enough technical background, in simple terms, to better understand the function of these systems.

Radar is an acronym for RAdio Detection And Ranging. It is a means for detecting the presence of objects, for determining their range and bearing and for recognizing their character. This is accomplished utilizing radio principles. A series of pulses of radio wave signals is produced in a high-powered Ultra-High-Frequency (UHF) radio transmitter and sent to an antenna. The antenna confines the pulses of radio frequency energy into a narrow beam, which is directed over the area to be searched. When a pulse strikes an object in its path, energy (an echo) is reflected. Some of the echo is returned toward the antenna and is picked up by a sensitive radio receiver which detects the object. The receiver amplifies the echoes and reproduces them as video pulses which are displayed visually on a screen. Since radio waves travel at the constant velocity of light, the timing can be accurately measured when used in conjunction with the antenna direction, this provides range, bearing and relative shape of an object on the display or screen.

SEARCH RADAR

The requirements for each type of radar differ widely. The primary function of air search radar is the detection of aircraft at extreme ranges. It must determine the range, bearing and altitude of targets with reasonable accuracy. It does not, however, require the precision of surface search radar which must determine range and bearing with sufficient resolution to show separate targets so they may be indicated to the fire control systems. Fire control radar, on the other hand, must be precise enough to produce accurate gunfire. Air, surface search and fire control radars, therefore, have fundamentally

Radar, electronics and communications systems have become increasingly more important to warfare at sea. The ability to gather information and disseminate and process selected data, results in the delivery of maximum performance from the various weapons systems. This photograph of the *Iowa*, taken in early-1986, shows a great deal of the sophisticated gear which she now carries. In the foreground is a portion of the discone/cage array of the NTDS antenna at the bow. The two inboard whip antennas at the bridge level are receivers and the two outboard are AS-2537A/SR transmitter antennas. The two antennas for the SLQ-32(V)3 electronic countermeasures system are at the air defense level. The antenna for the long range SPS-49 radar is on the foretop. On the foretopmast above the SPS-49 radar is an array of AS-1735/SRC communications antennas and on the very top is the AS-3240/URN-25 antenna for tactical air navigation. (Courtesy FCCM (SW) Stephen Skelley, USNR.)

different characteristics which enable them to perform their primary functions best and usually at the expense of other functions.

When the *Iowas* were originally completed during World War II, the requirements for battleship search radar were relatively fundamental, and consisted of air and surface search sets. The primary difference between air and surface radar is the different wavelength range on which they operate. The long-range air search sets, such as the SK series, operated in the longer wavelengths of about 100cm. The shorter range surface search sets, such as the SG series, operated in the shorter wavelengths of about 10cm or microwave range. The wavelength, therefore, usually determined the characteristics and geometry of the antenna. The longer the wavelength meant a more open antenna, and the shorter the wavelength meant a more solid antenna. For example, the SK antenna was a large, open bedspring

The original radar installation of the *Iowa* is shown in this photograph, taken in November 1943 at the Boston Navy Yard. The SK air search antenna was mounted atop a plain pole foretopmast. The forward SG surface search set can be seen on a platform just below the air defense level. The displays were located directly below in the primary conning station to avoid a long and complex waveguide arrangement. Although not an ideal location for generating a search pattern, the transmission loss was held to a minimum. Note that the longer wavelength SK antenna is a large open mesh, while the shorter wavelength SG antenna is solid. An IFF BK-7 'steering wheel' transponder antenna can be seen just forward of the SG set.

while the SG antenna was a small, solid band. The same basic operating considerations are true with current equipment.

For the battleships, radar equipment added to the weight problem which had already become a concern due to the increase in the number of additional light anti-aircraft batteries, men to man them, etc. The need to place antennas and associated equipment as high as practical in and above the superstructure further complicated the problem. Original battleship design had not reckoned on this new science but radar was definitely here to stay.

In addition to the basic air and surface search units, other units and equipment which operate in conjunction with them must also be considered. These include the height-finding and low-angle search radar sets along with the recognition equipment used with them.

For the purpose of this discussion, radar equipment aboard the *Iowa* class battleships will be considered in the following categories:

The *Missouri* in drydock on 23 July 1944 at the New York Navy Yard. The *Missouri* is the only ship of the class completed with the new SK-2 air search radar which was fitted to the foretop. The second dipole inside the SK-2 dish is a BM interrogator for the Mark III IFF system. Note the BK-7 'ski pole' transponder antenna on the yardarm. By the time the *Missouri* was completed, the waveguide transmission problems had been resolved and the SG set was placed in a better position on the foretopmast.

Air search radar equipment
Height-finding and low-angle search radar equipment
Surface search radar equipment
Recognition equipment for use with radar

See Appendix A for radar equipment tables

Air search

Air search radar equipment is designed to perform the following functions: warn of approaching aircraft before they can be sighted visually and bring anti-aircraft defenses to a proper and timely degree of readiness; allow continuous observation of enemy aircraft; provide security against attack at night, during poor visibility or from behind a smokescreen; scout; and range on land 150 to 250 miles or more.

The large air search antennas, characteristic of radars operating in the longer wavelengths, contributed more to the topside overweight problem than any of the other radar and electronics equipment. Each of these antennas and its operating gear had to be supported aloft. Structures, masts and yards had to be greatly strengthened to carry the additional loads. In the design of new radar equipment, an important goal became the reduction in the total antenna package weight.

The *Iowa* is shown entering ASBD-2 at Ulithi on 27 December 1944. Most of her radar and electronics suites are visible. At the foretop is the large SK 'bedspring' air search radar and her two SG surface sets appear on the fire control tower just below the air defense level and at the main top. Recognition equipment of the Mark III IFF system includes the small BL 'bedspring' interrogator atop the SK antenna, two BK-7 'ski pole' transponders on the foreyard and one BK-7 on the afteryard. There is an unusual mixture of ECM gear, probably the result of field installations and modifications. The DBM radar direction-finders are hidden by the air defense level, but two TDY jammers are clearly visible, one on each side of the fire control tower. An AS-56 receiver antenna is on the starboard foreyard and AS-37 'wagon wheel' receivers are at the air defense level.

The original air search sets were in the SK series. When first completed, the *Iowa*, *New Jersey* and *Wisconsin* were equipped with SK, and the *Missouri* with SK-2 radar sets. The antennas for the *Iowa* and *New Jersey* were mounted atop the pole foremast while those for the *Missouri* and *Wisconsin* were on a foretop platform. This difference was

due to the new location of the SG sets on the last two ships (see SG Search Radar below). When the *Iowa* and *New Jersey* were fitted with the SK-2 they also received foretop platforms as in the *Missouri* and *Wisconsin*. The SK used a 17ft square antenna with an array of dipoles and could distinguish targets up to 100nm at 10,000ft. The radiating beams, or lobes, from this flat reflector produced a side lobe effect which was duplicated in the returning signal. The SK-2 was designed to reduce this effect using a 17ft parabolic mesh reflector. It had the additional advantages of a stronger structure resulting in a reduction in weight over the SK bedspring installation. The *New Jersey* received the SK-2 in 1945, followed by the *Iowa* and *Wisconsin* in 1946.

Although the SK series had great range, the search beams reflected by these large antennas were relatively low (10,000ft at 100nm). The SR was a new design for long-range air search that attempted to improve the altitude capability. Later in World War II, the height capability of the SK series became a serious problem due to attacking aircraft approaching at very high altitudes. The SR used a 15ft x 6ft rectangular bedspring antenna with a diapole array. Targets could be distinguished at approximately 20,000ft and 80nm. The SR was used with the SK/SK-2 set for long-range searching and higher altitude detection. The SR was mounted on the mainmast, which required additional bracing and the addition of a maintop platform for the new antenna. Only the *Iowa* and *Wisconsin* carried the SR sets, which were fitted in 1945.

The SR-3 was under development at the end of World War II as a replacement for the SK series. As designed, it had a 17ft x 5ft parabolic antenna. It did not perform as expected however, having a range of only 20 to 30nm. Modifications, making the model an SR-3c, included replacing the antenna with an SPS-6 reflector. The use of the successor (SPS-6) antenna, which considerably improved the overall performance, often caused it to be mistakenly identified in photo-

The post-World War II changes in radar and electronics are visible in this photograph of the *Iowa*, taken on 22 May 1947, at anchor off the Naval Air Station at Alameda in San Francisco Bay. Surface search radar includes a new SK-2 on her foretop and an SR on the maintop. Her after SG surface search set remains, but the foward set has been replaced by one TDY ECM jammer. A DBA radio direction-finder is on the foretopmast. The outermast dipole in the SK-2 is the antenna for her BM IFF. The SR also used the BM, but its antenna was integral with the SR antenna and could be distinguished by the four vertical dipoles in the top half of the 'bedspring'. Other ECM gear visible includes two DBM radar direction-finders. One is on the aft side of the air defense level and the other is on the foretop aft of the topmast. An AS-56 receiver antenna is fitted on a brace aft of the air defense level. A TBS ship-to-ship radio antenna can be seen just forward and above the DBA.

graphs. Only the *New Jersey* and *Missouri* carried the SR-3/3c sets which were installed on the foretop platform in 1948. The *New Jersey*'s was replaced with an SPS-6 in 1952, but the *Missouri* went into reserve in 1955 with the only remaining SR-3 series set.

The SPS-6 was the direct successor to the SR-3 and was the first post–war air search radar set. The antenna used an 18ft × 5ft parabolic reflector which was horn fed from the front and had a wind balancing vane on the back. This was a very successful set and could distinguish fighter planes at 80nm and 25,000ft. Later versions, the SPS-6A and 6B, could detect a fighter at 80nm and over 40,000ft. The *Iowa* and *Wisconsin* were fitted with the SPS-6 in 1951, followed by the *New Jersey* in 1952. The antennas were installed on the existing foretop platforms. The *New Jersey* went into reserve in 1957 with the SPS-6 and when she was refitted for Vietnam service, the set was updated to the SPS-6C version. The *Missouri* retained her SR-3c set.

With the success of the SPS-6, the natural follow-on was an improved version with greater capability. The new set, designated SPS-12, became available in 1953 and was installed on the foretop platform on the *Iowa* and *Wisconsin* during their 1955 refits. Both ships

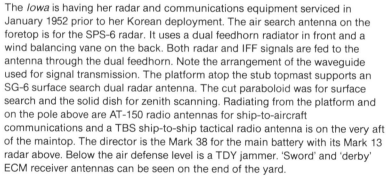

The *Iowa* is having her radar and communications equipment serviced in January 1952 prior to her Korean deployment. The air search antenna on the foretop is for the SPS-6 radar. It uses a dual feedhorn radiator in front and a wind balancing vane on the back. Both radar and IFF signals are fed to the antenna through the dual feedhorn. Note the arrangement of the waveguide used for signal transmission. The platform atop the stub topmast supports an SG-6 surface search dual radar antenna. The cut paraboloid was for surface search and the solid dish for zenith scanning. Radiating from the platform and on the pole above are AT-150 radio antennas for ship-to-aircraft communications and a TBS ship-to-ship tactical radio antenna is on the very aft of the maintop. The director is the Mark 38 for the main battery with its Mark 13 radar above. Below the air defense level is a TDY jammer. 'Sword' and 'derby' ECM receiver antennas can be seen on the end of the yard.

Another view of the *Iowa* in January 1952 shows the rest of her radar and electronics suites. The 18ft × 5ft parabolic reflector of the SPS-6 antenna is nearly full front as are the dual antennas of the SG-6 radar. The 8ft dish antenna of her SP height-finding radar is on the platform at the maintop. IFF equipment includes a BK-7 'ski pole' to starboard on the forward yard and two BK-7s on the afteryard using 'steering wheel' antennas. The SP used a BO interrogator fed by the outer dipole in the center. Two DBM radar direction-finders are located on the after stack and the TDY jammer is on the platform below the air defense level. Other ECM gear, the 'sword' and 'derby', are on both ends of the foreyard.

were placed in reserve in 1958 with this set. The SPS-12 antenna was also a horn-fed parabolic reflector, measuring 17ft × 6ft, but without a wind balancing vane. Discrimination of aircraft could be made at 90nm and over 40,000ft.

When modernized and fitted for service in the 1980s, all four ships were fitted with the new SPS-49 radar. A heavy new tripod foremast was fitted to accommodate these antennas and other electronic gear. The antenna is a horn-fed parabolic reflector approximately 24ft × 14ft. The SPS-49 is capable of extremely long-range, high-angle detection and discrimination. It has Electronic Counter-Counter-measures (ECCM) features and is designed to operate in the Automatic Detection and Tracking (ADT) mode.

Height-finding and low-angle search

Height-finding and low-angle search radar equipment is designed to perform the following functions: obtain accurate range, bearing and altitude data on enemy aircraft; detect low-flying aircraft; act as high-power surface search radar; and range on land 80 miles or more.

Because of their wide beams, early search radars did not provide accurate target elevation information. The radiation pattern also left a conical shaped void in the zenith above the antenna. The SP and SPS-8 sets were developed to resolve the target elevation and zenith search problems. (Also see SG-6 and SPS-4 below and Mark 22 fire control radar, Chapter 6.) They functioned together with the search radar to furnish an accurate target location for hostile aircraft so that friendly aircraft could be directed to a favorable intercept position. They also served as an early warning for the air defense fire control radar. Their very narrow 'pencil beam' had almost no side lobe or fade effect from signal reflection off the sea, but the narrow beam was unsuited for search. Accurate altitude angle measurement depends on the surface of the sea as a reference plane; therefore, some form of stabilization is necessary. This can be accomplished by stabilizing the antenna or by a moveable feed to the antenna reflector.

The first height-finding set used aboard the *Iowa*s was the SP. It was developed late in World War II and used an 8ft dish antenna, which was stabilized for accurate target attitude angle measurement. The SP could range on larger aircraft to 70nm at 10,000ft, smaller aircraft at 40nm and 10,000ft and a battleship at 35nm. To mount the SP, a new tripod mainmast was fitted to the after stack and the antenna was installed on the maintop platform. The *New Jersey* received her SP in

1945 and the *Iowa* and *Missouri* received theirs in 1948. The *Wisconsin* retained her SR radar in this position and was not fitted with the new set.

The SPS-8 was solely a height-finder and replaced the SP radars used aboard the *Iowa* class. The antenna featured a large 14ft × 4ft 'orange peel' type reflector, a horn feed well in front and a wind

Below left: The *Iowa*'s radar, electronics and communications antennas seen here, on 18 February 1956, at the Norfolk Navy Yard. She was decommissioned two years later in this configuration. There is a new air search radar, the SPS-12, on the foretop and the standard SG-6 surface zenith set is located as before. The new Mark X recognition equipment is labeled AS-177/upx. Note the new TDY-1a jamming transmitter which was installed in 1952. The TDY was removed during the 1955 refit but the *Iowa* used both jammers for three years. There was another TDY-1a located opposite on the port side. Unlike the earlier model, the new transmitter was installed much lower with the optimum height for battleships being 34ft to 54ft above the waterline. The DBM antennas were also relocated. The 'sword' is identified as 66132 and the 'derby' as 66131.

A view aft, taken on 18 February 1956, shows the *Iowa*'s new quadrapod and kingpost mainmast, maintop and SPS-8 height-finding radar.

balancing vane extending well behind. The antenna was not stabilized as in the SP but, instead, featured a moving feed to obtain accurate target angle measurement. In addition to zenith search capabilities it was credited with furnishing accurate target elevation data at over 80nm and 10,000ft. All four units were equipped with the larger, heavier SPS-8 radar and, therefore, required a new mainmast arrangement. In 1953, the tripod mainmast on the after stack of the *Missouri* and *Wisconsin* was reformed into a quadrapod with the after legs extending down to the 02 level of the superstructure. The *New Jersey* received a similar modification in 1954. The *Iowa* had a somewhat different arrangement fitted in mid-1955. The tripod mast on the after stack was also reformed into a quadrapod, but its after legs terminated on the mainbrace spreader for the kingpost tops. (Kingposts with 65ft booms were fitted on the 02 level to handle the large boats nested on the main deck abeam the after main battery fire control director.) In late-1955, kingposts were also fitted to the *Wisconsin* and her quadrapod was modified to be similar to that of the *Iowa*. The *New Jersey* and *Missouri* were not fitted with kingposts.

Surface search

Surface search radar equipment is designed to perform a number of functions. It warns of the presence of enemy surface craft beyond visible range at night, during poor visibility or from behind a smokescreen, and makes appropriate disposition of assets to attack

the enemy or defend against an attack. It also assists fire control radar to make quick target acquisition; acts as auxiliary fire control radar; facilitates station keeping and assists in navigation; and ranges on land 50 miles or more.

The early surface search radar sets were under-powered and plagued with waveguide transmission losses. The waveguide was a rectangular tube which transmitted the radio waves from the power source to the antenna, and the received echo from the antenna to the displays via the receiver. The run had to be relatively straight, for any hard bends could cause reflections within the waveguide itself which would further reduce the quality of the transmission. This required that the antenna be located near enough to the power source and the receiver so that all of the signal would not be lost. Another problem was the accumulation of moisture from the damp sea air which eventually would cause an electrical breakdown. By 1944, the major problems had been eliminated by increasing the power and pressurizing the waveguide to keep the moisture out. There were also improvements in waveguide design which helped to increase transmission efficiency.

The first surface search radar sets were in the SG series. Under development in late-1940, the prototype was tested at sea in June 1941, and the first production models were delivered in April 1942. The SG antenna used a small, waveguide-fed, solid reflector, characteristic of radars operating in the microwave range. The SG could detect large ships at over 20nm and aircraft at 15nm and 500ft.

Its displays of vessels, as well as land masses, made it useful to navigation. The original installation called for two SG sets per ship. When first completed, the *Iowa* and *New Jersey* had their forward sets placed on a platform on the fire control tower just above the primary conning station where their displays were located. Although not an ideal location for generating a search pattern, it avoided a long, complex waveguide arrangement. By the time the *Missouri* and *Wisconsin* were completed, the waveguide transmission problems had been worked out and their forward sets were fitted to the foretopmast. All four ships had their after sets mounted atop the pole mainmast on the after stack. When the *New Jersey* was overhauled in

antenna mounted on a stabilized platform and enclosed in a 30in dome 35in high. Its performance was comparable to that of the SG and with its considerable savings in weight, it was an attractive package for larger units. The *Iowa* and *New Jersey* received an SU in 1945 and the *Wisconsin* in 1946, but the *Missouri* did not have a set installed. Because of their small size and light weight, they could be conveniently spotted in almost any high topside location. Those on the *Iowas* were fitted in the foremast platform area.

The SQ was a portable, lightweight radar set designed for emergency use in case the surface search radars were disabled. The antenna consisted of a vertical dipole-fed paraboloid reflector

1945, her foremast was reconfigured and her forward SG set was relocated similar to the *Missouri* and *Wisconsin*. The *Iowa* underwent a similar rework of her foremast in 1946, however, the forward SG set was landed in favour of a DBA radio direction finder. The forward sets were later replaced by the new SG-6 as described below and the after sets were removed when the SPS-8s were installed as described previously.

The SG-6 was an attempt to combine SG surface search and zenith search capabilities in the same radar set. The antenna had two reflectors, a 7ft × 2ft cut paraboloid for surface search and a 5ft solid dish for zenith scanning. Transmission signals could be switched from one reflector to the other for the search mode desired. This was an interim solution for searching the void space directly above the ship before the SPS-8 radar became fully operational. All four ships had SG-6 sets fitted to their foretopmasts replacing the SGs or the DRB as in the *Iowa*. The *Iowa* and *Missouri* had theirs installed in 1948, followed by the *New Jersey* in 1950 and the *Wisconsin* in 1951.

In 1953, the *Wisconsin*'s SG-6 set was replaced by an SPS-4 radar which was nearly identical to it functionally and in physical appearance. It operated on a slightly longer wavelength than the SG-6 and could detect large ships at over 20nm and aircraft at 20nm. The SPS-4 was fitted only to the *Wisconsin* and she went into reserve in 1958 with this set.

Originally developed for the destroyer escort program, the SU was a small, lightweight surface search radar using a 24in paraboloid

The *New Jersey* underway in the Delaware River, on 18 April 1968, *en route* to sea trials. There is an SPS-6C air search radar on her foretop and an SPS-10 surface search set on a platform just above. The large radomes aft of the foretopmast enclose AS-570/SLR and AS-571/SLR ECM antennas. It is difficult to distinguish the ULQ-6 ECM system on the side of the fire control tower at the air defense level. Note the discone/cage array on the bow and the AS-1018 radio antennas on the mainmast.

measuring about 2ft × 4ft. It could detect a battleship at 8nm and a surfaced submarine at nearly 3nm. The SQ allowance was one for the *Iowa* and two each for the *New Jersey*, *Missouri* and *Wisconsin*. All deliveries were in 1944 and use of the sets was discontinued by 1946.

The SPS-10 became the most widely used post-World War II surface search radar. Operational since late-1953, hundreds of sets are currently still in use. The antenna has an 11ft × 3ft parabolic small mesh reflector and can effectively range on the horizon. In service, it has proven excellent in detecting and tracking submarine periscopes up to 16,000 yards distant depending on the mode of operation and sea state. The SPS-10, often referred to as the 'old standby', is considered the most reliable surface search set in current US Navy service. The *New Jersey* received the SPS-10 radar during her 1968 reactivation for Vietnam service and retained it when modernized in 1982. The *Iowa* was fitted with a set when modernized in 1984. It was mounted on the new foremast platform. The *Missouri* and *Wisconsin* are fitted with the new SPS-67.

The SPS-67 is essentially a re-engineered, solid state version of the SPS-10 using the same antenna. Most SPS-10 sets will be converted to the new SPS-67, which has additional capabilities. The modular concept of the new set is expected to increase its reliability and simplify maintenance and repair. The *Iowa* was fitted with the SPS-67 during her 1985 overhaul, the *Missouri* received hers when modernized in 1986, the *New Jersey*'s installation was made during her 1987 overhaul and the *Wisconsin* was fitted during her modernization in 1988.

RECOGNITION EQUIPMENT

Recognition equipment for use with radar is designed to perform several IFF functions. It identifies returning signals from friendly ships and aircraft sending back a coded response and indicates range and bearing of friendly aircraft at distances greater than those from which echoes can be returned. It acts as a beacon to indicate contact with the enemy and upon which friendly aircraft can home. The equipment also follows friendly aircraft through areas of antenna null or clutter, assists in navigation and indicates distress.

Though IFF itself is not radar it is a system integrated with many radars, because it is essential to provide a means of direct recognition/identification at the point where the target is detected by the radar. In the various IFF systems, ships and aircraft are provided with equipment to allow them to establish their friendly character, either directly through the primary radar antenna, or through other devices associated with the radar.

The basic IFF system is composed of an interrogator, a transponder and a responsor. The interrogator is a radio transmitter which emits signals in the IFF band which must be recognized by its associated radar. A transponder is a combined receiver-transmitter fitted in all friendly ships and aircraft. When it receives a challenge pulse from an interrogator, it automatically returns a friendly coded signal. The responsor is a radio receiver, associated with the radar equipment, which receives the reply returned from the transponder. It translates the reply into a suitable form for the display system. The responsor and interrogator are usually combined in a single unit.

The Mark III IFF system

When first completed, the *Iowa* class was equipped with a Mark III IFF system, which was the first to employ an interrogator and transponder operating independently of the radar. The system consisted of BK transponders and BL, BM, BN and BO interrogator-responsors. The arrangement of these components varied between ships. Signals from these units could be sent out using one of several free-standing antennas. The one most commonly used was referred to as the 'ski pole'. The BL, BM and BO could also use an antenna which was

Opposite: The *New Jersey* on transit through the Panama Canal to the Pacific on 4 June 1968. Antennas or the ULQ-6 ECM system are supported by the framework, extending from the large boxes added to each side of the forward fire control tower at the air defense level. AS-1750/S1 antennas are on top and bottom for transmitting and receiving. The center array is an AS-1751/SLA receiver stacked on an AS-1341/ULQ jammer. The large antenna on the bow is the discone/cage for the NTDS system.

Right: This stern view of the *New Jersey*, taken on 4 June 1968, shows the communication antennas on the mainmast and the main deck level at the helicopter landing area. The deck edge antennas were hinged and would be turned outboard during flight operations and the crane on the stern would be rotated directly aft.

integral with a search radar antenna.

All four of the *Iowa*s carried three BK antennas which resembled 'ski poles' and were installed vertically on the yards. In this arrangement, two units were located on the fore yard and the third unit was located on the main yard as an emergency standby.

The *New Jersey*, *Missouri* and *Wisconsin* were each equipped with two BNs which could use either the 'ski pole' or 'steering wheel' antennas installed on the yards or high in the superstructure. Both the BK and BN were omni-directional antennas.

The *Iowa* and *New Jersey* were fitted with one BL each. The BL was a small rectangular bedspring providing four vertical dipoles and mounted atop the large SK radar antenna. The *Wisconsin* used a BM with her SK radar. The BM was an improved unit, functionally interchangeable with the BL and using the same antenna. The *Missouri* also used the BM, but with the SK-2 radar. The BM antenna was a second dipole, mounted in front of the feed dipole for the SK-2 antenna. When the *New Jersey* was fitted with the SK-2 in 1945, followed by the *Iowa* and *Wisconsin* in 1946, their installations were comparable to the *Missouri*'s.

In 1945, the *Iowa* and *Wisconsin* were fitted with an additional air search radar, the SR. It also used a BM interrogator and its integral antenna was distinguished by four vertical dipoles protruding from

the top of the SR antenna.

The model SP height-finding radar was mounted on the *New Jersey* in 1945 and the *Iowa* and *Missouri* in 1948. The SP dish antenna used a BO interrogator fitted as a second dipole similar to the SK-2 installation. The BO was a large unit similar to the BM, but differing in frequency ranges.

Between 1948 and 1952, when the SK-2 radars were replaced by the SR-3 and SPS-6 models, the BM equipment operated through the dual feed-horn radiators of the SR-3 and SPS-6 antennas.

The Mark X IFF system

The Mark III IFF remained in service for some time after World War II, but the system's slow coding technique ws unsatisfactory for tracking high-speed aircraft. The system was also completely compromised, because it had been widely distributed to Allied forces, including the Soviet Union. Therefore, the Mark X IFF system was developed to replace the Mark III. The Mark X was installed on the *Iowa* and *Wisconsin* during their 1955 overhauls when the SPS-12 air search radar was fitted. The BK, BM and BN were all replaced with the new AS-177/UPX-72, AS-177/UPX-27 and AS-177/UPX-23 antennas respectively. The Mark X system was fitted to the *New Jersey* to operate with her SPS-6 antenna when she was reactivated for Vietnam service.

The system was efficient in resolving friendly aircraft congestion, but it lacked security. A coder unit was added to the IFF transponder system which enabled it to generate many variable coded replies. This coding capability was termed Selective Identification Feature (SIF). The SIF feature was not available before the vessels were mothballed in the late-1950s. It is not clear if the *New Jersey* had SIF in 1968-1969, since the refit was austere and she was not indended to control aircraft.

The Mark XII IFF system

The Mark XII identification system is the first major equipment/sub-system program involving tri-service implementation. It is sometimes referred to as AIMS, an acronym broken down as follows:

A – ATCRBS (Air Traffic Control Radar Beacon System)

Cont.

The *New Jersey* on sea trials, 20 April 1968. The new ULQ-6 ECM antennas can be seen projecting from the side of the forward fire control tower. The system detected incoming missiles and initiated jamming signals to confuse their active radar guidance. Zuni rocket launchers have been installed in the former 40mm gun tubs amidships. The ULQ-6 worked in conjunction with the rocket launchers to fire chaff-loaded Zunis to further confuse the missiles' guidance. Note the Mark 56 fire control director over and between the launchers. Two other Mark 56s can be seen under cover, one just foward of the Mark 37 director at the forward stack and another aft below the Mark 38 director's rangefinder.

This photograph of the *Iowa* shows the typical elements of the radar and electronics suite currently aboard the class. On the very top of the foremast is the AS-3240/URN-25 TACAN antenna for tactical air navigation. Directly below the TACAN is a red dual task light, two dual AS-1735/SRC transmitter antennas, a white dual task light, another pair of AS-1735/SRC antennas and another red dual task light. In the center of the foretop is the SPS-49 surface search radar antenna. The SPS-49 is a stabilized, long-range two-dimensional radar which is widely used in the US fleet. Near the forward end of the top is the SPS-67 surface search radar antenna. The SPS-67 is a solid state replacement for the SPS-10 radar using the same antenna. Note the port antenna for the SLQ-32(V)3 electronic countermeasures system at the air defense level. (Courtesy FCCM (SW) Stephen Skelly, USNR.)

The new enclosure around the forward portion of the air defense level houses the equipment for the SLQ-32(V)3 ECM system and serves as a mounting platform for the two system antennas which are an array of sensors and receiving and transmitting antennas. The SLQ-32(V)3 system can detect and identify hostile weapons and their launching platforms and initiate defensive and evasive action against them. The round dish antenna in the center of the platform is an OE-82 of the satellite communications relay system. (Courtesy FCCM (SW) Stephen Skelley, USNR.)

I – IFF (Identification Friend or Foe)
M – Mark XII Identification System
S – Systems (reflecting many configurations)

The program is managed by the Department of Defense and participates in air traffic control of the national air space during peacetime. Much of the Mark XII equipment is similar to the Mark X equipment. The primary advantage is the much wider range of capabilities for military use.

The system currently installed in the *Iowa*s consists of four AS-177 type antennas. The transponder unit is an AS-177/UPX-72 and the interrogator is an AS-177/UPM-137. The SPS-10 radar uses an AS-177/UPX-27 and the SPS-49 radar is associated with an AS-177/UPX-23. The primary IFF interrogator for the SPS-49 is an AS-2188/U bar feeder in front of the antenna feed–horn radiator.

ELECTRONICS

The great technical advances made in the development of radar and electronics during World War II also ushered in the age of electronic

warfare. The same radar signals which can detect an enemy can also alert him to your presence. With the proper receiving equipment, the enemy can also determine the direction of the transmission. Radar countermeasures, therefore, developed almost as rapidly as radar.

In this discussion, electronic equipment aboard the *Iowa* class battleships is divided into three areas, the first of which includes the Electronic Support Measures (ESM) which are passive devices used to intercept and to listen to enemy transmissions. The second is the ECM equipment which is used to jam and deceive enemy transmissions and the third takes in those ECCM devices and actions taken to negate the enemy's use of electronic countermeasures.

Electronic Warfare (EW) deals not only with radio, radar and electronic emissions, but with all electromagnetic energy including optical, infrared and laser systems. Because of the highly classified nature of EW, many areas cannot be covered and this discussion, of necessity, is incomplete.

ECM equipment 1944 to 1956

In 1944, the *Iowa* class was equipped with SPT-1 and SPT-4 ECM equipment for direct noise amplification and signal jamming. The various components were fitted to the yards and masts and as high up in the superstructure as possible to avoid obstructions. The number and location of the components varied between ships.

Typically, the passive part of the system used a pair of DBM radar direction finders and three types of intercept receiving antennas, the AS-56, AS-57 and AS-37. The two DBMs were used to cover the different frequency ranges and provide an approximate fix for the

The *New Jersey* maneuvers off the Pacific Missile Test Center range in California on 23 March 1983. The doors just below the ship's name on the stern are for streaming the SLQ-25 gear for the Nixie torpedo countermeasures system. A device, which can generate noise equivalent to the acoustic signature of a ship, is towed at a specific distance and depth from the ship. Sufficient noise can be generated at the proper frequencies to divert an acoustic homing torpedo away from the ship.

highly directional jammers. They were a low radome-enclosed antenna. The other antennas were also used in pairs, each on either side of the ship for full directional coverage. They fed the intercepted signals to broad band receivers and pulse analyzers which identified and classified the transmissions. The AS-56 antennas were long, heavy dipoles used to cover the upper frequencies, while the AS-57s were encased, double cones which resembled a field drum and covered the lower frequencies. The AS-37 antennas were in the mid to upper frequency range and were referred to as 'wagon wheels' because of their rotating, ground plane dipoles. On some ships, the ground plane was a solid sheet.

After World War II, the AS-56s and AS-57s were replaced with CAGW-66132 and CAGW-66131 antennas respectively. Both antennas used a fan of ground plane dipoles forming half a 'wagon wheel'. The 66132 used a long, thin dipole in the center of the fan and was called the 'sword'. The 66131 used a series of cones in the center, encased in a small radome cup and was referred to as the 'derby'.

The active portion of the system used the high-powered TDY antenna and transmitting equipment. The antenna radiated a wide band, random noise signal on a carrier frequency being used by enemy communications and radar systems. Unavoidable reception of sufficient amounts of this signal by the enemy equipment would render his own signals useless. The useless enemy signals were also monitored and analyzed to determine the effectiveness of the jamming. Four different antenna reflectors could be used to cover beam patterns of from 55 degrees to 180 degrees and frequency ranges of from 90mc to 1,250mc, depending on the tactical situation. The antenna reflectors were a flat rod structure, angled widely at the center and located behind the dipoles.

All four ships were still using this ECM gear when they were deactivated and placed in the reserve fleet between 1955 and 1958. In 1952 the Iowa had two TDY-1a jamming transmitters installed. One was located on each side of the superstructure just below the base of the side MK 37 director barbettes. It was a smaller unit with a radome enclosed antenna which covered a wider range of frequencies. The TDY-1a system normally used a third, receiving, antenna for analyzing the jammed signals but the *Iowa*'s installation used the existing TDY receivers for this purpose. Both systems were used until the TDY transmitter was removed during a 1955 refit.

The ULQ-6 ECM system

When the *New Jersey* was reactivated for Vietnam service, she was outfitted with the ULQ-6 ECM system. A new pair of radar direction finders was fitted to the aft side of the foremast. They were the AS-570/SLR for the higher range and the AS-571/SLR to cover the lower frequencies. The 'sword' and 'derby' antennas were still in use for monitoring. The new gear associated with the ULQ-6 was supported by a framework extending from the large boxes added to each side of the fire control tower at the air defense level. The equipment on each side was identical. The top and bottom antennas were AS-1750/SLs, transmitters and receivers respectively. The center array was stacked with an AS-1751/SLA receiver over a AS-1341/ULQ jammer.

The system was used to detect a number of threats, including the Soviet-made Styx missile. Signals from the AS-1341 jammer were intended to confuse the active radar guidance of the Styx. Chaff could also be sent aloft, as an additional evasive measure, with modified Zuni missiles. The *New Jersey* carried four Zuni launchers, one in each of the four remaining 40mm gun tubs between the stacks.

A close-up of the Mark 36 Super RBOC (Rapid Bloom Offboard Chaff) launcher aboard the *Iowa*. The *Iowa*s are fitted with eight sextuple Mark 36 launchers, four on each side of the superstructure around the barbettes for the Mark 37 directors. The launchers are integrated with, and can be fired by, the SLQ-32(V)3 ECM system. The Mark 36 launchers fire a cartridge which dispenses chaff at a specific distance from the ship. The chaff quickly changes the electrical properties of the air between the missile and the target creating decoys and false targets causing the missile to be diverted. (Courtesy FCCM (SW) Stephen Skelley, USNR.)

The SLQ-32(V)3 ECM system

As part of the 1980s reactivation and modernization, the *Iowa* class was outfitted with the latest ECM and ECCM equipment. The SLQ-32(V)3 is a defense against anti-ship cruise missiles and their launching platforms. It incorporates both ESM and ECM capabilities.

The system uses an array of receiving antennas, sensors and a transmitting antenna to exploit the energy radiated by the presence and activity of an enemy. It can detect and identify his weapons and launching platforms and can initiate evasive and defensive actions as appropriate. It is able to identify all known radars and present this information in a usable manner to the receiver display and classify contacts as friendly, suspected, unknown or definite enemy.

Its high-powered emissions can be used against the search radars on reconnaisance aircraft to disrupt targeting of tactical fleet units and can also be directed against missile carrying ships and aircraft to interfere with target acquisition and launch sequences. It can, for instance, mimic a specific Soviet radar. For defense against incoming missiles it can transmit emissions to deceive and divert the missile's

The radome mounted on the mast platform on the forward side of the second stack encloses the communications antenna for the Pioneer RPVs. This antenna transmits control signals to, and receives transmissions from, the RPVs. This radome was installed in August 1986 but was too sensitive to blast overpressure from the 16in guns. It was replaced in November of that year. The OE-233/WRN-5 antenna on the port yard is used with the satellite communication relay system. To starboard is a CCTV and other RPV communications antennas. The heavy dual pole antenna just forward of the Tomahawk launchers is the receiver for the WLR-1 radar warning system. The second OE-82 dish antenna for the satellite communications relay system can be seen on a platform on the after side of the stack. (Photograph by the author.)

active radar guidance. There is a quick reaction mode that will jam an incoming emission before its characteristics have been established. This is intended to protect against attacks from small craft obscured by coastal clutter as well as submarine-launched missiles.

There are two SLQ-32(V)3 combination antennas installed. One is located on each side of the new enclosure around the air defense level on the fire control tower.

The system is also integrated with the Mark 36 Super Rapid Bloom Offboard Chaff (RBOC) launchers. Chaff, in effect, changes the electrical properties of the air between the missile and the target causing the missile to be diverted. The Super RBOC can be launched either manually or semi-automatically by the SLQ-32(V)3 operator. The system provides the operator with launcher selection and launch timing recommendations. There are eight, sextuple Mark 36 launchers. Four launchers are located on each side of the forward stack at the 05 level.

In August 1987, the WLR-1 radar warning receiver was installed aboard the *Iowa* for evaluation. The receiver provides instantaneous frequency measuring for rapid analysis of ship missile threats. The installation may also be made on the other ships in the class.

The SLQ-25 Nixie torpedo countermeasures system

The 1980s modernization also provided for defense against torpedo attack with the installation of the SLQ-25 Nixie torpedo counter-measures system. The Nixie uses a towed device containing a sensor package which can generate noise equivalent to the acoustic signature of a ship. When streamed astern at the proper distance and depth, the noisemaker produces sufficient random noise at correct frequencies to divert an acoustic homing torpedo away from the ship.

The helicopter control station is located at the aft end of the 02 level just above and forward of Turret No. III. This is the control and communications center for all flight operations, including the RPVs. Note the covered periscopes for Turret No. III in the foreground and the open ports for the trainer's and pointer's telescopes of the after Mark 37 director above. (Photograph by the author.)

COMMUNICATIONS

No element is more vital to the success of naval operations than fast and reliable communications. The ability to communicate makes possible effective command and control, ensuring that every unit in the fleet is responsive to the tactical and strategic needs and services of other units. This discussion deals with radio communications which fall into three categories; ship-to-shore, ship-to-ship and ship-to-aircraft.

Long-range ship-to-shore communications provide the main channel of information from the operating forces to the CNO and the command centers. These communications concern vital movement information such as the composition, operational control, departure, destination, route of travel, arrival and location of all units. Also included in this mode are certain short-range functions such as the control of shore bombardment and fire support for amphibious operations.

The shorter range ship-to-ship communications are usually limited to those ships tactically linked together. Ship commanders must be able to communicate whenever necessary among ships operating in close company as well as over-the-horizon, depending on the tactical combinations of action groups and task forces. Most ship-to-aircraft communications are handled in a similar manner.

It is essential that each ship be able to quickly handle and process information in order to conduct strike warfare, engage in amphibious operations and provide for an effective AAW and ASW defense. By the end of World War II, it was apparent that shipboard combat information centers had reached the limit of their data handling capability. The development of high-performance jet aircraft created the need for fast and accurate methods of tracking and identifying air contacts.

The naval tactical data system

The advent of the digital computer led to the development of the Naval Tactical Data System (NTDS). It first became operational in the fleet in the early-1960s and was of great value for target detection, tracking, evaluation and weapons selection. However, there was no rapid method of incorporating weapons designations and acquisition into the computerized system. This was accomplished by the development of various data links which are fully integrated with the NTDS.

The NTDS Link 11

The Link 11 weapons direction system provides for a quick, effective single ship and fleetwide defense against all types of enemy targets. It provides a crypto-secure, two-way flow of target information between NTDS-equipped ships and a one-way transmission of target information to non-NTDS equipped ships. Its operation is automatic and under program control; therefore, it receives all tactical data available in its area. Currently the *Iowas* have a Link 11 receive only capability to the Tomahawk weapons control system.

The NTDS Link 14

The Link 14 is a crypto-secure, one-way data link that provides for data transfer fom an NTDS computer to a teletype on a non-NTDS ship. The tactical data must then be plotted on the vertical plot in the SWC. Since the non-NTDS ship could easily become saturated with technical data, only selected information is transmitted. When

The *Missouri* is shown entering the Gatun Locks of the Panama Canal on 10 December 1986 *en route* to Long Beach on the final leg of an around-the-world shakedown cruise. Note the large discone/cage antenna array for the NTDS on the bow. The array consists of two antennas, the conical portion below the disc is an AN/SRA-57 and the disc is an AS/SRA-58. Note the SLQ-32(V)3 ECM antennas on the sides of the air defense level. The SPS-67 surface search radar can be seen on the foretop directly below the IFF bar of the SPS-49 air search radar.

reactivated for Vietnam service the *New Jersey* was equipped with Link 14 and during the current modernization, the system was installed on the *Iowa*, *Missouri* and *Wisconsin*.

NTDS antennas

Certain special antennas are the only visual signs that ships have an NTDS capability. The large discone/cage array on the bow is actually two antennas, the conical portion below the disc is an AN/SRA-57 and the disc is an AN/SRA-58. The *Iowas* have an OE-82 satellite communication relay system which uses a pair of 8ft AN/WCS-3 dish antennas. One antenna is located on the forward end of the air defense level and the other is located on the after side of the second stack.

Chapter 8

PROTECTION

A battleship's ability to survive an attack is one of the most important considerations in its design and construction. It must be protected against the weapons that are expected to be used against it and this is one of the more complex areas of battleship construction.

This overview of armor and protection, while by no means complete, is intended to provide the reader with sufficient background to better understand the complex factors in the *Iowa* class design. For the purpose of this discussion, armor provides protection against gun fire and aerial bombing. The side protective and triple bottom systems, which comprise the underwater protection, are designed to protect the vessel from the effects of torpedoes, mining and near miss aerial bombing.

The *Wisconsin* leaves the Philadelphia Navy Yard on 24 September 1944 to join the Pacific Fleet. This aerial photograph clearly shows the large side and massive deck areas which had to be protected. The armored citadel of the vessel ranged from just forward of Turret No. I to just aft of Turret No. III. The viewing angle is near that of an approaching shell, close to the far side of the immune zone. The shell might penetrate some of the deck armor but because of the inclination of the side armor, it would probably glance off the main belt. On the other hand, a shell approaching near the inner end of the zone would have a flatter trajectory. It would probably glance off the deck armor but would confront the main belt at a more favorable angle for penetration.

In this photograph of the *Kentucky*, looking aft on 26 March 1946, the lower belt has been completed to the forward armor bulkhead. It can be distinguished by the holes for the upper belt alignment pins. The upper belt backing plate has been extended forward to the front of Turret No. I. The outer tanks of the torpedo defense system are visible outboard of the lower armor belt. The carrier in the background is the *Lake Champlain* (CV 39).

Left: The forward end of the armored citadel is beginning to take shape on the *Kentucky* in this photograph taken on 4 February 1946. The Class A forward armor bulkhead, which rises to the second deck, is just forward of the stool for Turret No. I. On the *Iowa* and *New Jersey* this bulkhead was 11.3in thick at the top and tapered to 8.5in at the bottom. On the other four ships the bulkhead tapered from 14.5in to 11.7in. It consists of six pieces, five of which can be clearly seen. These five pieces rest on one horizontal piece which is not visible. Installation of the Class B lower armor belt has progressed to about the center of Turret No. I on the port side and to about halfway between the forward turrets on the starboard side. The lower barbette for Turret No. II can be seen below the partially plated second, or main armor deck, and fabrication of the lower barbette for Turret No. I has begun just aft of the stool. A close look at the edges of the forward-most plates of the main armor deck will indicate the 4.75in Class B armor laid over the 1.25in STS plate.

All vital equipment necessary for a battleship's operation and survival during battle, such as magaines, machinery, plotting rooms, etc., are protected by heavy armor. The armor can be visualized as a box, or citadel, extending from just forward of Turret I to just aft of Turret III. The sides of the citadel consist of the heavy armor belt which is covered over by the lighter layers of deck armor and closed forward and aft by heavy armor bulkheads. The bottom of the box is not ballistically protected. Other items outside the box requiring protection, such as turrets, barbettes, conning tower, fire control directors and stearing gear, are armor appendages connected to the box.

IMMUNE ZONE

Contrary to popular belief, protection is not specified in armor thickness, but rather by an immune zone. In theory, immunity is desired against a specific weapon, usually that of the main armament of the vessel to be protected. Operationally, a ship would overpower a weaker adversary and avoid contact with a more powerful one. Within this context, the immune zone can be considered as an expression of the expected battle ranges. The inner edge is the shortest range at which the side belt and deck armor cannot be penetrated. The outer edge is the shortest range at which plunging fire will penetrate the deck armor. The inner and outer edges of the immune zone are determined by the size and performance of the belt and deck armor.

For example, consider a vessel mounting 16in guns, with their best performance at between 20,000 and 30,000 yards. Those distances would describe the preferred or expected battle ranges. Side armor thickness would then be selected to defeat the armor piercing shell fired by that gun between those ranges. Similarly, deck armor thickness would be selected to protest against that same shell within the same ranges.

ARMOR PRODUCTION

Beyond purpose and design, there are other considerations to be taken into account in any study of the armor and protection systems of the *Iowa* class battleships. Not to be overlooked are the treaty limitations on warship construction that had been in effect since the 1920s.

Following the Washington Treaty of 1922 and the cancellation of

160,000 pounds and measure 12.1in×126in×360in.

These heavy armor plates were formed by either forging or rolling. Plate that was less than 4in thick was rolled in a mill. On the other hand, large plates thicker than 4in were forged. It was thought that rolling would work the thicker plates less uniformly than forging. American steel-producing equipment was geared to this theory; therefore, rolling mills were limited to the size of ingots that could be worked. In this discussion, armor less than 4in thick is referred to as Special Treatment Steel (or STS) plate.

Included in the manufacturing cycle was the requirement for testing before the heavy armor could be delivered to the shipbuilder. Testing required that one plate from each group of armor (with a maximum group weight of up to 800 tons) be tested by the Naval Proving Ground at Dahlgren, Virginia. The results of the testing could require the armor to be given additional treatment and could even result in the rejection of the entire armor group. There was at least one exception. Early in 1942, several of the groups of armor tested slightly below standards, but considering the urgency of the wartime building program, they were accepted. The armor's quality was not evaluated to be low enough to justify the delay that would have been caused by rejection, retreatment and retesting.

ARMOR TYPES

The types of armor used in the construction of the *Iowa* class battleships consisted of Class A, Class B, STS and cast. The definitions, as applied in the US Navy to these types of armor, are as follows:

Another view of the *Kentucky*, looking forward on 26 March 1946. The lower belt has been completed to the after armor bulkhead, the sides of which are visible just aft and outboard of Turret No. III. Note the double layer of plating on the main armor deck. Clearly visible is the extension of the horizontal armor aft of Turret No. III on the third deck showing 5.6in Class B armor being laid over the 0.75in STS deck. Not visible is the extension of the lower belt which is below the edge of the 0.75in STS deck. This extension of the armor citadel is to protect the steering gear leads and equipment. The after portion of the torpedo defense system can be defined in this photograph.

the battleship and battlecruiser programs, the only armor produced was for the Treaty Cruisers, which was an insignificant amount compared to that required for a battleship. Heavy armor was not produced for some sixteen years, until well after the replacement of over-age capital ships was authorized in 1934.

In 1939, when heavy armor was required for the *Iowa* class, the United States was the world's largest manufacturer of steel, with the capacity to produce 75,000,000 tons per year. The capacity to produce steel, however, could not be compared to the capacity to produce armor. The many special manufacturing processes required to produce armor meant that during the same year, 1939, the nation's steel mills could produce only a little more than 19,000 tons.

The magnitude of the many problems involved in the production of heavy armor is not generally understood. Designed, manufactured and delivered to a specific vessel, the production of heavy armor plate, from design to finish machining, could take as long as nine months for Class A (face hardened) armor. A plate of Class B (homogenous) armor of equivalent size, which required less heat treatment, could be produced in about seven months. A typical ingot for a single plate of Class A belt armor weighed about 200,000 pounds and measured about 26in×132in×200in. When finished, the plate would weigh about

This photograph shows the construction progress of the *Kentucky* on 7 September 1945. The 3in STS plate of the lower barbette for Turret No. II is being fitted to the third deck. Note the scalloped butt straps vertically joining the 0.625in plates of the holding bulkhead as the torpedo defense system begins to take shape forward. The shipyard workers in the center of the photograph are sitting on the webbing which forms the shallow splinter deck. The splinter deck at the bottom of the webbing is 0.625in STS plate and the lower course of 1.25in STS plate for the main armor deck will be laid on top of the webbing.

These two photographs show the installation of the Class B lower belt armor on the *Kentucky* on 4 July 1945. The assembly is lower belt group 8 consisting of plates L.B. 22-P, 23-P and 24-P. Each plate is approximately 10ft across the top and 28ft deep; therefore, this group is 30ft by 28ft. Note the vertical keys and keyways for aligning the individual plates and adjoining groups and the scalloped butt straps joining the plates. The Class A upper belt plates were approximately 30ft across at the top and 10ft 6in deep so that one upper belt plate fits atop three lower belt plates or one lower belt group. The armor belt was installed at an angle of 19 degrees sloping outboard. The two sets of three holes in the top of each plate are for securing the pads of the lifting bolts. They are also for the alignment pins when fitting the upper Class A belt. This pin arrangement was used on the *Kentucky* and *Illinois* but the *Iowa*, *New Jersey*, *Missouri* and *Wisconsin* aligned the upper and lower belts with keys as in the vertical alignment of the lower belt group shown here. The shipyard workmen are standing on the third deck shelf. As can be seen from these photographs, internal armor is difficult and expensive to install and repair.

Class A

An armor with a hard, non-ductile face and a ductile back. The purpose of the hard face is to break up the attacking projectile, while the soft and tougher back is designed to prevent the plate from shattering. If Class A armor succeeds in breaking up the projectile, it is superior in penetration resistance to all other types of armor. The hard face is produced by case carburizing or decremental hardening, or both.

Class B

An armor which is substantially uniform in composition and physical properties throughout the cross-section of the plate. Class B armor is often referred to as homogeneous armor and it relies on its strength and ductility to resist impact by spreading the force over a wider area.

STS

Special treatment steel is Class B armor and is used in ship structures. This gives additional protection which would not be obtained if mild steel were used.

Cast

Cast armor is cast directly in its final shape. It is usually homogeneous, but can also be face hardened. Casting is useful in fabricating small armored housings such as rangefinders and sight hoods.

Class A armor is usually not used as a structural member and, therefore, is not considered as contributing to the strength of the ship's structure. Class B armor, however, is usually worked into the ship's structure and becomes a strength member. In some cases the lighter plates can be welded but the heavier plates are usually secured by bolting and riveting similar to Class A armor.

Extensive use was made of STS plating. It could be integrated with the ship's structure and used in combination with both Class A and Class B heavy armor in areas such as turret faces, the main belt and the armored deck. The ballistic performance of divided, multiple and laminated armor is, in general, inferior to that of a single plate of equivalent total thickness (see Figure 1). The use of STS did, however, afford considerably more protection than would have been obtained if mild steel had been used.

The upper, or main barbettes, are assemblies of segments of Class A heavy armor. The barbette for Turret No. II of the *New Jersey* is shown here on 12 January 1943. The heaviest segments, which are directly abeam, are 17.3in thick. They taper to 14.8in on the quarters and taper further to 11.6in dead ahead and astern. This photograph was taken just prior to the turret being set in place and the blocks are spacers which will be removed when the upper and lower roller tracks are perfectly aligned. Note the buffers inside the barbette to keep the gun pit bulkhead from scuffing when being lowered into position.

ARMOR DESIGN

The design of the *Iowa* class armor protection system is essentially the same as that of the *South Dakota* class. Both feature an internal main belt which represents a significant change from the *North Carolina*s and was adopted only with reluctance. In the first place, an internal belt is difficult and costly to install and secondly, it is difficult to reach for repairs. The *North Carolina*s were designed with an external belt, inclined to 15 degrees for protection against a 14in shell. In this arrangement it was possible to maintain a beam of 108ft that would pass through the Panama Canal. In the *South Dakota* class, the solution for protection against the 16in shell had been to further incline the belt to 19 degrees. An external belt inclined at the steeper angle would have required a wider beam to maintain stability due to the loss of waterplane area, but would preclude passage through the Panama Canal. Therefore, an internal belt was adopted. This condition was also accepted for the *Iowa* class. Not until the *Montana* class did the Bu C & R return to the exterior belt. It was also inclined at 19 degrees which gave the ships a waterline breadth of 115ft. This increase in beam was acceptable and consistent with the *Midway* class design studies at that time and plans to provide a wider set of locks for the Panama Canal.

Contract plans for the *Iowa* class were completed in January 1939 and appropriations for BB 61 and BB 62 were made in Fiscal Year 1939. The armor system was designed to resist the weapon in use at

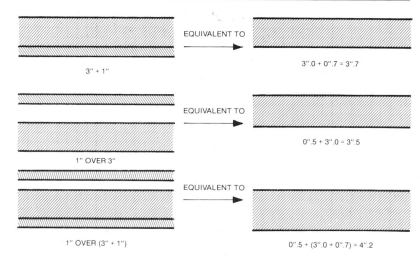

3".0 + 0".7 = 3".7

1" OVER 3"

0".5 + 3".0 = 3".5

1" OVER (3" + 1")

0".5 + (3".0 + 0".7) = 4".2

Figure 1. EQUIVALENT PLATE THICKNESS
In estimating the solid plate equivalent of laminated armor, such as the upper and lower courses of the armor deck, 0.7 of the thickness of the lighter course is added to the full thickness of the heavier course. For estimating separated armor, such as a lighter deck over a heavier deck, the solid plate equivalent is 0.5 of the lighter deck added to the full thickness of the heavier deck. A combination of laminated and separated armor is estimated in the same manner.

that time, which was the 16in/45cal Mark 6 gun, firing the 2,240 pound Mark 5 projectile, between 18,000 and 30,000 yards.

Nearly a year after the design had been fixed, the Bu Ord proposed a new shell weighing 2,700 pounds. In June 1939, this new more powerful shell was adopted. The *Iowa* class design could not be changed at this point and armor for BB 61 and BB 62 was already on order. Any major increases in armor size would have drastically

Looking down on the forward turrets of the *Kentucky* on 22 October 1945. The lower armor belt can be seen installed to halfway between the turrets. The 3in STS lower barbette of Turret No. II is completed and erection of the lower barbette for Turret No. I is just beginning. The turret stools appear complete and ready for bolting down the lower roller track and training rack. The second, or main armor deck, will be laid over the lower barbettes and the main barbette will extend from the second deck up to the turret gun houses.

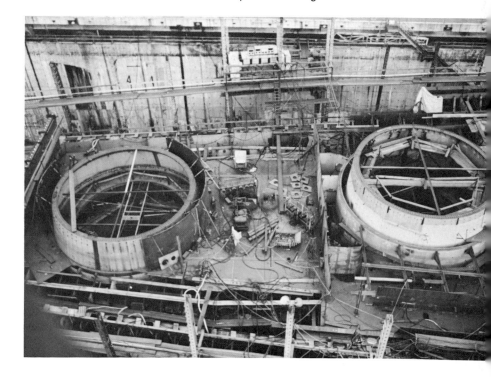

The *New Jersey*'s gun house No. 2 and pit is lowered into place on 12 January 1943. The gun house is partially fabricated with the 0.75in STS side backing plates in place. The numerous holes are for armor bolts which will attach the 9.5in Class A armor side plates. Approximately one bolt for every 5sq ft of armor surface is provided. A portion of the plate in the upper rear end of the gun house will be cut out for the projection of the rangefinder.

increased displacement. (However, some moderate increases were made in BB 63–66 which are discussed under Armor Distribution below.) The new shell, designated the Mark 8, caused the immune zone to shrink to between 20,200 and 25,500 yards when fired from the Mark 6 gun. The new 16in/50 cal Mark 7 gun firing the Mark 8 shell was yet another situation. The *Iowas* were almost completely vulnerable to this combination as shown in the table below.

IMMUNE ZONE COMPARISON

| Gun/Caliber | Projectile | | | Immune Zone | |
	Weight in pounds	Type	Mk	Inner Range in yards	Outer Range in yards
16in/45, Mk 6	2,240	AP	5	17,600	31,200
16in/50, Mk 7	2,240	AP	5	21,700	32,100
16in/45, Mk 6	2,700	AP	8	20,200	25,500
16in/50, Mk 7	2,700	AP	8	23,600	27,400

ARMOR DISTRIBUTION

The vertical side armor consists of an upper and lower belt on the outboard side of Torpedo Bulkhead No. 3 which is inclined to an angle of 19 degrees. The total depth of the belt is 38ft 6in and extends from frame 50 forward of No. 1 barbette to frame 166 aft of No. 3 barbette. The upper belt is Class A armor 12.1in thick and 10ft 6in deep. The lower belt is Class B armor 12.1in thick at the top and tapered to 1.62in at the bottom. The lower belt is 28ft deep and extends down to

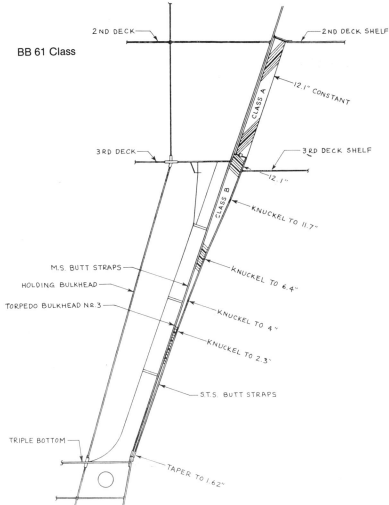

Figure 2. ARRANGEMENT OF VERTICAL SIDE ARMOR, BB 61 CLASS
The arrangement of the vertical side armor is shown at a typical web frame of Torpedo Bulkhead No. 3.

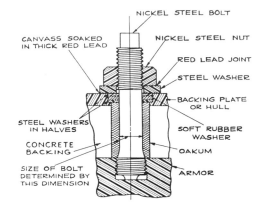

Figure 2B. ARRANGEMENT OF ARMOR BOLT
A typical watertight armor bolt used for securing the Class A upper belt to its STS backing plate. One bolt is provided for every 5sq ft of armor surface.

the inner bottom. The 12.1in upper belt inclined at 19 degrees is considered equivalent to 13.5in of vertical armor. Extending the lower belt down to the inner bottom is intended to protect against shells falling short and continuing underwater (see Figures 2 & 2B).

Two heavy strakes of 1½in STS plate form part of the shell between the second deck and the third deck shelf. They run from frame 50 forward to frame 171-1/2 aft. This is designed to be a de-capping plate for heavy projectiles. It has enough resistance to start the time delay on a base-detonating type fuze and if it dislodges or knocks off the armor piercing cap of the projectile the resistance of the main belt is enhanced by as much as 30 per cent.

A portion of the lower Class B armor belt was continued aft from frame 166 to frame 189 to protect the steering gear leads. It is 17ft ⁹/₃₂in deep at frame 166 and tapers to 15ft 4⁷/₈in deep at frame 189. Between frame 166 and 172 the belt is 13in thick tapering to 5in at the bottom and from frame 172 to frame 189 it is increased to 13.5in thick continuing the same degree of vertical taper. At frame 189 the belt is continued aft to frame 203 with 13.5in Class A armor of constant thickness protecting the steering gear equipment. It is 8ft 3⁵/₈in deep forward and 7ft 7in deep aft. All of this armor carried aft is also inclined at 19 degrees.

Heavy Class A armored transverse bulkheads protect the forward and aft ends of the citadel and the aft end of the extension for the steering gear. In the original *Iowa* class design, these bulkheads were 11.3in thick which was only marginal protection at expected battle ranges and then at considerable obliquity. In 1940, when Treaty restrictions were no longer in effect, consideration was given to increasing the thickness of these bulkheads. Armor for BB 61 and BB 62 had been ordered and the urgency of the building program did not warrant the delay which would be incurred by reordering the armor. On BB 63–66, however, there was ample time for ordering armor and these bulkheads were increased to 14.5in which afforded greater protection at a wider range of target angles.

The horizontal armor is distributed in a system of armored decks which includes protection against aerial bombs. The deck armor is homogeneous and consists of Class B armor, STS plate and a combination of both. In this system of decks, the main deck is designated the bomb deck, the second deck is the main armor deck and the splinter deck is a flat fitted just below the second deck only for the length of the citadel. The bomb deck is 1.5in STS plate, the main armor deck is 4.75in Class B armor laid on 1.25in STS plate and the splinter deck is 0.625in STS plate. The bomb deck is designed to detonate general purpose bombs on contact and arm armor piercing bombs so they will explode between the bomb deck and the main armor deck. Within the immune zone, the main armor deck is designed to defeat plunging shells which may penetrate the bomb deck or enter the side above the top of the de-capping plate and the main belt. The splinter deck is designed to contain any spall and pieces of armor which might be broken off from the main armor deck. The third and first platform decks also use STS plate of varying sizes which affords additional ballistic protection, mainly against splinters.

Horizontal armor continues aft on the third deck and covers the main belt extension protecting the steering gear leads and equipment. From frame 166 to frame 189, 5.6in Class B armor was laid over a course of 0.75in STS deck. The steering gear equipment, between frame 189 and frame 203, was covered by 6.2in Class B armor.

The turrets were constructed using a combination of Class A and Class B armor and STS plate. The turret faces are 17in Class B armor over 2.5in STS plate, which is the equivalent of a single plate 18.75in thick, inclined 36 degrees, 10 minutes and 18 seconds from the vertical. The side plates are 9.5in Class A armor on 0.75in STS plate. The back plates are 12in Class A armor and the roof plates are 7.25in Class B armor. The first roof plate is interlocked with the face plate by a unique hook and scarf joint.

Empirical data indicates that the 16in/50cal Mark 7 gun, firing the Mark 8, 2,700 pound shell, could penetrate the turret face up to about 25,000 yards. Between 25,000 and about 36,500 yards there would be a slight margin of immunity. Beyond 36,500 yards the turret face would possibly be vulnerable to plunging fire. This is a good indication why the US Navy considered this gun and shell combination adequate

In this photograph of the *Iowa*, taken in July 1941, the various tanks of the torpedo defense system are clearly visible. The view is looking forward from the No. 2 boiler room. Note the foundation bulkhead, or stool, for Turret No. II. Armor installation has just begun and the first plates of the lower belt can be seen on either side of boilers No. 3 and 4. They can be distinguished from other plates with scalloped butt straps by the keyway at the top of the plate. The lower armor belt formed Torpedo Bulkhead No. 3.

and did not push for development of the 18in gun.

The barbettes are assemblies of segments of Class A heavy armor extending from the turret shelf plate to the armor of the second deck. The heaviest segments are 17.3in and directly abeam. On the quarters they taper to 14.8in. Dead ahead and astern they taper to 11.6in. They are continued between the second and third decks by 3in of STS plate. The turret foundation bulkhead, or stool, which supports the turret within the barbette, is 1.5in STS plate.

The conning tower is elliptical in shape and assembled from segments of Class B armor 17.3in thick. In BB 61, the tower is three levels, the highest being the fire control station housing the Mark 40 director. The mid-level is the ship control station and the lower level accommodates a flag control station. In BB 62 through BB 66, the lower, or flag level, is omitted. The roof plates are 7.25in Class B, the floor is 4in STS and the decks inside are 1in STS plate. The conning tower is connected to the armor citadel by a communications tube with an inside diameter of 16in and a wall thickness of 16in Class B armor.

During the current modernization, exterior armor was provided to protect the SWC which is located on the 03 level just aft of the conning tower. Information on the thickness and type of armor is not currently available.

The secondary batteries and their ready service handling rooms directly below are protected with a 2.5in of STS armor plate. The directors and their communication tubes are armored with various STS plate sizes including 1.5in, 2in and 2.5in depending on their location in the superstructure.

Lighter STS splinter protection was afforded the 40mm and 20mm anti-aircraft batteries spotted around the main deck and in the superstructure. Their gun tubs were of 0.75in and 0.375in STS plate respectively.

ARMOR INSTALLATION

The installation of the heavy armor plates was no small task and the various methods of fastening them to the ship's structure are worth noting. Tests at the Philadelphia Navy Yard had indicated that homogeneous armor could be welded together and with mild steel. The procedures for installing the side and deck armor are good examples. The lower Class B belt was installed first. A typical plate is 10ft at the top and 28ft deep. It is keyed across the entire top and

down each side approximately 12ft 6in. Extending from the third deck down to the third skin, it forms Torpedo Bulkhead No. 3. It is made tight by scalloped butt straps of STS plate on the outboard side and mild steel inboard welded directly to the armor as shown in Figure 8–2. (The scalloping provides a greater linear distance of welding.)

The upper Class A belt was installed atop the lower belt plates. A typical plate is 30ft at the top and 10ft 6in deep. It is keyed on the sides and along the entire bottom and fits directly over three of the lower belt plates. The upper belt extends from the third deck up to the second deck and is bolted to a 0.875in STS backing plate with specially designed watertight bolts. Since it is impossible to fit the belt snugly against the backing plate, the bolts stand the armor off about 2in creating a small void space between the belt and the plate. After the armor installation is complete this void space is filled with concrete which provides support for the armor over its entire surface. One bolt for every 5sq ft of surface is provided and spaced as the framing behind the backing plate will permit.

The main armor deck (second deck) is composed of 4.75in Class B armor over 1.25in STS plate. It runs the full length between the forward and after armor bulkheads and lies between the upper armor belts. The heavier Class B plates are butt welded together and attached to the undercourse of STS plating with heavy rivets and armor bolts. *(See Appendix B for armor diagrams.)*

UNDERWATER PROTECTION

Protection against the effects of torpedoes, mining and near-miss bombing is provided by the side protection or torpedo defense and the triple bottom systems. Both systems are multi-layered and intended to absorb the energy from an underwater explosion equivalent to a 700 pound charge of TNT. This loading was determined as a result of an intelligence survey from the mid-1930s and, when the *Iowa* class was designed, the US Navy was unaware of the advances the Japanese had made in torpedo technology. One of the unpleasant surprises of the Pacific War was the Japanese 24in 'long lance' torpedo, carried by most of their surface craft. The Japanese were also able to pack a considerably larger explosive charge, by US standards, into their aerial and submarine torpedoes.

TORPEDO DEFENSE SYSTEM

The side protection system consists of four tanks on the outboard side of the hull extending approximately from the third deck down to the bottom of the ship. As previously indicated, the third torpedo bulkhead is formed by the lower armor belt and inclined to an angle of 19 degrees. The first and second torpedo bulkheads and the holding

In mid-1943 the *Missouri*'s hull begins to take shape at the New York Navy Yard. The side tanks, which form the multi-layered torpedo defense system, are clearly visible. Torpedo Bulkhead No. 4, formed by the lower armor belt is inclined outboard at 19 degrees. The other torpedo bulkheads are not quite so steeply angled. The two outboard tanks are liquid loaded and the two inboard tanks are kept void which is intended to absorb the energy from an underwater explosion. Note the portion of the bow being fabricated in the foreground.

Opposite: The construction progress on the stern of the *Kentucky*, photographed here on 4 February 1946, shows the inner bottom framing and housings for the rudder stocks. The torpedo defense system aft can be clearly defined. The edge of the extension of the lower armor belt can be seen on the port side between the third deck and the first platform deck.

bulkhead are not as steeply inclined. The full tank system ranges from frame 50 forward of No. 1 barbette to frame 166 aft of No. 3 barbette. The two outboard tanks are liquid loaded with fuel oil or ballast and the two inboard tanks are kept void. The liquid layers are intended to deform and absorb the shock from the explosion and contain most of the shards from the damaged structure. The first void is expected to contain any leakage, and the belt, on its inboard side, is intended to stop fragments which penetrate the second torpedo bulkhead. The second void and holding bulkhead should remain intact protecting the machinery spaces. (See Figure 3)

The system is the shallowest at No. 1 and No. 3 barbettes because of the fineness of the hull form. This defect had to be accepted, for any increase in hull volume, especially around the forward barbette, would have resulted in an unacceptable reduction in speed.

As previously indicated, the torpedo defense system was virtually the same as in the *South Dakota* class. The Navy was not able to conduct caisson tests until after all of the *South Dakotas* had been laid down. In 1939, results of the tests conducted at the Philadelphia Navy Yard proved to be disappointing. The lower belt, which formed Torpedo Bulkhead No. 3, was too rigid. Even though it tapered to 1.75in at the bottom, it did not deform properly to absorb the energy from an explosion. By this time, the *Iowa* class design was too far along for any major changes to be made. It was at this point that the decision was made to liquid load the outer tanks instead of the inner tanks. Since the outboard tank had considerably greater capacity than the other tanks, the larger liquid shock absorber reduced the load on the armor bulkhead. (See Figure 3)

Caisson tests were again conducted in 1943 at Philadelphia. The system was under study for the *Midway* class carriers. Results of the tests indicated certain structural defects, and improvements were made to BB 65 and BB 66. It was estimated that these changes might improve the performance of the system by as much as 20 per cent. Neither ship, of course, was ever completed. (See Figure 4.)

TRIPLE BOTTOM SYSTEM

The triple bottom system consists of two layers of tanks on the very bottom of the hull between the third torpedo bulkheads of the torpedo protection system. The tanks are formed by the shell at the bottom of the hull and the inner bottom and third bottom flats. The inner bottom runs the entire length of the ship but the third bottom is spread essentially under the vitals of the ship from frame 36 well forward of No. 1 barbette to frame 173 well aft of No. 3 barbette. The inner bottom tanks are liquid loaded with fuel oil, reserve feed and potable water, except near the ends where they are kept void. The third bottom tanks are all kept void. The system is intended to absorb the shock of an underwater explosion and function similarly to the torpedo defense system.

SURVIVABILITY

The *Iowa* class battleships were never subjected to the kind of attack that they were designed to resist. None of them were torpedoed, bombed or hit with heavy shell fire. In 1944, the Bu Ships conducted an analytical study to determine the effects of certain weapons on various types of US Naval vessels. The report of that study, *Vulnerability of US Naval Vessels to Attack by Air-Borne Weapons*, was issued 11 May 1944 and edited portions pertaining to the *Iowa* class ships are discussed here.

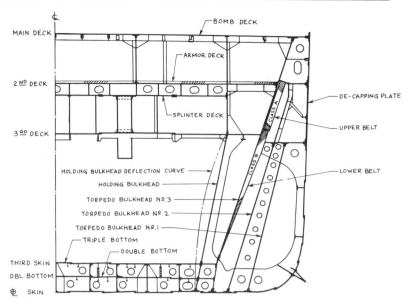

Figure 3. MIDSHIP SECTION, BB 61–64
Showing the arrangement of protection for the torpedo defense and triple bottom systems.

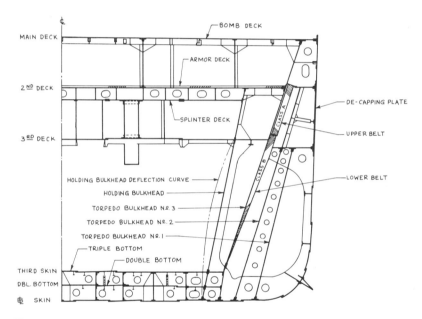

Figure 4. MIDSHIP SECTION, BB 65 and 66
Showing the alterations to the arrangement of protection for the torpedo defense and triple bottom systems.

The *Iowa* class battleships have an efficient torpedo defense system and excellent stability characteristics. In general, a 660 pound TNT warhead is not expected to rupture the holding bulkhead. The chief danger from torpedo attack involves an extensive fore and aft rupture of the inner voids of the torpedo defense system. About 360ft of inner voids must be flooded to produce a list which would put the main deck at the waterline on the damaged side. War experience with torpedo hits indicated that about four torpedoes, spaced at 60ft intervals along the side, would be required to cause this condition. Even if this should occur, the damage control facilities provide means for quickly removing the list, unless other damage disrupts damage control facilities. It is estimated that at least five, well-spaced hits, all on the same side and striking almost simultaneously would be required to place the vessel in jeopardy.

The decks have an equivalent thickness of about 6in of armor and,

This photograph of the *Kentucky*, taken on 7 September 1945, shows the detail of construction of the torpedo defense system forward. A portion of the holding bulkhead can be seen just aft of the forward armor bulkhead. The edge of the lower armor belt, forming Torpedo Bulkhead No. 3 has been installed to about the center of the forward turret. One more group of lower armor belt plates will be needed to close the armor citadel. Just outboard of the armor belt is Torpedo Bulkhead No. 2 and farther aft the framing for Torpedo Bulkhead No. 1 is visible.

A section of the *Kentucky*'s triple bottom, looking forward on 11 January 1945 shortly after work was resumed on the vessel. The triple bottom lies between the third torpedo bulkheads and consists of two layers of tanks formed by the shell at the bottom of the hull and the inner bottom and third bottom flats. The lower portion of the holding bulkhead is in place and the next shell strake will start the turn of the bilge. The bulkhead in the foreground is at frame 119 and the foundations are for boilers No. 5 and 6 in No. 3 boiler room. The inner bottom tanks are liquid loaded and the third bottom tanks are kept void. This system is intended to function similar to the torpedo defense system and absorb the shock from an underwater explosion.

for penetration, AP bombs have to be dropped from an altitude in excess of 10,500ft; GP bombs will probably not penetrate the 1.50in STS main deck prior to detonation, although deflagration may result in rupture of the main deck. Much of the topside structure is also of STS in sufficient thickness to limit the blast effect and fragment damage.

The probabilities of loss from typical weapons in general use are presented in the table below. Probabilities for the GP bombs pertain to putting the ship out of action rather than sinking.

Since the *Iowa* class has a fully developed torpedo defense system, the probability of sinking from near misses is very small and not feasible to predict.

Penetration of the side belt armor was not addressed in the study, but since the probabilities were based on hits which penetrated the armored citadel, the effects of large caliber hits from AP and HC projectiles can be considered similar to those from AP and GP bombs.

The *Iowa*s remain among the most survivable ships afloat and this was an important consideration for their reactivation. There are very few conventional weapons which can penetrate their heavy armor except for special-shaped charges which can be adapted for use with cruise missiles. Although the major powers have issued a number of cruise missiles to Third World countries, it is unlikely that the export version would contain such advanced warhead technology. As in the case of heavy projectiles, the Bu Ships analysis can be applied to cruise missiles as well.

VULNERABILITY TO ATTACK

Weapons Torpedo/Bomb	Equivalent Charge Weight	Probability of Sinking/No. of Hits					
		1	2	3	4	5	6
Torpedo	660 lb TNT	0.01	0.02	0.10	0.40	0.70	0.90
1,000 lb AP	150 lb TNT	0.23	0.41	0.55	0.66	0.73	0.79
1,600 lb AP	240 lb TNT	0.23	0.41	0.55	0.66	0.73	0.79
		Probability to Disable/No. of Hits					
1,000 lb GP	500 lb TNT	0.01	0.05	0.10	0.18	0.40	0.70
2,000 lb GP	1,000 lb TNT	0.02	0.10	0.20	0.40	0.55	0.90

NOTES: 1. The effects of large caliber hits from A.P. and H.C. projectiles can be considered similar to those from A.P. and G.P. bombs.
2. The same effects apply to cruise missiles with standard warheads. Special shaped charge warheads do not apply.

Chapter 9

ENGINEERING AND DAMAGE CONTROL

The *Iowa*s are the fastest battleships ever built. Their machinery was designed for extreme performance to produce the specified speed and endurance. The desired 33 knot speed at full load displacement is attainable with the plant's 212,000 plus horsepower. Their enormous fuel storage capacity enables them to easily meet the required endurance of 15,000nm at 15 knots.

About one-third of the ship is devoted to engineering areas which contain the main engines, boilers, generators, evaporators, air compressors, steering engines, anchor windlass, deck winches, repair lockers, etc., together with their auxiliaries and equipment. This discussion cannot include all of the machinery aboard the *Iowa* class ships; therefore, only the main propulsion and auxiliary units usually associated with moving the vessel and supplying necessary services are covered. These units are all operated and/or maintained by the ship's engineering department.

MACHINERY

The design and weight of the machinery installation depended on the arrangement of the machinery within the hull. The propulsion machinery was distributed in an alternating fire room, engine room arrangement and the location of the propellers had been fixed by the design of the hull form. Therefore, the first step was the location of the main engines and the run of the propeller shafts. This having been decided, the rest of the machinery in both the fire rooms and engine rooms could be located to accommodate the shafting. There were two auxiliary machinery spaces, one forward and one aft of the main spaces, to accommodate machinery not directly associated with the propulsion machinery.

Boilers, turbines and reduction gearing were all of the latest design, incorporating metallurgical advancements as well as improvements in

Opposite: The extremely fine lines of the *Iowa* class can be fully appreciated in this photograph of the *New Jersey* in dry dock at the Philadelphia Navy Yard, only a few days prior to her commissioning. The clipper bow, which fairs into a straight stem below the waterline, features a moderate-sized bulb which improves resistance at high speeds. The chain at the bow, running from the bull nose to the bottom of the bulb, is for hauling paravanes.

The primary consideration in the design of the hull and machinery for the *Iowa* class was high speed. Externally, this meant fine hull lines and extreme length. Both of these features can be fully appreciated in this aerial photograph of the *New Jersey* taken on 23 May 1968. Note the smoke rings from firing her 5in battery.

turbine nozzles and blading over previous designs. In comparison, the *Iowa*'s weight to horsepower ratio was 8.79 pounds less than that in the *South Dakota*.

	South Dakota	Iowa	net
Designed horsepower	130,000	212,000	+ 82,000
Machinery weight in tons*	3,236	4,444	+ 1,208
Pounds per horsepower	55.75	46.96	− 8.79

*dry weights and 2,240 pounds per ton

The main propulsion machinery was designed for an overload of 20 per cent or a maximum of 254,000 horsepower. Self-propelled model tests were run in January 1945, but full speed and standardization trials do not seem to have been conducted for any of the class. Although data was taken a number of times from all units, it was usually following a refit and conducted in shallow water near the overhaul yard. High-speed trials in shallow water are not considered representative because of the ground effect on the hull. The condition of the bottom with regard to marine growth and fouling can also be a factor. Representative horsepower curves derived from all data suggest that 32.5 knots can be attained with 212,000 horsepower on 53,900 tons and that a change in displacement of 1,000 tons would be the equivalent of 0.25 knots in speed. During the Bicentennial celebration in July 1986, the Secretary of the Navy, John F. Lehman, claimed the *Iowa* was capable of 35 knots. It is not known if this speed was actually attained or if he was quoting horsepower curves. The displacement was not cited for 35 knots.

Fuel consumption curves before the conversion of the plant to burn standard naval distillate or DFM, indicate a cruising radius of 20,000 miles at 15 knots. It should be noted, however, that when operating in a task force, battleships usually refuel their escorts until replenishment ships can refuel the force. The endurance figure is, therefore, more hypothetical than realistic since a battleship rarely operates alone. Oil storage and consumption data are not currently available for DFM.

Propulsion plant

Steam for the plant is furnished by eight boilers and delivered to four sets of geared turbines. They are direct-coupled to double reduction gears which drive the shafts. Superheated steam is supplied to each main steam line from the two boilers in each fire room. The main steam system is divided into two groups. The forward group consists of No. 1 and No. 2 fire and engine rooms; the after group consists of No. 3 and No. 4 fire and engine rooms. The two groups cannot be cross-connected; however, each space can be cross-connected within its group. The operation of the forward and after groups is controlled by Main Engine Control located in engine room No. 3 of the after group.

The shallow, cut-away stern is supported during dry-docking by a twin skeg arrangement. The skegs also house the inboard shafts forming a tunnel between them which helps to direct a clean flow of water to the propellers and twin rudders improving their efficiency. This photograph was taken at Philadelphia but during the *New Jersey*'s reactivation for Vietnam service.

The turbine group consists of one high-pressure turbine, one low-pressure turbine and one double reduction gear. The high-pressure turbine is coupled to the high-speed high-pressure pinion of the reduction gear. The low-pressure turbine is coupled to the gear's high-speed low-pressure pinion. The low-pressure turbine contains an astern element in each end which can reverse the shaft rotation for backing down. The reduction gear reduces the high-speed input from the turbines in two stages furnishing 202rpm to the shafts to make 33 knots.

The high-pressure turbine is of the impulse reaction, single flow type with one double row first stage impulse element and eleven single row stages of reaction blading. At 4,905rpm and a propeller speed of 202rpm, the output is 24,400 rated horsepower at the low-speed gear coupling. The low-pressure turbine has six single row stages of reaction blading arranged for double steam flow. At 3,913rpm and a propeller speed of 202rpm, the output is 28,600 rated horsepower at the low-speed gear coupling. The astern section of the turbine consists of a single three row stage of impulse blading mounted on each end of the low-pressure turbine rotor. At 2,375rpm and a propeller speed of 123rpm, the output is 11,000 rated horsepower at the low-speed gear coupling. The reduction gear is a double helical, double reduction gear unit with reduction ratios of 24.284:1 for the high-pressure side and 19.369:1 on the low-pressure side. All ancillary machinery for the main engines is located in the same space as the equipment it serves.

Two boilers are located in each fire room together with all of their auxiliaries and supporting equipment. The boilers are three-drum, divided furnace, doubled cased, single uptake express type, with a designed working pressure of 634psi and an operating pressure of 565psi. They are fitted with integral, separately fired superheater, economizer, soot blowers and oil burners. There are nine burners in all; five under the saturated side and four under the superheater side. The temperature of the superheated steam is 850 degrees.

An improvement to the main propulsion plants made during the 1980s modernizations was the conversion of the boilers from burning black oil to naval distillate fuel or DFM. The fuel oil storage and transfer tanks were thoroughly cleaned and coated inside with epoxy. The fuel oil piping system was cleaned, refurbished and modified for use with the new fuel. The fuel tank heating system for the old bunker fuels was not required for the new, lighter fuel so the tank heating coils and their piping were either removed or blanked off.

The four shafts which transmit the power to the propellers vary in length because of the staggered locations of the main engines. They are numbered from starboard to port and have the following approximate lengths: Shaft No. 1, 340ft; Shaft No. 2, 243ft; Shaft No. 3, 179ft; and Shaft No. 4, 277ft. Each shaft is divided into a number of sections which include the thrust shaft at the reduction gear, various sections of line shafts, the stern tube shaft and the propeller or tail shaft. The sections of shafting are joined together with integral flange-type couplings and are supported by a number of main line shaft bearings. A main thrust bearing is mounted at the reduction gear casing to absorb the axial thrust transmitted through the shaft from the propeller. The shafts penetrate the hull through the stern tube and are supported at each end of the tube by the stern tube bearings. The inboard shafts penetrate the hull at the aft end of the skegs where the propellers are immediately fitted. Therefore, the last length of shafting is a combination stern tube, tail shaft piece. The tail shaft pieces of the outboard shafts are supported at the propellers by the strut bearings, each of which is secured to the hull by two heavy struts.

Inside the tunnel stern of the *Missouri*. The shipyard workers are preparing to remove the shoring just prior to launching. Note how the skegs slope slightly outboard. The centerline skeg extends past the after armor bulkhead as an additional support under Turret No. III.

The twin skeg arrangement of the *Iowa* class is clearly shown in this photograph of the *Kentucky*, taken on 16 January 1950 just prior to flooding her building dock for launching. Note the huge castings for the rudder posts and the stern tubes for the inboard shafts.

Four screw-type, fixed pitch propellers are fitted to convert the horsepower into thrust. The two inboard propellers are five-bladed with a diameter of 17ft and the outboard propellers are four-bladed with a diameter of 18ft 3in. Two semi-balanced streamlined-type rudders, with a projected area of 340sq ft each, are located aft and slightly inboard of the center propellers to take the best advantage of the flow of water through the tunnel and the wash from the propellers.

Auxiliary machinery plant

The purpose of the auxiliary machinery is to furnish power for the operation of all ship functions except the main propulsion. The various services include the power for lighting, ventilating, heating, cooking, drinking, cleaning, refrigeration and air conditioning, operating electrical, including radio and other electronic, equipment, and the power for loading, aiming and firing the ship's guns.

The ship's service electrical plant consists of eight separate 1,250 KW, AC turbo-generators. For maximum reliability, they are interconnected by bus ties which make split-plant operation possible. The plant is arranged in four units, with one unit in each engine room. Each unit consists of two turbo-generators with their own switch gear for control of the generators to supply power to the ship's service power and lighting systems. When required, all four units may be connected in a ring-bus system using any or all eight generators operating in parallel. The generators are rated at:

AC Generator: 1,250 KW, 0.80 power factor, 3 phase, 60 Hertz 450 volts, 2005 amperes, 1,200rpm
DC Exciter: 120 volts, 16 KW, 1,200rpm, direct connected

The emergency electrical plant consists of two independent, self-contained 250 KW, AC diesel generators with individual distribution systems. One generator set is located in the Forward Diesel Generator and Evaporator Room and the other is in the After Diesel Generator Room. There is no provision for parallel operation of the emergency plants and they cannot be paralleled with the ship service generators. The two emergency generators are identical and are rated at:

AC Generator: 250 KW, 0.80 power factor, 3 phase, 60 Hertz 450 volts, 401 amperes, 900rpm
DC Exciter: 120 volts, 5.5 KW, 900rpm, direct connected

During the current modernization, provision was made to provide 400 Hertz power for the operation of new electronics equipment and the NTDS. The equipment consists of three 100 KW solid state frequency converters which were installed in a former radio area aft of No. 2 barbette.

The distilling plant consists of three triple-effect evaporator units. Two of the units are located on the upper level in the Forward Diesel Generator and Evaporator Room and the third unit is on the upper level in engine room No. 3. They are of the standard 20,000 gpd type using three horizontal cylinder shells set side-by-side in parallel. Together, the units can produce up to 60,000 gallons of fresh water a day for boiler feed water and crew consumption. At sea, the boilers have priority over any other uses.

Refrigeration for perishable stores is furnished by three 5/2.5 ton units. During the current modernization, eight 125 ton units were installed to air condition most of the crew living areas and selected office spaces.

Since 1972, all US Naval vessels have been equipped with a marine sewage CHT system. The CHT system prevents the discharge of sewage into rivers, harbors and coastal waters. It is designed to accept soil and waste drains from water closets, urinals, showers, laundries and galleys. In the system aboard the *Iowa*, three large tanks store the soil and waste material until it can be discharged at sea or transferred into an industrial sewage system ashore.

The general arrangement of the rudders and propellers is shown in this photograph of the *Missouri* taken on 23 July 1944, during her post shakedown overhaul at the New York Navy Yard. The propellers convert the 212,000 shaft horsepower into thrust. Note the five-bladed inboard and four-bladed outboard propellers. The two semi-balanced streamlined type rudders are located slightly inboard of the center propellers to take advantage of the flow of water through the tunnel and the wash from the propellers.

The massive port side propellers of the *Missouri* are shown in dry-dock on 23 July 1944. The stern tube for the center propellers is offset slightly outboard to be flush with the inboard side of the tunnel. The outboard shafts are supported in their strut bearings by two heavy struts set deep within the hull. Note the leading edge of the rudder assembly.

DAMAGE CONTROL

The engineering department is also responsible for the organization and administration of damage control procedures and practices. Damage control encompasses all efforts directed toward keeping a ship in action despite the effects of any damage which may be sustained. Damage control is not only concerned with battle damage but also non-battle damage such as fire, collision, grounding, weather damage and explosion. The importance of damage control cannot be over-stressed, for the ship's ability to inflict damage upon or destroy the enemy or carry out any mission could very well depend upon its effectiveness.

The damage control organization is divided into two separate, but related functions: damage control and engineering casualty control. Damage control is concerned with the preservation of stability and watertight integrity, the control of fires and flooding, the repair of structural damage and the control of Nuclear, Biological and Chemical (NBC) contamination. Damage control is an all-hands responsibility which is controlled by the engineering department. Engineering

The two large stacks are the only visible external indication of the massive main propulsion plant required for the *Iowa* class to meet the 33 knot speed. The main propulsion machinery required 256ft of hull space below the third deck, which is nearly the full length of the superstructure topside. Each stack intakes air and exhausts flue gasses for the boilers. (Courtesy Robert DeGast.)

casualty control is concerned with the effects of operational and battle casualties to the machinery and related systems. It is vital that all engineering services remain intact under all operating conditions.

One of the most important aspects of damage control is the preventive phase or, maintaining the material readiness of the vessel and its machinery before combat. Most damage can be effectively contained; therefore, doors, hatches, scuttles, etc., must be watertight and in good working order or they cannot be expected to stop progressive flooding from damage in other areas of the ship. The same is true of machinery and its related equipment, for if it is not maintained in a state of maximum efficiency and reliability, it will be useless in combat.

Damage Control Central

Located on the third deck forward of the machinery spaces near the centerline of the ship, Damage Control Central (DCC) exercises control over all repair parties and inport emergency teams. Information concerning battle damage or other casualties under the responsibility of the repair parties is collected and evaluated so the condition of the ship is known at all times. There are lighted status panels indicating various engineering conditions and liquid loading. Damage control diagrams and charts are plotted with stability, structural casualty and engineering casualty information. Publications which contain pertinent damage control information such as damage control and engineering casualty control manuals and booklets of ships' plans, machinery plans and machinery operating data are maintained.

A set of damage control diagrams and charts is also kept at each repair locker and is maintained by repair party personnel in communication with DCC. The damage control diagrams and charts are a series of expanded isometric drawings for each deck and level in the ship and present all of the information from the manual in graphic form. There is a set of charts for each major system in the ship, such as liquid loading, compartmentation, ventilation, firemain, fuel oil, etc.

The extent and status of all damage and flooding is plotted on the charts as reports are made by the repair parties so that immediate action can be taken to isolate damage and make emergency repairs. The effect of flooding on stability and buoyancy can be estimated using the liquid loading diagrams. The necessary corrective measures can then be determined. Counterflooding, if necessary, can be accomplished very rapidly, for the *Iowa*s have an enormous capacity to move large quantities of liquids very quickly.

Main Engine Control is located with the after engineering group in engine room No. 3. It exercises complete control over all main propulsion and auxiliary machinery.

In the damage control organization of the *Iowa* class ships, there are seven repair parties stationed at repair lockers strategically located throughout the ship. Each is assigned a specific area of responsibility.

*Repair 1F—main deck and above from the bow to the forward stack and second deck from barbette No. 2 to aft of the forward stack. Cont. p. 142

The main machinery plant of the *Wisconsin*, looking forward on 8 July 1942. The vessel on the shipway to the right is the *New Jersey*. The boilers are all in place and the main engines, in the spaces between the boilers, have already been covered over. The minute sub-division of the spaces within the hull is of primary importance for the control of flooding after damage. Lists can be corrected by counterflooding to keep the vessel on an even keel and maintain stability.

Right: Access to the machinery spaces was via 'Broadway', the main fore and aft passageway on the third deck, photographed here aboard the *Iowa* in 1986. Access to the 5in magazines was also gained from this passageway and 16in projectiles could be transferred between Turret No. II and Turret No. III on the overhead monorail. 'Broadway' was entirely within the armor citadel and portions of the monorail were removable, as shown here, to allow transverse watertight closures to be made. The repair lockers for the forward and aft engineering group repair parties were located off this passageway. (Photograph by the author.)

Opposite: The *Iowa* suffered a failure of the stern tube bearing on the starboard inboard shaft in December 1944. Emergency repairs were made in ABSD 2 to enable her to return to Hunters Point Shipyard in San Francisco for a general overhaul.

In No. 3 boiler room on the *Iowa* in May 1943, looking to port. Note the burners in the face of No. 6 boiler and the gear to control the operation of the boiler. No. 5 boiler is located on the opposite side of the room. The *Iowa*'s have eight of these boilers which furnish high pressure, superheated steam to four sets of geared turbines which drive the four shafts.

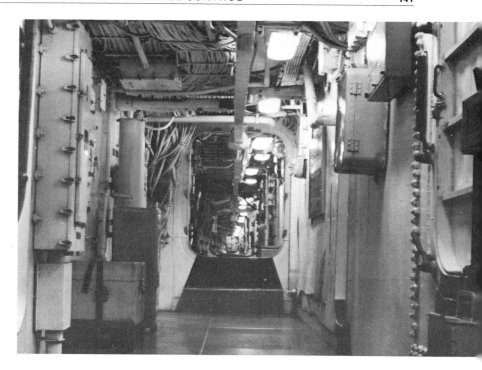

*Repair 1A—main deck and above from the forward stack to the
   stern and second deck from the forward stack to aft of the
   second stack.
*Repair 2—second deck from barbette No. 2 to the bow and third
   deck and below from the main machinery rooms to the bow.
*Repair 3—second deck from the after stack to the stern and third
   deck and below from the machinery spaces to the stern.
*Repair 4—forward engineering group, consisting of No. 1 and 2
   fire and engine rooms.
*Repair 5—after engineering group, consisting of No. 3 and 4 fire
   and engine rooms.
*Repair 6—incorporated with Repairs 2 and 3 and responsible for
   ordnances forward and aft respectively.
*Personnel battle dressing stations—located near Repair 1F, 3 and
   4.
*Personnel decontamination station—located at Repair 1A.

Each repair party has an officer in charge assisted by a chief or senior

Except for the carriers, the vessels of the *Iowa* class are the largest US Navy
ships afloat today. Even with their extreme overall length of 887ft, they can still
be docked in a ten-section ABSD for emergency repairs to the hull, shafting
and rudders as shown here. The *Iowa* is docked in the ABSD 2 at Mancus
Island, Ulithi Atoll on 28 December 1944.

petty officer and about twenty ratings. Typical damage control
equipment stored in the repair lockers includes access tools for
forcible entry, cutting torches, patching kits for broken piping,
plugging and patching kits for structural repairs, shoring to reinforce
weakened structures, an electrical repair kit and radiological defense
equipment. This material is used only by the repair parties and is
never removed from the lockers for other uses.
   When damage occurs, survivability can depend on the effectiveness
of damage control efforts. It is important to limit the effects of
damage by quickly establishing fire and flooding boundaries. Repairs
can only be made after the damage has been contained and is under
control.

Chapter 10

THE *IOWA* CLASS TODAY

The US Navy's *Iowa* class battleships are unique among the world's navies. The four *Iowa*s are the only surviving battleships in active naval service today. Each is the central and primary combatant of a battleship battle group (BBBG) and occupies a singular place in the United States' military strategy.

Their mission is to conduct prompt and sustained combat operations at sea, taking full advantage of their capability to destroy hostile surface, air and shore targets. In carrying out their mission the *Iowa*s can be projected into a number of roles. They can operate with carrier battle groups (CVBG), as the principal ship of an independent surface action group (BBBG) and in support of amphibious groups.

To understand the role of the battleship and BBBG in today's Navy, it is necessary to look at several general areas considered critical in the development of a long-term national integrated military strategy.[1]

1 Excerpts from the report of the Commission on Integrated Long-Term Strategy to the Secretary of Defense, January 1988.

First, the United States must be capable of discriminate nuclear strikes in order to deter a limited nuclear attack on Allied or US forces, and if necessary to stop a massive invasion. A further objective of this strategy is to contain Soviet expansion in any region of the world, with forward deployed forces in critical, threatened areas. To help protect United States interests and allies in the Third World, America will need versatile, mobile forces, minimally dependent on overseas bases, that can deliver precisely controlled strikes against distant military targets. Finally, in certain cases, the United States must be ready to assist anti-communist insurgents who are resisting a

In areas of high threat, a battleship battle group is intended to operate offensively with a carrier battle group. Such a force has greatly increased surface action and long-range strike capabilities with nuclear and conventional cruise missiles and 16in gunfire. Presently, a two-carrier, carrier battle group reinforced with a battleship battle group would present an adversary with an almost unsolvable tactical problem. The *Missouri* in company with the *Dwight D. Eisenhower* in the Pacific in late-1986.

hostile regime imposed from the outside or democratic states threatened by neighboring communist regimes.

There are a variety of situations envisioned in current strategy considerations. They are grouped according to the different levels of threat that they present.

A situation presenting a high-level threat would probably come from confrontation with a major power where the opposing forces would commit substantial air/missile assets. With the present strength of the Soviet Navy, high-threat areas would probably be limited to the range and capability of land-based aircraft to properly support their surface forces. The addition of carriers now under construction will enable the Soviets to project their naval power to almost anywhere in the world.

Some client states of the Soviet Union are capable of posing a medium-level threat. While their weaponry is usually of export quality and it is unlikely that their sponsor would risk direct involvement, they can expect to be freely resupplied. Medium-threat areas are generally considered to be portions of the Middle East, Mediterranean and Caribbean.

Generally, Third World countries present the lowest areas of threat in regard to aggressive military behavior. Although many of these

areas are within the Soviet sphere of influence, the countries involved have few real military capabilities. Subversive and terrorist activities are typical threats and can best be countered with a strong naval presence.

THE BATTLESHIP BATTLEGROUP

The battleship and the BBBG are versatile assets in the United States' integrated strategy for a wide range of conflicts, from the lowest intensity and highest probability to the most apocalyptic and least likely. They are ideally suited for specific employment in a number of tactical and strategic situations and greatly increase the options of the US Navy's operating forces. Since all of the *Iowa*s have at least fifteen, and possibly twenty, years of service life remaining, the Navy expects

The battleship battle group is ideally suited for employment in a number of tactical and strategic roles which makes it one of the US Navy's most versatile assets. The battle group consists of a battleship, an Aegis cruiser and three destroyer types. The *Iowa* is shown here with her battle group in 1985. The lead ship is the frigate *Underwood* (FFG 36) and to the left is the destroyer *Conolly* (DD 979). To the right is the destroyer *Comte de Grasse* (DD 974). The *Iowa* is in the center and the cruiser *Ticonderoga* (CG 47) is astern.

The mission of the battleship in the modern US Navy is to conduct prompt and sustained combat operations at sea. They are capable of destroying surface, air and shore targets and can be used in a variety of tactical situations. The *Missouri* fires a broadside with her 16in guns during target practice in 1987.

to use them past the year 2000 and they figure prominently in the Navy's future force structure.

As planned, the BBBG will consist of one *Iowa* class battleship, one CG 47 class Aegis guided missile cruiser and three DDG 51 class guided missile destroyers. The CG 47 and DDG 51 types support the battle group, furnishing advanced AAW and ASW capabilities. The CG 47 Aegis cruisers are considered the world's most capable AAW ships. The DDG 51 destroyers are designed to supplement the Aegis cruisers in air and missile defense for the battle group. Both the CG 47 and DDG 51 types have the latest in bow mounted and towed array sonar and a full range of ASW weapons.

The first DDG 51 guided missile destroyers will not become operational before 1990 or 1991 and the current BBBGs operate with a mix of available destroyer and frigate types supporting the Aegis cruiser. Support vessels that have been used include DD 963 class destroyers, FFG 7 class guided missile frigates and FF 1052 class frigates. It is likely that some mix of supporting types will be in use for

several years.

The versatility and flexibility of the BBBG can be appreciated by examining some of their more important mission–capable tasks.

First, the BBBGs are intended to operate offensively with CVBGs in areas of high-threat. Carrier force-level objectives are for seven two-carrier CVBGs and one single-carrier CVBG. At present, a two-carrier CVBG reinforced with a BBBG presents an almost unsolvable tactical problem for an adversary. Alternatively, a BBBG can also replace one of the carriers and its escorts in a two-carrier CVBG. This new formation would have greatly increased surface action and long-range strike capabilities with nuclear and conventional cruise missiles and 16in gun fire. This type of formation would allow the force

When operating as an independent surface action group, the battleship battle group can move quickly against shore targets within range of 16in gunfire. A controlled 'surgical' strike can be executed with great precision. The 16in projectiles have considerably more penetrating power than any airborne weapons. They also have greater accuracy, which assures minimum damage to non-military targets. The *New Jersey* practising just such a maneuver in September 1982.

commander greater flexibility in the use of tactical aircraft. The relieved carrier could be used to form a new CVBG or could retire for overhaul and maintenance as required. The single carrier CVBG could be reinforced by the addition of a BBBG, thus upgrading it to the capabilities as described above. Used with CVBGs, the four BBBGs can greatly relieve the operational demands on the carriers, especially during extended deployments.

A BBBG can also operate independently in areas of medium or lesser threat. The group is capable of conducting offensive operations in forward areas against hostile surface forces and shore targets when a CVBG is not available or not appropriate. Operational demands on the carriers are thus relieved allowing them to remain in the higher threat areas. In dealing with surface threats, the BBBG can intercept hostile strike forces over the horizon with conventionally armed cruise missiles and at close range with 16in gun fire. Against hostile shore targets which are within range of the 16in guns, the battleship can execute a controlled, 'surgical', strike with great precision. The

16in projectiles have considerably more penetrating capability than any airborne weapons. They are also more accurate than airborne weapons in assuring minimum damage to non-military targets. The BBBG has the ability to launch long-range inland strikes with both conventional and nuclear armed cruise missiles.

During amphibious operations, the BBBG can provide the amphibious group with surface and air protection, pre-landing shore bombardment and gun fire support for the beachhead. Current amphibious tactics use a direct assault on the beach and an inland assault from the air which link up to establish a firm foothold. The effectiveness of the beach assault is improved by bombardment from the large caliber guns. These guns are more effective against fortifications than are airborne weapons and one battleship can deliver conventional munitions, in tons per hour, at a rate of about two and a half times faster than a carrier. The number of aircraft which would otherwise be committed for close support can be reduced if the landing is supported by a BBBG.

Opposite: The battleship battle group is capable of conducting offensive operations in forward areas against hostile surface forces. The *Iowa* launches a Harpoon RGM-84 anti-ship cruise missile during Fleet Exercise 2-86. In dealing with surface threats, the *Iowa* class can intercept hostile strike forces over-the-horizon up to 85nm with the Harpoon.

The battleship battle group can provide an amphibious group with surface and air protection, pre-landing shore bombardment and gunfire support for the beachead. The battleship itself is still unmatched in firepower, delivery rate and target precision. The *Missouri* photographed in 1987 conducting gunnery exercises to hone the precision of her 16in guns.

Battleships are ideally suited for establishing a naval presence and in the role of 'showing the flag'. It is the most impressive of all warships when standing off foreign shores or making port calls. The projection of her power is understood by allies, neutrals and adversaries alike. The *Missouri* is leaving Lisbon, Portugal on 28 November 1986 after a port visit.

Finally, the BBBG serves an important function in establishing a naval presence. Although not a mission in the truest sense, a naval presence can serve a number of ends. In the role of 'showing the flag', a battleship is the most impressive of all warships. When standing off foreign shores or visiting harbors, her size and armament are clearly visible and the projection of power is understood by allies, neutrals and adversaries alike. The knowledge that a battleship can take offensive action within sight of its target with almost complete immunity makes the mere presence of a battleship and its battle group in areas of unrest an effective deterrent during a time of crisis without the firing of a single shot. The same strong naval presence maintains control of the seas and protects maritime lines of communication.

The success of any battle group can be measured, at least in part, by its endurance or its ability to remain on station for extended periods of time. The *Iowa*s are the most self-sustaining surface vessels in the US Navy except for the carriers. They store large amounts of fuel, ammunition, food and other items required by the crew. They are capable of refueling all of the escorts in the BBBG and can operate and refuel all types of navy helicopters. They have medical facilities on

The battleship battle group has a long-range strike capability against surface and land targets with the Tomahawk BGM-109 series cruise missiles. The Tomahawk can reach surface targets up to 470nm and land targets up to 675nm. The Tomahawk also has a nuclear capability against land targets with a range of up to 1,500nm. The *Iowa* launches a conventional Tomahawk land attack missile on 2 August 1986.

Opposite: The effectiveness of any battle group is a function of its endurance and ability to remain operational for long periods of time. The vessels of the *Iowa* class can store large amounts of fuel and are capable of refueling all of the escorts in the battleship battle group. The *Iowa* refueling the *Halyburton*, one of the frigates of her battle group in September 1985. Depending on weather conditions, underway replenishment is usually conducted at between 12 and 16 knots.

Below: Underway replenishment equipment, photographed aboard the *Iowa* in 1986. The large outrigger is used for streaming the fueling lines to the receiving ship. The equipment is in the stowed position with the fuel line saddles secured by their whips and the probe secured to the A frame on deck. (Photograph by the author.)

The *New Jersey* entering Pearl Harbor on 24 May 1986. The modernized *Iowa* class battleships are among the most survivable ships afloat today and they bring back the dimension of survivability to surface warfare. Of course, no vessel is unsinkable but their heavy armor, torpedo defense system, watertight subdivision and systems redundancy would not be easily defeated by any conventional weapons, including newer missiles such as the Exocet.

Opposite: The battleship battle group is a highly mobile tactical unit which can be quickly shifted from the Atlantic to the Pacific Ocean via the Panama Canal. Carrier battle groups cannot be shifted as easily since the carriers are too large to pass through the locks of the Canal. Although a tight fit, the *Missouri* is shown passing through the Gatun Locks on 10 December 1986.

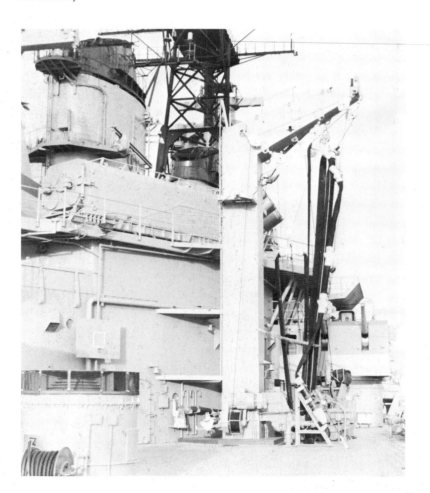

board which can accommodate the needs of the entire battle group and medical personnel who can be transferred between ships in the group as necessary.

Another dimension that the *Iowa*s bring back to surface warfare is survivability. With their ability to resist and withstand damage and their systems redundancy, they are ideally suited for strike warfare against an equal or even larger hostile force. This is not to imply that a battleship cannot be sunk, but their heavy armor, torpedo defense system and watertight sub-division would not be easily defeated by any conventional weapons, including newer missiles such as the Exocet. They are among the most survivable ships afloat today.

Originally designed to fight other battleships, the *Iowa*s have survived because they could be adapted to meet the needs of changing naval warfare. It appears that they will celebrate their fiftieth birthdays in active service and it may well be that their most important battles are yet to be fought. In remarks to the men of the pre-commissioning detail for the *Wisconsin* (BB 64), Admiral Carlisle A. H. Trost, USN, Chief of Naval Operations, stated: 'Put a battleship with an Aegis cruiser and you've got something that can operate anywhere in the world. Put a battleship battle group within a couple of hundred miles of a carrier battle group and you've something that no one in the world can beat!'

APPENDIX A
STATISTICAL DATA

ARMAMENT SUMMARIES

IOWA (BB 61)

Weapon	Feb 1943	Jul 1943	Apr 1945	Jun 1946	Jan 1947	Apr 1947	Oct 1951	Apr 1955	Apr 1984
16in/50cal 3 gun	9	9	9	9	9	9	9	9	9
5in/38cal twin	20	20	20	20	20	20	20	20	12
40mm quad	15	19	19	19	19	15	15	19	
20mm single	60	52	52	52					
20mm twin			8		16	16			
20mm CIWS									4
RGM-84 Harpoon									16
BGM-109 Tomahawk									32

NEW JERSEY (BB 62)

Weapon	Jun 1943	Apr 1945	Nov 1945	Jan 1947	Apr 1947	Oct 1951	Apr 1955	Apr 1968	Dec 1982
16in/50cal 3 gun	9	9	9	9	9	9	9	9	9
5in/38cal twin	20	20	20	20	20	20	20	20	12
40mm quad	20	20	20	20	16	20	18		
20mm single	49	49	41	10					
20mm twin		8	8	8	8	16			
20mm CIWS									4
RGM-84 Harpoon									16
BGM-109 Tomahawk									32

MISSOURI (BB 63)

Weapon	Jun 1944	Apr 1945	Sep 1945	Mar 1946	Jan 1947	Oct 1947	Apr 1951	Apr 1952	May 1986
16in/50cal 3 gun	9	9	9	9	9	9	9	9	9
5in/38cal twin	20	20	20	20	20	20	20	20	12
40mm quad	20	20	20	20	20	20	20	20	
20mm single	49	49	43	26	22				
20mm twin		8	8	8	8	16	32		
20mm CIWS									4
RGM-84 Harpoon									16
BGM-109 Tomahawk									32

WISCONSIN (BB 64)

Weapon	Dec 1944	Apr 1945	Jan 1946	Jun 1946	Jan 1947	Apr 1947	Oct 1951	Nov 1955	Jul 1988
16in/50cal 3 gun	9	9	9	9	9	9	9	9	9
5in/38cal twin	20	20	20	20	20	20	20	20	12
40mm quad	20	20	20	20	16	16	20	16	
20mm single	49	49	47	46					
20mm twin	2	8	8	2	18	16	16		
20mm CIWS									4
RGM-84 Harpoon									16
BGM-109 Tomahawk									32

This tabulation was taken from the Armament Summaries of the Bureau of Naval Ordnance, 1943 through 1955 and the current Ship's Allowance List.

ARMOR PENETRATION
2,700lb Mk & Projectile @ 2,425 f/s IV[1]

Armor Class	Range/ yards	Angle of Fall°	Striking Velocity f/s	Penetration in inches
Class 'A' Vertical	14,600	9.86°	1,682	22"
	17,850	13.29°	1,755	20"
	21,400	17.52°	1,661	18"
	25,000	22.43°	1,586	16"
	29,300	29.08°	1,530	14"
	34,300	37.88°	1,517	12"
	39,200	48.74°	1,583	10"
Class 'B' Horizontal	15,250	10.58°	1,839	3"
	19,800	15.54°	1,701	4"
	23,700	20.59°	1,610	5"
	27,000	25.42°	1,555	6"
	30,200	30.58°	1,523	7"
	32,700	34.92°	1,515	8"
	34,850	38.95°	1,519	9"
	36,700	42.73°	1,534	10"
	39,250	48.90°	1,583	12"

[1] Data from ORD 653(c) using initial velocity of a gun with a liner worn to the average life of the liner.

REINFORCED CONCRETE PENETRATION
Slab Concrete (5,000psi)

Projectile Type	Range/ yards	Angle of Fall°	Striking Velocity f/s	Thickness in ft Obiliquity 0°	30°
2,700lb AP Mk 8 @ 2,500 f/s IV[1]	10,000	6°	2,074	27.5'	20.5'
	15,000	10°	1,982	23.5'	17.5'
	20,000	15°	1,740	21.0'	15.5'
	25,000	21°	1,632	19.5'	14.5'
	30,000	28°	1,567	18.5'	14.0'
	35,000	36°	1,556	18.0'	13.5'
	40,000	45°	1,607	19.0'	14.0'
	42,345	53°	1,686	20.0'	15.0'
1,900lb HC Mk 13 @ 2,690 f/s IV[1]	10,000	5°	2,083	16.5'	13.0'
	15,000	10°	1,820	14.0'	11.0'
	20,000	16°	1,606	12.5'	9.5'
	25,000	23°	1,461	11.0'	8.5'
	30,000	32°	1,391	10.5'	8.0'
	35,000	41°	1,394	10.5'	8.0'
	40,000	51°	1,479	11.0'	9.0'
	41,622	57°	1,552	12.0'	9.5'

[1] Data from OP1172 using initial velocity of a gun with a new liner.

PAINTING AND CAMOUFLAGE MEASURES

VESSEL	PAINTING SYSTEM – CAMOUFLAGE MEASURE				
	21	22	32–1B	32–22D	HAZE GRAY
Iowa (BB 61)		02–1943 02–1945	01–1944		03–1946
New Jersey (BB 62)	05–1943	05–1945			01–1946
Missouri (BB 63)		01–1945		06–1944	03–1946
Wisconsin (BB 64)		04–1944			07–1946

During a September 1945 availability at Pearl Harbor the *Missouri* had her entire hull painted navy blue (5–N), eliminating the navy blue band parallel to the waterline from the lowest point of sheer down.

RADAR SUMMARY

	SEARCH RADAR																
	Air Search							Height-Finding		Surface Search							
	SK	SK-2	SR	SR-3	SPS-6	SPS-12	SPS-49	SP	SPS-8	SG	SG-6	SQ	SU	SPS-4	SPS-10	SPS-53	SPS-67
IOWA (BB61)	c 1943 f	1946 f	1945 a		1951 f	1955 f	1984 f	1948 a	1955 a	c 1943 f & a	1948 f	c 1943 p	1945 f		1984 f		1985 f
NEW JERSEY (BB62)	c 1943 f	1945 f		1948 f	1952 f		1982 f	1945 a	1954 a	c 1943 f & a	1950 f	c 1943 p	1945 f		f 1982	1968 f	1987 f
MISSOURI (BB 63)		c 1944 f		1948 f			1986 f	1948 a	1953 a	c 1944 f & a	1948 f	c 1944 p					1986 f
WISCONSIN (BB64)	c 1944 f	1946 f	1945 a		1951 f	1955 f	1988 f		1953 a	c 1944 f & a	1951 f	c 1945 p	1946 f	1953 f			1988 f

Key to letters: c, as completed; f, forward; a, aft; p, portable.

FIRE CONTROL SUMMARIES

DIRECTORS AND RADAR

Battery Gun Director (or gun sight) Radar	Main 16in/50 Mk 38		Secondary 5in/38 Mk 37			Anti-aircraft 40mm					20mm	Mk 15/16 CIWS	Missile (Strike) RGM-84	BGM-10 TASM	TLAM
	Mk 8	Mk 13	Mk 4	Mk 12/22	Mk 25	Mk 51	Mk 49 Mk 19	Mk 57 Mk 29	Mk 56 Mk 35	Mk 63	Ring/Mk 14	VPS-2	Active	Active	TERCOM
IOWA (BB 61)	c	f 1945 a 1946	c	1945	1955	c		1945	1955	1955	c/1945	1984	1984	1984	1984
NEW JERSEY (BB 62)	c	f 1945 a 1952	c	1945	L 1953 S 1954	c	P 1943	1945	1954		c/1945	1982	1982	1982	1982
MISSOURI (BB 63)	c	f 1946 a 1946	c	1948		c		1945			c/1945	1986	1986	1986	1986
WISCONSIN (BB 64)	c	f 1945 a 1952	c	1953		c		1945			c/1945	1988	1988	1988	1988

Key to letters: c, as completed; f, forward; a, aft.

SERVICE ROUNDS

Gun/Caliber Rounds/min	Item	Projectiles			Velocity (f/s)[2]	Propellant					Maximum Range	
		wt (lb)	Type	Mk		Powder	wt (lb)	Charge	Sections	Assy	E1	yards[3]
16in/50	[1] 1	2,240	AP	5	2,700	SPD	640	Full	6	Stacked	45°	47,000
Mk 7	2	2,700	AP	8	2,425	SPD	660	Full	6	Stacked	45°	40,185
2 rpm	3	2,700	T	9	2,500	SPD	660	Full	6	Stacked	45°	42,500
	4	2,700	AP	8	1,725	SPD/N	420	T	6	Stacked	45°	22,490
	5	2,700	T	9	1,800	SPD/N/CG	340	T	6	Stacked		
	6	2,700	AP	8	1,800	SPD/N/CG	305	Reduced	6	Dumped		
	7	2,700	T	9	1,800	SPD/N/CG	325	Reduced	6	Dumped		
	8	1,900	HC	13	2,690 2,615	SPD	660	Full	6	Stacked	45°	41,600 39,500
	9	1,900	HC	13	2,075 1,975	SPD/N/CG	305	Reduced	6	Dumped	45°	27,379 25,109
	10	1,900	HC	13	2,075	SPD/N/CG	325	Reduced	6	Dumped		
	11	1,900	HC	13	1,900	SPD	325	Reduced	6	Dumped		
	12	1,900	HE	14	2,690	SPD	660	Full	6	Stacked		
	13	1,900	HE/CVT	143[4]	2,690	SPD	660	Full	6	Stacked	5	5
	14	1,880	ICM	144[4]	2,690	SPD	660	Full	6	Stacked	5	5
	15	1,900	HE/ET	145[4]	2,690	SPD	660	Full	6	Stacked	5	5
	16	1,900	ICM	146[4]	2,690	SPD	660	Full	6	Stacked	5	5

NOTES: 1. The gun was originally designed to use the 2,240lb AP projectile. The 2,700lb AP projectile was adopted in 1939.
2. Where two velocities are given the first is for a gun with a new liner and the second is for a gun with average liner life wear.
3. Where two ranges are given the first is for a velocity of a gun with a new liner and the second is for a velocity of a gun with average liner life wear.
4. Projectiles Mark 143, 144, 145 and 146 use a modified Mark 13 body.
5. Altered ballistics depending on when/where munitions are dispensed. Impact of projectile body approx 2,000 yards down range from point where munitions are dispensed.
6. Two modified Mark 13 projectiles are in Limited use for target firing. They are 1900lb BLP rounds designated Mark 15 and Mark 16.

REPRESENTATIVE SERVICE ROUNDS

Gun/Caliber	Item	Projectiles			Velocity (f/s)[2]	Propellant			Maximum Range		Maximum Altitude	
		wt (lb)	Type	Mk		Powder	wt (lb)	Charge	E1	yards	E1	feet
5in/38[1]	1	53.3	HC	35	2,600	[2]	15.5–17[2]	Full	45°	18,200	85°	37,200
Mk 12	2	55.1	AAC	35	2,600	[2]	15.5–17[2]	Full	45°	18,200	85°	37,200
rpm: 15	3	54.3	ILLUM	50	2,600	[2]	15.5–17[2]	Full	45°	3	3	3
	4	54.5	WP	50	2,600	[2]	15.5–17[2]	Full	45°	18,200	3	3
40mm[4] (1.57in/60) MK 1 rpm: 160	5	1.96	AP	81	2,890	SPDN	300gms	Full	42°	11,000	90°	22,800
	6	1.985	AAC	1/2	2,890	SPDN	300gms	Full	42°	11,000	90°	22,800
20mm[5] (0.8in/70) Mk 4 rpm: 450	7	0.269	AP-T	9	2,740	SPDN	27.7gms	Full	35°	4,800	90°	10,000
	8	0.271	HE	3	2,740	SPDN	27.7gms	Full	35°	4,800	90°	10,000
	9	0.274	HE-T	7	2,740	SPDN	27.7gms	Full	35°	4,800	90°	10,000
20mm[6] CIWS Phalanx six-barrel rpm: 3,000	10		AP	149						2,000		

NOTES: 1. There were and are a large number of 5in/38 projectiles available for all purposes. The rounds represented are typical of World War II and current ammunition being used.
2. The types of powder in use for all service rounds listed is SPD, SPDN and SPDF.
3. Altered ballistics depending on when/where illumination or smoke is desired.
4. AP penetrates 1.7in max @ 1,000 yds. Tracer burns out @ 5,000 yds horizontal, 15,000ft vertical.
5. Tracer burns out @ 3,000 yds.
6. Sabot round with sub-caliber heavy metal penetrator of depleted uranium. No other data available.

REPRESENTATIVE MISSILE ROUNDS

Weapon/Desig	Item	Warhead			Speed (Mach)		Propellant		Range		Guidance
		Wt (lb)	Type	Mk	Cruise	Attack	Cruise	Boost	Mode	nm	
BGM-109	1	1,000	HE		0.50	0.75	Liquid	Solid	TSAM	470	Active Radar
Tomahawk	2	980	HE		0.50	0.75	Liquid	Solid	TLAM-C	675	TERCOM
	3	293	HE-N		0.50	0.75	Liquid	Solid	TLAM-N	1,500	TERCOM
RGM-84	4	510	HE		0.82	0.87	Liquid	Solid	RBL	64	Active Radar
Harpoon	5	510	HE		0.82	0.87	Liquid	Solid	BOL	85	Active Radar

16in DELIVERY RATE

					1,900lb High Explosive Projectiles				
No. of Rounds	Per Minute	No. of Guns	Rounds per Hour	Long Tons per Hour	30 Minute Gun Strike		2 Hour Gun Strike	
					Total Rounds	Total Long Tons	Total Rounds	Total Long Tons
1	1	3	180	153	90	77	360	305
1	1	6	360	305	180	153	720	611
1	1	9	540	458	270	229	1,080	915

NOTES: 1. *Nimitz* class carriers can deliver approximately 75 long tons of ordnance per strike. At an average of three strikes per day 225 tons of ordnance can be delivered per day. *Iowa* class battleships can deliver 229 long tons of high explosive and steel in a 30 minute gun strike.

2. *Nimitz* class carriers have an aviation ordance payload capacity of approximately 3,000 long tons. *Iowa* class battleships can carry an ordnance payload of 1,034 HE long tons or 1,470 AP long tons. A mix of 3 HE to 1 AP rounds is assumed per gun strike involving some hard targets of reinforced concrete. Aviation ordnance is assumed to have the penetration of the 1,900 pound HE projectiles. See penetration tables.

3. The cost to deliver ordnance on target is estimated to be $12,000 per long ton of aviation ordnance from a *Nimitz* class carrier and $1,600 per long ton of gun ordnance from an *Iowa* class battleship.

HULL DATA

	IOWA	NEW JERSEY	MISSOURI	WISCONSIN	ILLINOIS	KENTUCKY
Length Overall	887'-2.75"	887'-6.625"	887'-3"	887'-3"	887'-3" (Design)	887'-3" (Design)
Waterline Length	859'--5.75"	859'-10.25"	860'-0"	860'-0"	860'-0" (Design)	860'-0" (Design)
Maximum Beam	108'-2.063"	108'-1.375"	108'-2"	108'-2"	108'-2" (Design)	108'-2" (Design)
Design Waterline	34'-9.25"	34'-9.25"	34'-9.25"	34'-9.25"	34'-9.25"	34'-9.25"
DISPLACEMENT:						
Design	54,889 tons	54,889 tons	54,889 tons	54,889 tons	54,889 tons	54,889 tons
Standard 1945	45,000 tons	45,000 tons	45,000 tons	45,000 tons	45,000 tons	45,000 tons
Full Load 1945	57,540 tons	57,216 tons	57,540 tons	57,216 tons	55,250 tons	55,250 tons
Full Load 1988	57,500 tons	57,500 tons	57,500 tons	57,500 tons		
DRAFT/LOADING						
Design	34'-9.25" @ 54,889 tons	34'-9.25" @ 54,889 tons	34'-9.25" @ 54,889 tons	34'-9.25" @ 54,889 tons	34'-9.25" @ 54,889 tons	34'-9.25" @ 54,889 tons
Full Load 1945	37'-9" @ 57,540 tons	38'-0" @ 57,216 tons	37'-9" @ 57,540 tons	38'-0" @ 57,216 tons	35'-10" @ 55,250 tons	35'-10" @ 55,250 tons
Full Load 1988	37'-8.75" @ 57,500 tons	37'-8.75" @ 57,500 tons	37'-8.75" @ 57,500 tons	37'-8.75" @ 57,500 tons		
Tons/inch Immersion	154	154	154	154	154	154

Hull Design Characteristics @ Design Waterline: 1. Block Coefficient – 0.593. 2. Prismatic Coefficient – 0.596. 3. Midship Section Coefficient – 0.996. 4. Waterplane Coefficient – 0.69ft. 5. Wetted Surface – 113,600 sq ft. 6. GM (Metacentric Height) –.

STATISTICAL DATA

	IOWA	*NEW JERSEY*	*MISSOURI*	*WISCONSIN*	*ILLINOIS*	*KENTUCKY*
Hull Number	BB 61	BB 62	BB 63	BB 64	BB 65	BB 66
Builder	New York Navy Yard	Philadelphia Navy Yard	New York Navy Yard	Philadelphia Navy Yard	Philadelphia Navy Yard	Norfolk Navy Yard
Laid Down	27 June 1940	16 September 1940	6 January 1941	25 January 1941	15 January 1945	7 March 1942
Launched	27 August 1942	7 December 1942	29 January 1944	29 January 1944	Cancelled –	20 January 1950
Commissioned	22 February 1943	23 May 1943	11 June 1944	16 April 1944	11 August 1945	Suspended –
Decommisioned	24 March 1949	30 June 1948	26 February 1955	1 July 1948	Broken up –	August 1946
Recommissioned	25 August 1951	21 November 1950	10 May 1986	3 March 1951	September 1958	Resumed –
Decommissioned	24 February 1958	21 August 1957		8 March 1958		17 August 1948
Recommissioned	28 April 1984	6 April 1968		22 October 1988		Stricken –
Decommissioned		17 December 1969				9 June 1958
Recommissioned		28 December 1982				

MACHINERY DATA

	IOWA	*NEW JERSEY*	*MISSOURI*	*WISCONSIN*	*ILLINOIS*	*KENTUCKY*
Boilers:	8-Babcock & Wilcox	8-Babcock & Wilcox	8-Babcock & Wilcox	8-Babcock & Wilcox	8-Babcock & Wilcox	8-Babcock & Wilcox
Pressure	565psi	565psi	565psi	565psi	565psi	565psi
Temperature	850 deg. F.	850 deg. F.	850 deg. F.	850 deg. F.	850 deg. F.	850 deg. F.
Turbine Sets:	4-General Electric	4-Westinghouse	4-General Electric	4-Westinghouse	4-Westinghouse	4-General Electric
High Pressure	24,400 hp. @ 4,905 rpm.	24,400 hp. @ 4,905 rpm.	24,400 hp. @ 4,905 rpm.	24,400 hp. @ 4,905 rpm.	24,400 hp. @ 4,905 rpm.	24,400 hp. @ 4,905 rpm.
Low Pressure	28,600 hp @ 3,913 rpm.	28,600 hp @ 3,913 rpm.	28,600 hp @ 3,913 rpm.	28,600 hp @ 3,913 rpm.	28,600 hp @ 3,913 rpm.	28,600 hp @ 3,913 rpm.
Astern	11,000 hp. @ 2,375 rpm.	11,000 hp. @ 2,375 rpm.	11,000 hp. @ 2,375 rpm.	11,000 hp. @ 2,375 rpm.	11,000 hp. @ 2,375 rpm.	11,000 hp. @ 2,375 rpm.
Reduction Gears:	General Electric - Double Red.	Westinghouse - Double Red.	General Electrical - Double Red.	Westinghouse - Double Red.	Westinghouse - Double Red.	General Electric - Double Red.
High Pressure Ratio	24.284:1 rpm.	24.284:1 rpm	24:284:1 rpm.	24.284:1 rpm.	24.284:1 rpm.	24.284:1 rpm.
Low Pressue Ratio	19.369:1 rpm.	19.369:1 rpm.	19.369:1 rpm.	19.369:1 rpm.	19.369:1 rpm.	19.369:1 rpm.
Shafts	4	4	4	4	4	4
Shaft rpm	202	202	202	202	202	202
Shaft Horsepower	212,00 fwd.-44,000 ast.	212,00 fwd.-44,000 ast.	212,00 fwd.-44,000 ast.	212,00 fwd.-44,000 ast.	212,00 fwd.-44,000 ast.	212,00 fwd.-44,000 ast.
Speed	33 knots	33 knots	33 knots	33 knots	33 knots	33 knots
Propellers:	4	4	4	4	4	4
Inboard	2, 5-bladed 17'-0" dia.	2, 5-bladed 17'-0" dia.	2, 5-bladed 17'-0" dia.	2, 5-bladed 17'-0" dia.	2, 5-bladed 17'-0" dia.	2, 5-bladed 17'-0" dia.
Outboard	2, 4-bladed 18'-3" dia.	2, 4-bladed 18'-3" dia.	2, 4-bladed 18'-3" dia.	2, 4-bladed 18'-3" dia.	2, 4-bladed 18'-3" dia.	2, 4-bladed 18'-3" dia.
Rudders:	4, semi-balanced, streamlined	4, semi-balanced, streamlined	4, semi-balanced, streamlined	4, semi-balanced, streamlined	4, semi-balanced, streamlined	4, semi-balanced, streamlined
Projected Area	340 sq.ft. each	340 sq.ft. each	340 sq.ft. each	340 sq.ft. each	340 sq.ft. each	340 sq.ft. each
Turbo-Generators	8, 1,250 KW	8, 1,250 KW	8, 1,250 KW	8, 1,250 KW	8, 1,250 KW	8, 1,250 KW
Diesel Generators	2, 250 KW	2, 250 KW	2, 250 KW	2, 250 KW	2, 250 KW	2, 250 KW
Fuel Oil (1945)	8,624 tons	8,624 tons	8,624 tons	8,624 tons	8,624 tons	8,624 tons
Diesel Oil (1945)	187 tons	187 tons	187 tons	187 tons	187 tons	187 tons
Gasoline (1945)	8,588 gal.	8,588 gal.	8,588 gal.	8,588 gal.	8,588 gal.	8,588 gal.
Distilling Plants:	3	3	3	3		
Evaporators	triple-effect	triple-effect	triple-effect	triple-effect		

	IOWA	*NEW JERSEY*	*MISSOURI*	*WISCONSIN*	*ILLINOIS*	*KENTUCKY*
Capacity	20,000 gpd. each	20,000 gpd. each	20,000 gpd. each	20,000 gpd. each		
Reserve Feed Water	491 tons	490 tons	490 tons	490 tons		
Potable Water	777 tons	776 tons	776 tons	776 tons		
Refrigeration	3,5/2.5 ton units	3,5/2.5 ton units	3,5/2.5 ton units	3,5/2.5 ton units		
Air Conditioning	8,125 ton units	8,125 ton units	8,125 ton units	8,125 ton units		

MANNING LEVEL - ACCOMMODATIONS

	IOWA	*NEW JERSEY*	*MISSOURI*	*WISCONSIN*	*ILLINOIS*	*KENTUCKY*
Complement–Design						
Officer	117	117	117	117	117	117
Enlisted	1,804	1,804	1,804	1,804	1,804	1,804
Total	1,921	1,921	1,921	1,921	1,921	1,921
Complement–1945						
Officer	151	161	189	173		
Enlisted	2,637	2,592	2,789	2,738		
Total	2,788	2,753	2,978	2,911		
Complement–1949						
Officer	166	234	151	169		
Enlisted	2,451	2,554	2,255	2,503		
Total	2,617	2,788	2,406	2,672		
Complement–1968						
Officer		70				
Enlisted		1,556				
Total		1,626				
Complement–1988						
Officer	65	65	65	65		
Enlisted	1,445	1,453	1,450	1,450		
Total	1,510	1,518	1,515	1,515		

APPENDIX B

GENERAL ARRANGEMENT DRAWINGS

USS *Iowa* (BB 61). Outboard Profile and Overhead View as
outfitted late-1943. *Drawing by Thos. F. Walkowiak*

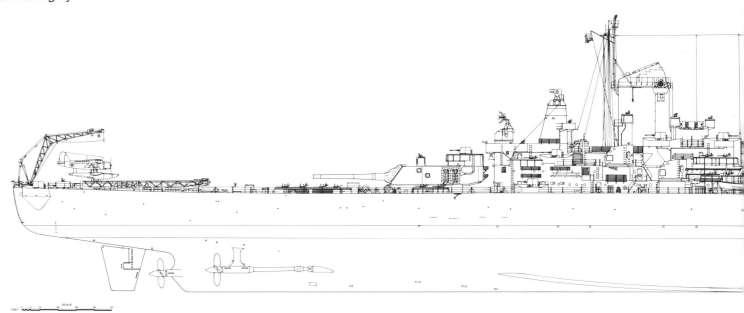

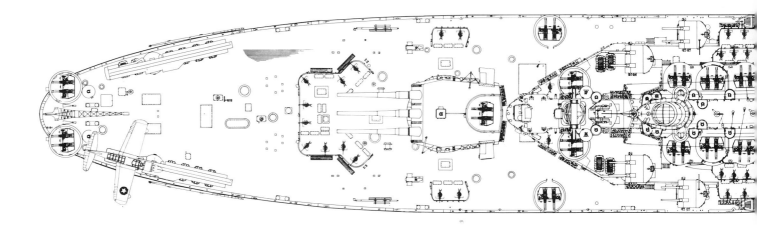

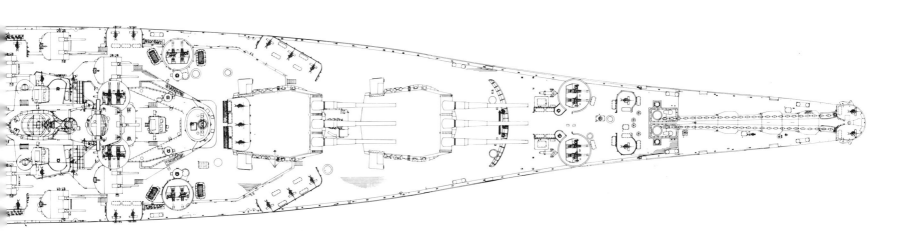

USS *Iowa* (BB 61). Outboard Profile and Overhead View as
outfitted early-1987. *Drawing by Thos. F. Walkowiak*

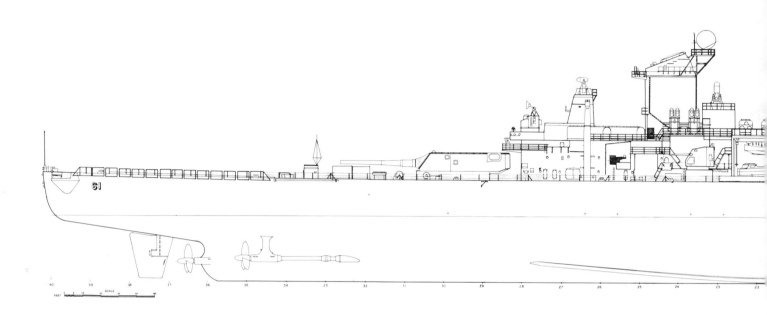

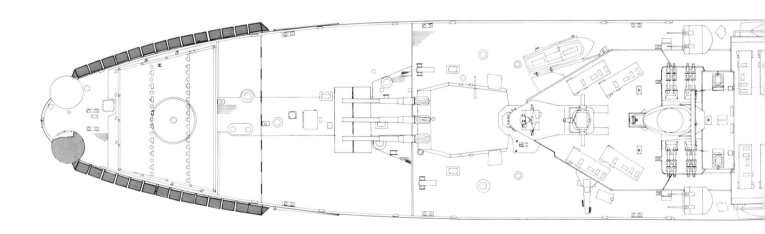

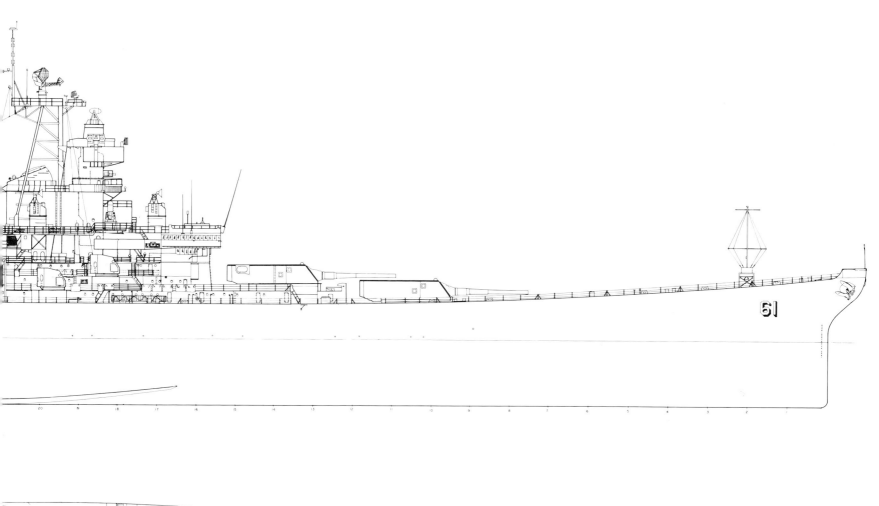

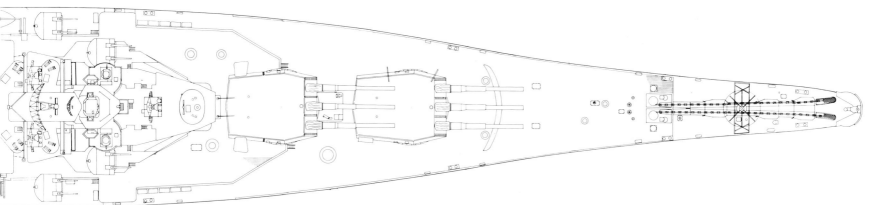

USS *New Jersey* (BB 62). Outboard Profile and Overhead
View as outfitted mid-1968. *Drawing by Thos. F. Walkowiak*

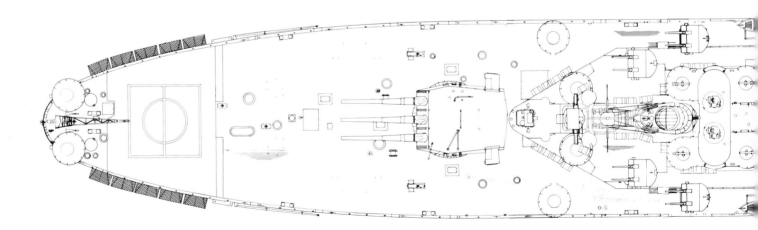

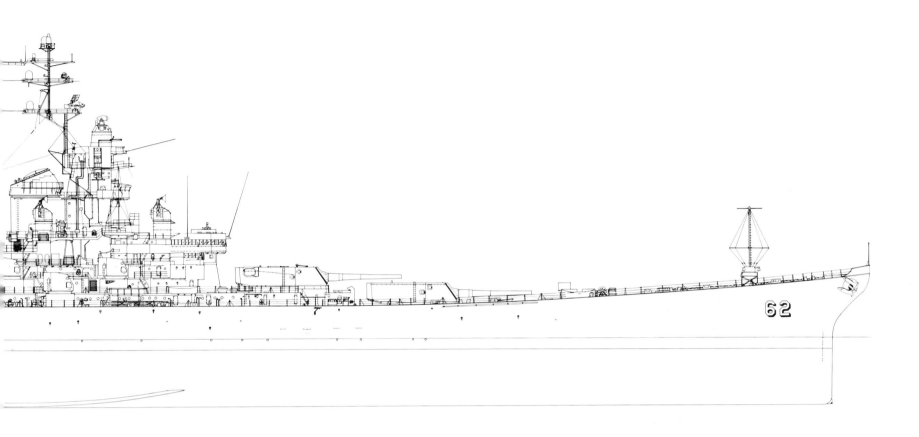

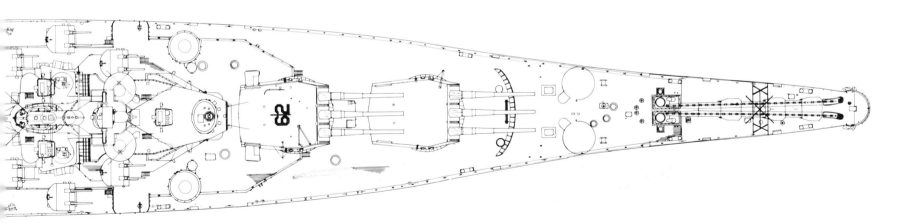

USS *Missouri* (BB 63). Outboard Profile and Overhead
View as outfitted mid-1945. *Drawing by Thos. F. Walkowiak*

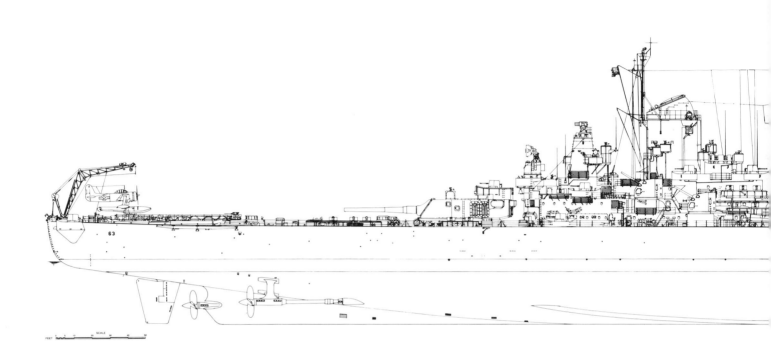

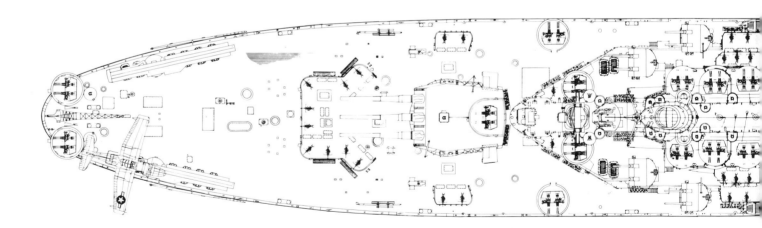

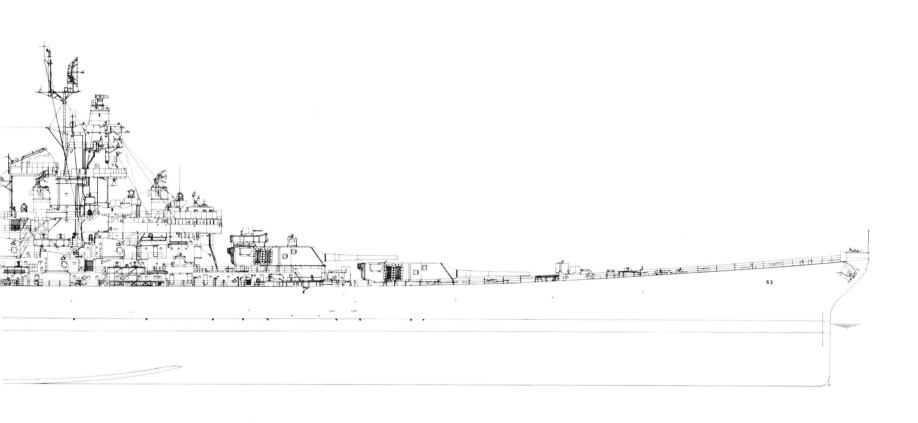

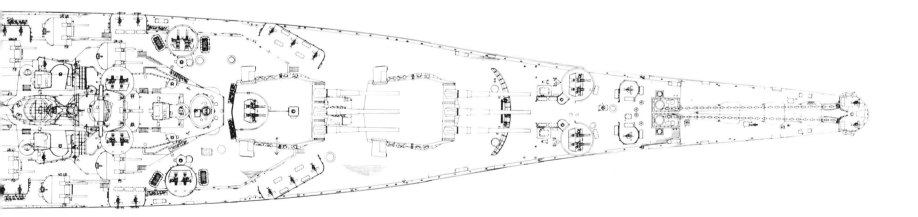

USS *Wisconsin* (BB 64). Outboard Profile and Overhead
View as outfitted early-1952. *Drawing by Thos. F. Walkowiak*

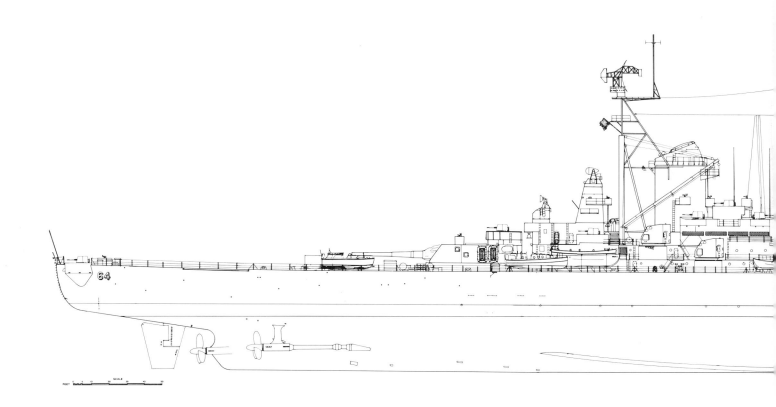

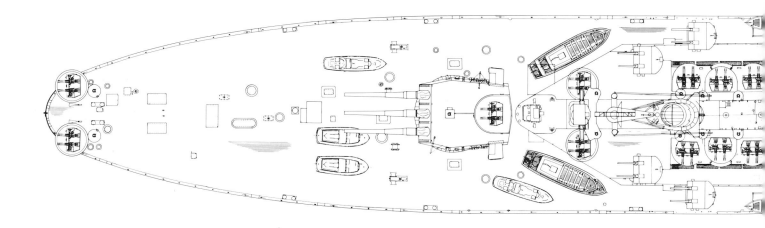

ARMOR DETAILS

SIDE ARMOR
Upper Belt Armor
From: FR 50 to FR 166.
From: 35'-0⅛ to 45'-7⅜" A.M.B.L. at FR 50.
  and 33'-10¼ to 43'-9" A.M.B.L. at FRS. 72½ to 166.
Normal thickness 12.1" class "A" armor.

Steering Gear Armor
From: FR 189 to FR 203.
From 28'-11⅝" to 37'-2⅝" A.M.B.L. at FR 189.
  and 31'-3⁵⁄₁₆ to 30'-10⁵⁄₁₀" A.M.B.L. at FR 203.
Normal thickness: 13.5" class "A" armor.

Lower Belt Armor
From: FR 50 to FR 189.
From: 7'-6" to 35'-0⅛" A.M.B.L. at FR 50,
  and 12'-6" to 33'-10¼" A.M.B.L. at FR 166 (for'd).
From: 17'-6" to 34'-6⁹⁄₃₂" A.M.B.L. at FR 166 (aft),
  and 21'-9¾" to 37'-2⅝" A.M.B.L. at FR 189.
Thickness: tapered from 12.1" to 1.62" FRS to 166 and
  from FRS 166 to 189 thickness varies from 13.5 to 5⅝ at FR 166
    to 13.5 to 7⅛ at FR 189.

S.T.S. Shell Plating
Varies from 25# to 35# between main & second dks FRS 52½ to
  173½ 60# between second & third dks FRS 50 to 171¾

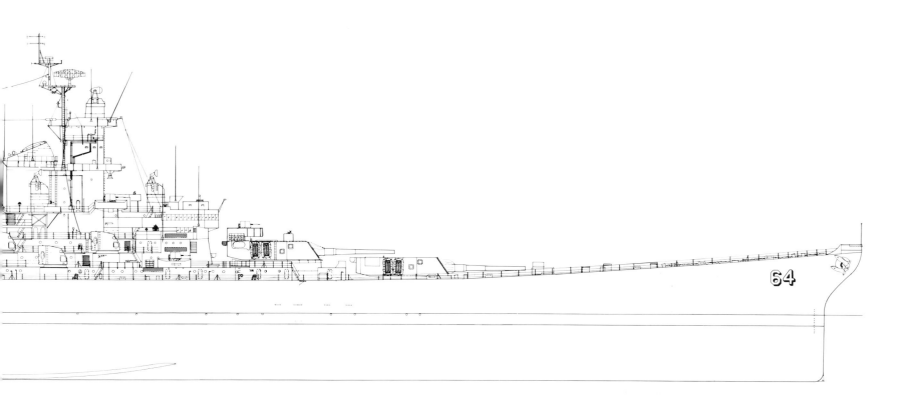

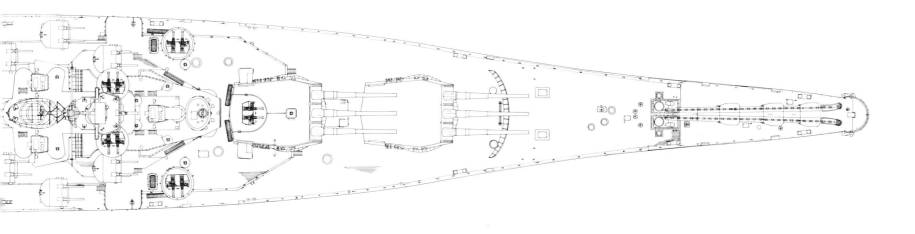

See following pages for armor diagrams

S.T.S. DECK PLATING

Main Deck
30# to 60# from FRS 33½ to 41½ and from FRS 172 to 191½
60# from FRS 41½ to 172.

Second Deck
30# to 50# from FRS 34 to 50 and from FRS 166 to 181.
4.75" PLUS 50# from FRS 50 to 166.

Splinter Deck
25# from FRS 79 to 156.

Third Deck
40# from FRS 50 to 82½ between BHD #3 (P&S).
20# to 25# from FRG 82½ to 151, and 40# from FRS 151 to 166
between BHD #3 (P&S).
5.6" plus 30# from frs 166 to 189 between BHD #3 (P&S).
6.2# from FRS 189 to 203 between BHD #3 (P&G).

First Platform
60# from FRS 189 to 204 — 19'-10" P/S off ₵ FR 189 to
18'-9" P/S off ₵ FR 204.

The ship represented is the *Iowa* with the inboard general arrangement as outfitted in 1945. Spaces along the center line have been given a letter designation which is explained in the adjacent key. *Drawing by Thos. F. Walkowiak*

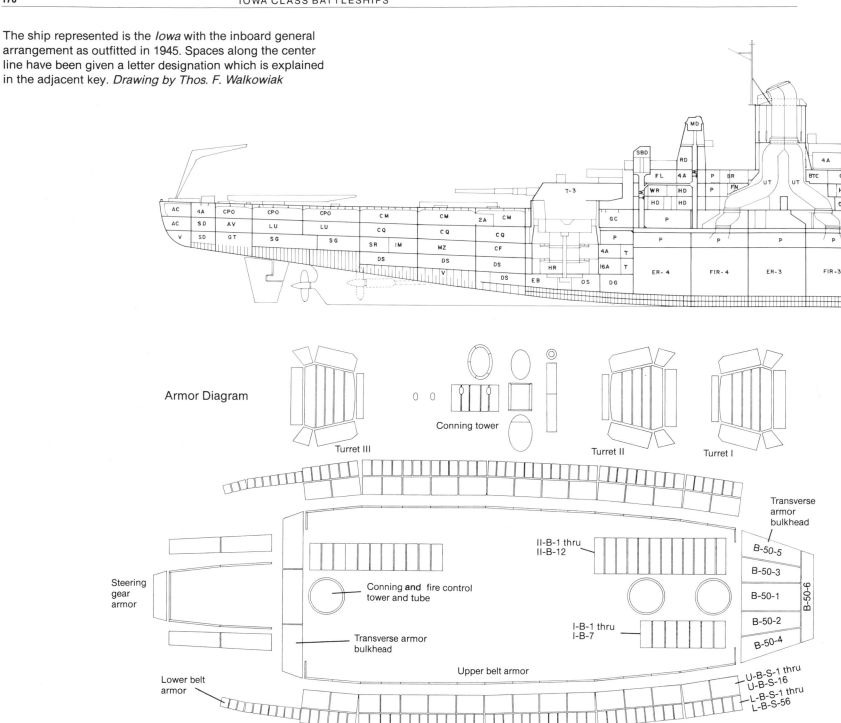

Armor Diagram

Turret III

Conning tower

Turret II

Turret I

Transverse armor bulkhead

Steering gear armor

II-B-1 thru II-B-12

B-50-5

B-50-3

B-50-1

B-50-6

Conning and fire control tower and tube

B-50-2

I-B-1 thru I-B-7

B-50-4

Transverse armor bulkhead

Upper belt armor

Lower belt armor

U-B-S-1 thru U-B-S-16
L-B-S-1 thru L-B-S-56

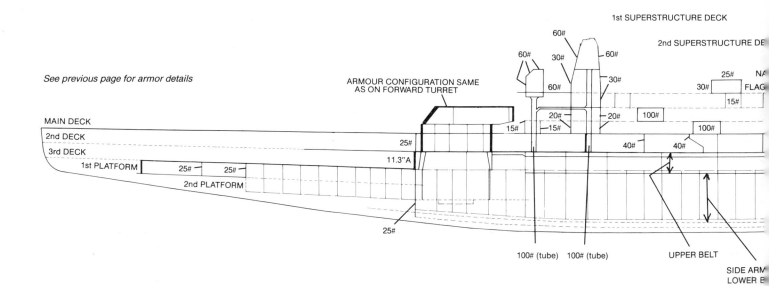

See previous page for armor details

1st SUPERSTRUCTURE DECK

2nd SUPERSTRUCTURE DE

60#

60#   60#

30#

60#   30#

ARMOUR CONFIGURATION SAME AS ON FORWARD TURRET

25#   NA

30#   FLAG

15#

20#   20#

100#

MAIN DECK

15#   15#

100#

2nd DECK

3rd DECK

25#

40#   40#

11.3"A

1st PLATFORM   25#   25#

2nd PLATFORM

25#

100# (tube)   100# (tube)   UPPER BELT

SIDE ARM
LOWER B

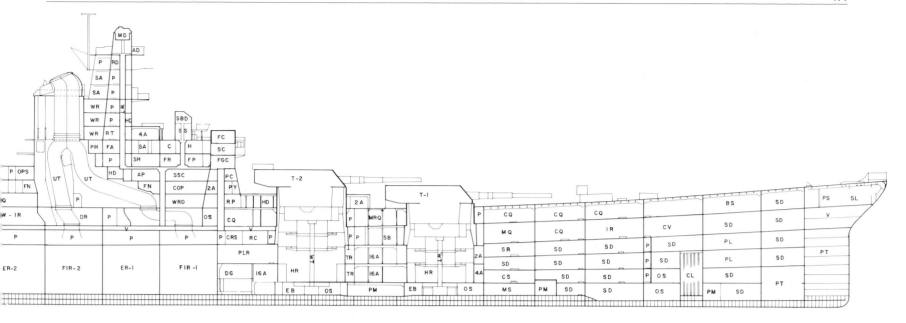

This diagram shows each piece of heavy armor which was manufactured for the *Iowa* class ships and its position in the armor citadel. This diagram represents BB 62 through BB 66. BB 61 is identical except for an additional level in the conning tower. *Drawing by the author*

Key: Typical Inboard Profile

AV	Aviation Stores	FN	Fan Room	RC	Radio Control Room
AC	Air Plane Crane Machine Room	FP	Flag Plot	RD	Radar Room
		FR	Flag Radio	RP	Repair Locker
AD	Air Defense Station			RS	Radio Trans. Room
AP	Admiral's Pantry	GC	Gun Cleaning Room		
		GT	Gas Tank	SA	Sea Cabin
BR	Boat Repairs	GW	General Workshop	SB	Sick Bay
BS	Boatswain's Stores			SC	Ship's Control
BTC	Battery Charging Room	HD	Head	SD	Store Room – Stewards'
		HR	Handling Room	SBD	Secondary Battery Director
CF	Chill Box – Fruit			SG	Steering Gear Room
CL	Chain Locker	IM	Ice Machinery Room	SH	Signal Shelter
CM	Crew's Mess	IR	Issue Room	SL	Sand Locker
COP	Captain's Pantry			SR	Store Room
CPO	Chief Petty Officers' Mess	LU	Laundry	SS	Switching Station
CQ	Crew's Quarters			SSC	Senior Staff Cabin
CRS	Central Station	MD	Main Battery Director		
CS	Captain's & Admiral's Storeroom	MQ	Mess Attendants' Quarters	T	Turret
		MRQ	Marine Quarters	TR	Watertight Trunk
CV	Canvas & Awning Storeroom	MS	Marine Stores		
		MZ	Meat Freezer	UT	Uptake
DG	Diesel Generator				
DR	Drying Room	OPS	Optical Shop	V	Void
DS	Dry Stores	OS	Ordnance Stores		
				WRD	Wardroom
EB	Electrical Booth	P	Passage	WR	Stateroom
ER	Engine Room	PC	Plenum Chamber	WS	Windlass Room
		PH	Photo Lab	WT	Wiring Tube
FA	First Aid	PL	Paint Storeroom		
FC	Fire Control	PLR	Plotting Room	2A	20mm Magazine
FGC	Flag Conning Station	PM	Pump Room	4A	40mm Magazine
FIR	Fire Room	PS	Paravane Spares	16A	16in Magazine
FL	Film Locker	PT	Peak Tank		
		PY	Pyrotechnic Locker		

This drawing shows the longitudinal distribution of heavy Class A and B armor, STS deck armor and other primary STS protection. This drawing represents BB 61. BB 62 through BB 66 are identical except for having only two levels in the conning tower. For BB 63 through BB 66 the forward armor bulkhead is 14.5in tapering to 11.7in and the after armor bulkhead is 14.5in straight. *Drawing by Thos. F. Walkowiak*

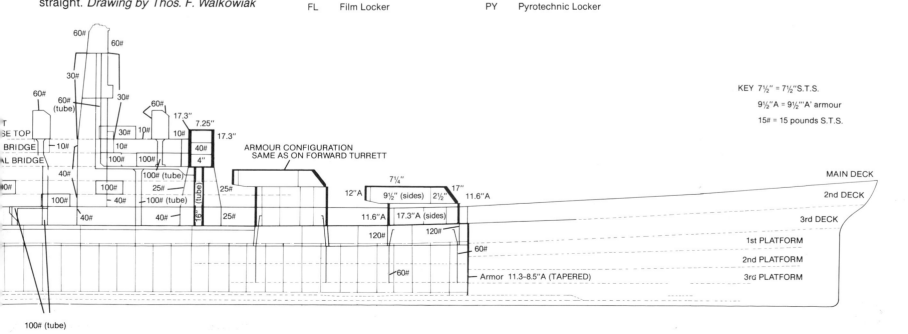

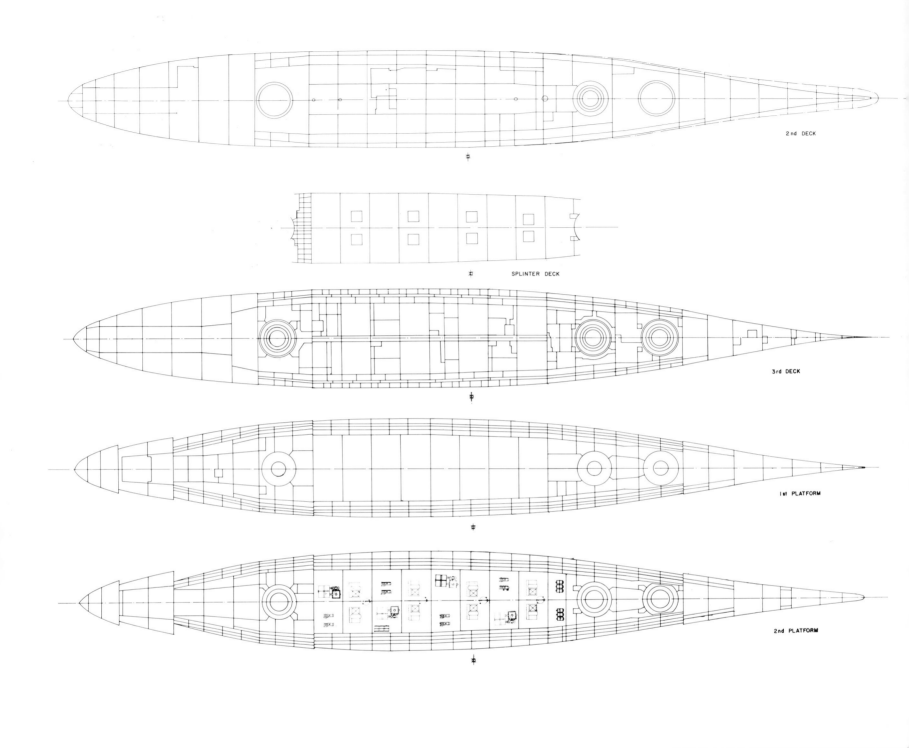

2nd DECK

SPLINTER DECK

3rd DECK

1st PLATFORM

2nd PLATFORM

Sheer, Half Breadth and Body Plans.   CE

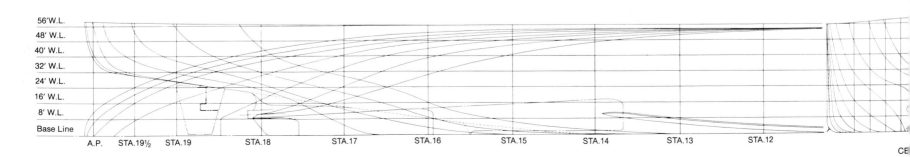

| 56' W.L. | 48' W.L. | 40' W.L. | 32' W.L. | 24' W.L. | 16' W.L. | 8' W.L. | Base Line |

A.P.   STA.19½   STA.19   STA.18   STA.17   STA.16   STA.15   STA.14   STA.13   STA.12   CE

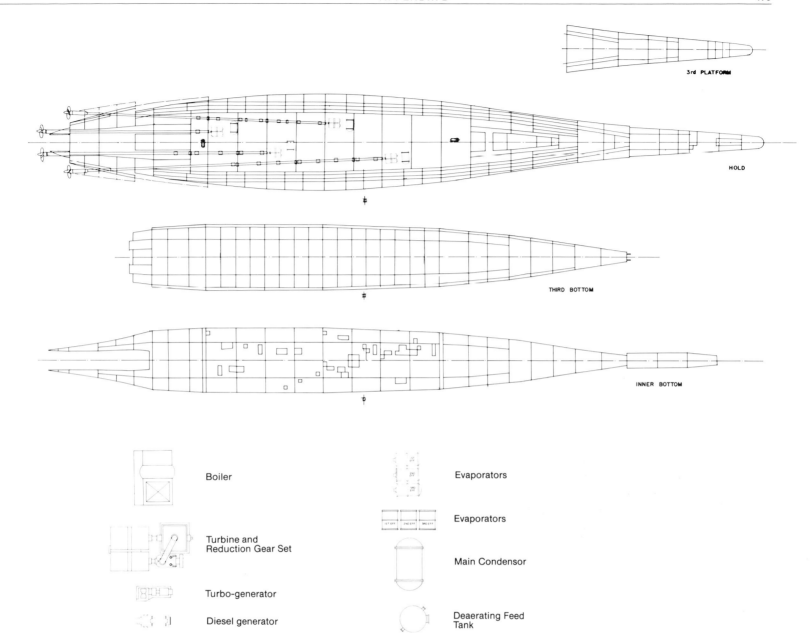

3rd PLATFORM

HOLD

THIRD BOTTOM

INNER BOTTOM

Boiler

Turbine and
Reduction Gear Set

Turbo-generator

Diesel generator

Evaporators

Evaporators

Main Condensor

Deaerating Feed
Tank

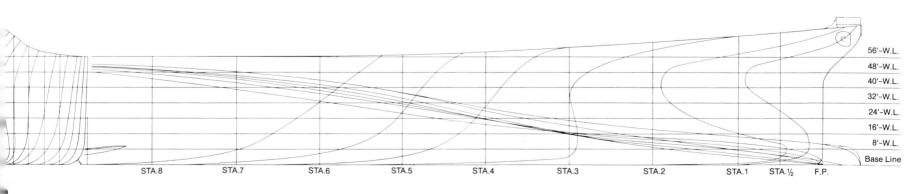

56'-W.L.
48'-W.L.
40'-W.L.
32'-W.L.
24'-W.L.
16'-W.L.
8'-W.L.
Base Line

STA.8   STA.7   STA.6   STA.5   STA.4   STA.3   STA.2   STA.1   STA.½   F.P.

PAINTING AND CAMOUFLAGE MEASURES

All painting systems for US Naval vessels have met specific operational requirements and in effect can be considered a form of camouflage. The haze gray system normally used in peacetime, for example, is the least visible under the widest range of light conditions. During war and in other emergencies it may be desirable to use a painting system for confusion rather than for low visibility.

During World War II, the US Navy had a wide range of camouflage measures and painting systems. However, only a few were used with the vessels of the *Iowa* class.

Measure 21, Navy Blue System. All vertical surfaces were painted navy blue (N–5) without exception. All decks and horizontal surfaces were painted deck blue (20–B).

Iowa, Measure 32, Design 1B.

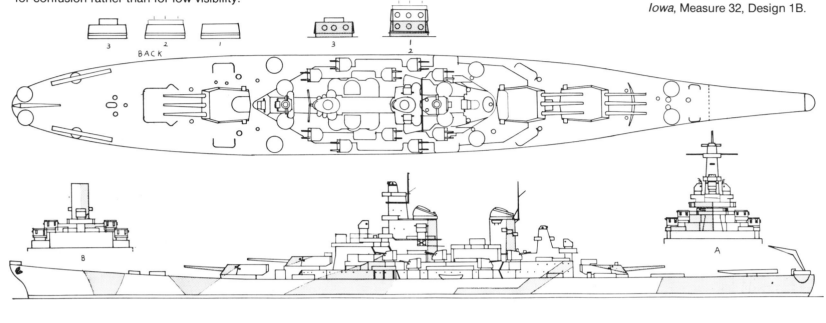

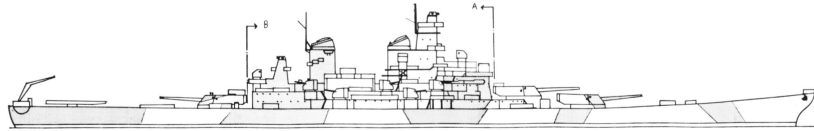

Measure 22, Graded System. All vertical surfaces were painted haze gray (5–H) with a navy blue (5–N) band on the hull parallel to the waterline from the lowest point of sheer down. All decks and horizontal surfaces were painted deck blue (20–B).

Measure 32, Medium Pattern System.

Design 1 B. Colors on the vertical surfaces were navy blue (5–N) and light gray (5–L). All decks and horizontal surfaces were painted deck blue (20–B) (see note 1). Design 7 A. Colors on all vertical and horizontal surfaces were the same as Design 22 D below (see note 2).

Design 22 D. Colors on the vertical surfaces were dull black (BK), ocean gray (5–O) and light gray (5–L). All decks and horizontal surfaces were painted deck blue (20–B) for areas of pattern which were ocean gray (5–O).

NOTES

1. No specific reference was found for this design number. It is believed that this is the first design in Measure 32 for a battleship or 1 B. The system has, therefore, been referred to as Measure 32, Design 1 B.
2. Design 7 A was prepared for the *Iowa* class but there was apparently no opportunity to apply it to a vessel before the use of Measure 32 was discontinued.
The table on page 155 indicates the approximate time frame of the painting systems and camouflage measures used on the four *Iowa* class ships.

DULL BLACK

OCEAN GRAY 5-O

LIGHT GRAY 5-L

ALL DECKS DECK BLUE 20-B EXCEPT 5-O FOR PATTERN

Missouri, Measure 32, Design 22 D.

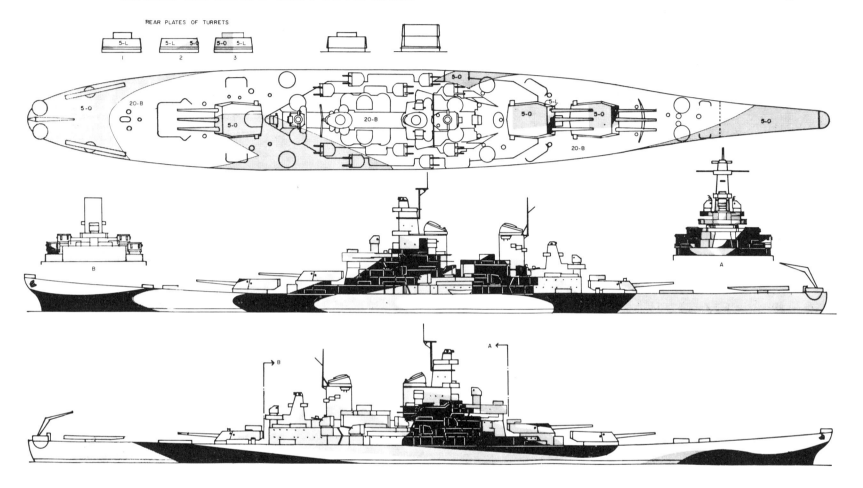

APPENDIX C

CHRONOLOGY OF SERVICE

The following chronology is taken from the ships' histories that are on file at the Naval Historical Center, Washington Navy Yard, Washington, D.C. It is intended as a quick reference to provide the reader with general information as to each of the four *Iowas*' areas of operation, their periods of active service, overhaul and maintenance, as well as their time in the reserve fleet. The chronology is an arbitrary selection of significant events and does not necessarily represent a complete list of the ships' activities.

USS *Iowa* (BB 61)

17 May 1938	Congress authorized construction of first two fast battleships of their class, USS *Iowa* and USS *New Jersey*.
27 June 1940	Laid down at New York Navy Yard.
27 August 1942	Launched at New York Navy Yard. Sponsored by Mrs Henry A. Wallace, wife of the Vice-President.
22 February 1943	Commissioned.
24 February 1943	To see for shakedown in Chesapeake Bay and along Atlantic Coast.
27 August 1943	*En route* to North Atlantic to neutralize threat of German battleship *Tirpitz* in waters off Newfoundland.
25 October 1943	To Norfolk Navy Yard for two weeks of maintenance in preparation for taking President Roosevelt to North Africa for Tehran Conference.
13 November 1943	*En route* to Mediterranean with FDR and other high-ranking members of American delegation to Tehran.
16 December 1943	Completion of mission with return of FDR to United States.
2 January 1944	*En route* to Pacific as flagship of Battleship Division 7, in company with USS *New Jersey*.
7 January 1944	Transit of Panama Canal.
23 January 1944	First Pacific campaign in support of carrier air strikes against Kwajalein and Eniwetok Atolls.
16 February 1944	First firing of weapons in combat in attack on Japanese naval base at Truk in Caroline Islands. In action off Truk, the *Iowa* sank light cruiser *Katori*.
18 March 1944	First shore bombardment against Mili Atoll in Marshall Islands. *Iowa* received her first hit when she was struck by two Japanese 4.7 projectiles, neither of which caused significant damage.
30 March 1944	In support of Task Group 58 air strikes against Palau and Woleai Islands, followed by further strikes against Hollandia, Aitape and Wake Islands.
22 April 1944	Supporting Army landing at Aitape and Tanahmerah and Humbolt Bays.
1 May 1944	Bombardment of airfield, bombs wharf and other enemy facilities at Ponape.
13 June 1944	Shelled Saipan and Tinian and blew up an ammunition dump.
19 June 1944	In action throughout Battle of the Philippine Sea. Downed at least three attacking planes.
September 1944	A unit of Fleet-Admiral William F. Halsey's Third Fleet in support of carrier strikes against Philippine and Caroline Islands.
10 October 1944	Participating in air strikes against Ryukyu Islands, Taiwan and Luzon.
23 October 1944	Headed for Battle of Leyte Gulf.
25 November 1944	Kamikaze attack on Third Fleet. The *Iowa* claimed two Jills and a Judy.
17 December 1944	At Ulithi for replenishment and maintenance. Lost plane, washed over during typhoon. Damage to shaft caused by storm required *Iowa* to return to the States for overhaul at Hunters Point Shipyard in San Francisco.
15 January 1945	In drydock until 19 March 1945.
15 April 1945	Arrives off Okinawa to relieve *New Jersey*.
25 May 1945	Supported air strikes against Kyushu.
1 July 1945	*En route* to northern Honshu and Hokkaido.
15 July 1945	*Iowa*, *Missouri* and *Wisconsin* attacked Muroran on Hokkaido inflicting significant damage on Nihon Steel Company and Wanishi Ironworks.
17 July 1945	The three battleships bombarded industrial city of Hitachi Miro. During this action, *Iowa* served as flagship for Rear-Admiral Oscar Badger.
29–30 July 1945	Bombarded island of Kahoolawe.
27 August 1945	In company with *Missouri*, *Iowa* put into Sagami Bay to effect surrender of Yokosuka naval district.
29 August 1945	*Iowa* and *Missouri* entered Tokyo Bay in support of landing of occupation forces to take place next day.
20 September 1945	Underway for United States.
15 October 1945	Arrived in Seattle, Washington and from there, went on to Long Beach where she engaged in training operations along West Coast.
27 January 1946	Arrived again in Tokyo Bay to serve as flagship of Fifth Fleet until March.
25 March 1946	Returned to Long Beach to operate along West Coast conducting drills, maneuvers and naval reserve and midshipmen training cruises.
September 1948	Inactivation begun at San Francisco.
24 March 1949	Placed out of commission in reserve.
25 August 1951	Recommissioned due to escalating level of hostilities in Korea.
1 April 1952	Underway for Far East to relieve *Wisconsin* and become flagship of Vice-Admiral Robert T. Briscoe, Commander, Seventh Fleet operating in support of United Nations Forces in Korea.
8 April 1952	Conducted gun strikes against enemy supply routes in Wonson-Songjin area.
9 April 1952	Joined bombline to strike enemy troop concentrations, supply areas and suspected gun positions in vicinity of Suwon Dan and Kojo.
13 April 1952	Bombardment in support of I ROK Corps, killing 100 enemy troops, destroying six gun emplacements and seriously damaging divisional headquarters.

14 April 1952	In Wonsan Harbor to bomb warehouses, observation posts and railroad marshalling yards and then back to bombline to support UN forces in Konsong area.
20 April 1952	Operating north of 38th Parallel, *Iowa* closed four railroad tunnels near Tanchon.
25–26 April 1952	Bombardment of Chindong and Kosong.
25 May 1952	In action against North Korean industrial and rail transportation center at Chongjin. Not since *Missouri* bombarded Chongjin in November 1950 had a battleship operated that far north, just forty-eight miles from Russian border. She effectively destroyed Chongjin's industrial center.
27 May 1952	Bombardment of Songjin, closing railroad tunnels and seriously damaging area bridges.
28 May 1952	Again on bombline in support of X Corps, followed by gun strikes on islands in Wonsan Harbor.
1 June 1952	Underway for Sasebo and replenishment.
June 1952	Gunstrikes against Mayang-do, Tanchon, Chongjin, Chodo-Sokto and ports of Hungnam and Wonsan.
9 June 1952	*Iowa*'s helicopter rescued downed pilot from USS *Princeton*.
16 July 1952	Second *Princeton* pilot is rescued by *Iowa*'s helicopter.
20 August 1952	Went to aid of destroyer *Thompson* off Songjin, taking aboard her casualties and covering her escape to safer waters.
23 September 1952	Gunstrikes in Wonsan area observed by General Mark Clark, USA, Commander in Chief of United Nations Forces who was aboard. *Iowa*'s gunfire destroyed a major ammunition dump.
25 September 1952	Gunstrikes against railroad and thirty-car train.
14 October 1952	Participated in Operation Decoy, an attempt to draw enemy troops under fire at Kojo.
16 October 1952	Provided anti-aircraft support for *Mount McKinley* during Kojo action.
17 October 1952	*En route* to Norfolk for overhaul, followed by training operations in Caribbean.
July 1953	Serving as flagship of Second Fleet, *Iowa* was a participant in Operation Mariner, a major NATO exercise in Northern Europe.
June 1954	On midshipman training cruise, rendezvous with the three other *Iowas* in Guantanamo Bay, Cuba.
1954 and 1955	Visited Mediterranean becoming first battleship regularly assigned to Commander of Sixth Fleet.
June 1955	To Norfolk for a four-month overhaul, followed by training cruises and operational exercises.
December 1955	Re-gunned for first time.
January 1957	Returned to Mediterranean for duty with the Sixth Fleet.
13 June 1957	Participated in International Naval Review off Hampton Roads, Virginia.
September 1957	Participated in NATO's Operation Strikeback in North Atlantic.
24 February 1958	Decommissioned at Philadelphia Navy Yard.
1 September 1982	In tow from Philadelphia to New Orleans and Avondale Shipyard, Inc. for modernization and reactivation. Subsequently towed to Ingalls Shipbuilding, Pascagoula, Missouri for completion of work.
28 April 1984	Recommissioned, ahead of schedule and within budget.
30 April 1984	Underway to Autec Range for Naval Gun Fire Support training.
May 1984	Two weeks refresher training at Guantanamo Bay.
21 May 1984	Off Vieques Island, Puerto Rico, for NGFS qualifications for *Iowa*'s 16in and 5in batteries.
19 June 1984	Underway for Caracas, Venezuela conducting a number of systems checks and gunnery exercises *en route*. *Iowa* also made stops at ports *en route* in support of 'Naval presence' operations designed to back up friendly states in Central America and Caribbean.
Mid-July 1984	Off Vieques Island for gunnery exercises.
8 August 1984	Underway to begin Pacific Coast operations.
12 August 1984	Two US Army UH-1 helicopters from *Iowa* were used when medical and dental assistance was needed in Guatemala.
13 August 1984	SAR communications drill.
14 August 1984	Engaged in surveillance of thirteen miles of Nicaraguan coast in conjunction with embassy contingency communication exercises.
26 August 1984	Nicaraguan surveillance completed and *Iowa* returned to Balboa, Panama for trip back through Canal.
17 September 1984	Arrived in Norfolk.
October 1984	Week-long visit to New York.
1–20 November 1984	Participated in COMPUTEX 1–85 in Puerto Rican Operations area.
December 1984	In port at Norfolk.
January 1985	Sea trials.
February 1985	Underway for deployment in Central America. Completed several civic action and humanitarian projects in Costa Rica and Honduras. Participated in encounter exercises with Battleship Surface Action Group.
March 1985	Engaged in Battle Force integrated training and post-shakedown availability training operating out of Norfolk. Offloaded ammunition at Yorktown's Naval Weapons Station.
26 April 1985	Into drydock at Norfolk Navy Yard at Portsmouth.
31 July 1985	Out of drydock to load gun ammunition while in Whiskey Anchorage in Hampton Roads. This was followed by a demonstration of her Tomahawk Handling System, then ten days of sea trials and ammunition onload at Yorktown.
22 August 1985	Received Battenburg Cup Award as best all-around ship in Atlantic Fleet for 1984.
27 August 1985	Underway for Ocean Safari as part of Battleship Surface Action Group providing protection for convoy of supply ships *en route* from Boston to Northern Europe.
20 September 1985	Operation Ocean Safari completed following rendezvous with USS *America* Battle Group. *Iowa* went on through English Channel to Le Havre, France, then Copenhagen and Aarhus, Denmark and Oslo, Norway.
12 October 1985	Underway for Baltic Operations (BALTOPS) 85 in Baltic Sea. Part of US Task Unit conducting multilateral exercises with allied vessels in Baltic area.
18 October 1985	BALTOPS 85 concluded with *Iowa* inport at Kiel, West Germany.
26 October 1985	Underway for Norfolk, conducting numerous drills and exercises *en route*.

5 November 1985	In Norfolk for preparations for INSURV/UMI and final contract trials.
February 1986	In Central America as peaceful presence in support of friendly countries.
March 1986	Continued presence in Central American waters.
4 July 1986	Carried President Reagan for Liberty Weekend's International Naval Review in Hudson River.
August 1986	Underway along Florida coast and in Gulf of Mexico conducting operational and training exercises.
17 August 1986	Underway for North Atlantic and NATO operation Northern Wedding.
September 1986	Participated in Operation Northern Wedding off southern coast of Norway. Following operations at sea, *Iowa* visited Portsmouth, England and Bremerhaven, West Germany.
2 October 1986	Underway for return trip to United States.
9 December 1986	Underway for sea trials off Virginia Capes. First launch, flight and recovery of a Pioneer RPV was made.
14 December 1986	*Iowa* fired 1,000th round of 16in ammunition since being recommissioned in 1984.
9 January 1987	Departed Norfolk *en route* to Caribbean.
10 January 1987	Participated in exercise BLASTEX 1–87 in Caribbean.
18 January 1987	Operations in Caribbean with port visits in Honduras, Columbia, and Virgin Islands.
11 February 1987	Arrived GTMO, Guantanamo Bay, Cuba for ORI (Operational Readiness Inspection).
13 February 1987	Departed GTMO for gunnery exercises Vieques Island, Puerto Rico.
26 February 1987	Arrived Norfolk.
27 February 1987	In restricted availability at Norfolk.
March 1987	Independent ship exercises.
30 March 1987	In service restricted availability at Norfolk.
25 April 1987	Departed Norfolk *en route* to Caribbean.
4 May 1987	Conducted SACEX in Puerto Rican operations area.
25 May 1987	Independent ship exercises.
8 July 1987	Participated in exercise FLEETEX 3–87 in Western Atlantic.
26 July 1987	Arrive Yorktown Naval Weapons center for loading ammunition.
28 July 1987	Arrive Norfolk. In service restricted availability.
17 August 1987	Independent ship exercises.
10 September 1987	Departed Norfolk *en route* to Mediterranean.
20 September 1987	INCHOP (enter Mediterranean. Join Sixth Fleet).
22 September 1987	Participated in Exercise Display Determination.
8 October 1987	Port visit Istanbul.
22 October 1987	OUTCHOP (leave Mediterranean. Detach from Sixth Fleet).
26 October 1987	Began North Sea operations.
30 October 1987	Arrived Trondheim, Norway.
8 November 1987	INCHOP.
25 November 1987	Transited Suez Canal.
4 December 1987	Arrived Diego Garcia to commence Persian Gulf Presence Operations.
7 December 1987	Depart Diego Garcia for operations in Indian Ocean and North Arabian Sea.
1 January 1988	In Gulf of Oman. Operations included escorting convoys through the southern Strait of Hormuz and protecting convoy assembly areas off Masirah Island and Muscat, Oman.
20 February 1988	Transited Suez Canal.

29 February 1988	OUTCHOP.
10 March 1988	Arrived Norfolk. In service restricted availability.
20 April 1988	Departed Norfolk *en route* to New York City to celebrate Fleet Week, 21–25 April.

USS New Jersey (BB 62)

17 May 1938	Congress authorized construction of first two fast battleships of their class, USS *Iowa* and USS *New Jersey*.
7 December 1942	Launched at Philadelphia Navy Yard under sponsorship of Mrs Charles Edison, wife of Governor of New Jersey and former Secretary of the Navy.
23 May 1943	Commissioned at Philadelphia.
May–December 1943	Fitting out and initial training completed in Western Atlantic and Caribbean.
7 January 1944	*En route* to Pacific through Panama Canal with USS *Iowa* as Battleship Division 7.
22 January 1944	Reported to Funafuti, Ellice Islands for duty with Fifth Fleet.
29 January 1944	First Pacific campaign in support of carrier air strikes against Kwajalein and Eniwetok Atolls.
31 January 1944	In support of troops in invasion of Eniwetok.
4 February 1944	Became flagship of Admiral Raymond A. Spruance, commanding Fifth Fleet.
16 February 1944	First firing of weapons in war action in attack on Japanese naval base at Truk in Caroline Islands. In action off Truk *New Jersey* sank minesweeping trawler *Shonan Maru* No. 15 and destroyer *Maikaze*.
18 March 1944	First shore bombardment against Mili Atoll in Marshall Islands.
13–22 April 1944	Screened carrier strike force which supplied air support for invasion of Aitape, Tanahmerah Bay and Humboldt Bay, New Guinea.
29–30 April 1944	Bombed shipping and shore installations at Truk. She and her formation splashed two enemy torpedo bombers in action at Truk.
1 May 1944	Pounded Ponape with her 16in guns, destroying fuel tanks and a headquarters building and badly damaging an airfield.
6 June 1944	Screened Admiral Mitscher's Task Force in air strikes prior to Marianas invasion.
12 June 1944	*New Jersey* downed an enemy torpedo bomber during her bombardment of Saipan and Tinian prior to landing of Marines on 15 June.
19 June 1944	Screened carriers during Battle of the Philippine Sea known as the Marianas Turkey Shoot in which the Japanese lost some 400 planes. *New Jersey*'s final action in Marianas was in strikes on Guam and Palaus Islands.
9 August 1944	Arrived at Pearl Harbor to become flagship of Admiral William F. Halsey, Commander, Third Fleet on 24 August.
30 August 1944	Sailed from Pearl Harbor to Ulithi.
September 1944	In support of fast carrier task force strikes against islands in Visayas and southern Philipines, Manila, Cavite, Panay, Negros, Leyte and Cebu.
20 October 1944	Screening carriers at opening of Battle of Leyte Gulf.
27 October 1944	With carrier strike force in attacks on Luzon.
29 October 1944	*New Jersey* and task force under kamikaze attack.

	Downed an attacking plane which struck carrier *Intrepid*'s port gun galleries. Three of *New Jersey*'s men wounded by machinegun fire from *Intrepid*.
25 November 1944	Shot down one attacker and scored hits on two others diving on task force.
14–16 December 1944	Screening *Lexington* task group for air attacks on Luzon. Caught in severe typhoon before returning to Ulithi on 24 December.
January 1945	Guarded carriers in strikes on Formosa, Okinawa, Luzon, Indo-China, Hong Kong, Swatow and Amoy.
27 January 1945	Admiral Halsey lowered his flag in *New Jersey*.
29 January 1945	Rear-Admiral Oscar Badger commander of Battleship Division 7 raised his flag in *New Jersey*.
19–21 February 1945	Screened *Essex* carrier group in air attacks on Iwo Jima.
25 February 1945	Screened carriers in first major raid on Tokyo.
14 March 1945	Screened carriers from beginning of conquest of Okinawa.
18–20 March 1945	Experienced intense enemy aircraft fire off Okinawa.
24 March 1945	*New Jersey*, *Missouri* and *Wisconsin* took part in bombardment of Okinawa.
16 April 1945	*New Jersey* is relieved by *Iowa* and returns stateside.
May–June 1945	In drydock at Puget Sound Naval Shipyard for overhaul.
4 July 1945	Left Puget Sound for San Pedro, Pearl Harbour, Eniwetok and Guam.
8 August 1945	Bombarded Wake Island, severely damaging main bridge on island and 8in gun emplacement on Peacock Point. The 5in rounds fired at Wake were last rounds fired by *Iowa*s in World War II.
14 August 1945	Became flagship of Admiral Spruance, commanding Fifth Fleet.
17 September 1945	Arrived in Tokyo Bay where she remained on duty in support of occupation forces until relieved by *Iowa* on 28 January 1946.
January 1946	Underway for United States with nearly 1,000 troops bound for home.
10 February 1946	Arrived in San Francisco for operations along West Coast and overhaul at Puget Sound.
23 May 1947	Returned to New Jersey and Atlantic coast.
7 June 1947	Became part of training squadron cruising Northern European waters with Naval Academy and NROTC midshipmen.
18 July 1947	Underway for exercises in Caribbean and Western Atlantic.
18 October 1947	Inactivated at New York Navy Yard.
30 June 1948	Decommissioned at Bayonne, New Jersey and assigned to New York Group, Atlantic Reserve Fleet.
21 November 1950	Recommissioned at Bayonne followed by her training cruise in Caribbean.
16 April 1951	Underway from Norfolk for Far East.
17 May 1951	Off east coast of Korea as flagship of Seventh Fleet under command of Vice-Admiral Harold M. Martin.
20 May 1951	Opened her first shore bombardment in Korea at Wonsan, serving as seaborne mobile artillery. During this first mission received only combat casualties of Korean War. One crew member was killed and two were wounded by fire from shore battery that hit her Turret No. I.
23–30 May 1951	Made gunstrikes against targets near Yangyang

	and Knasong, destroying a bridge and three ammunition dumps.
4 June 1951	Bombarded Wonsan.
6 June 1951	Fired on artillery regiment and truck encampment.
4–12 July 1951	In support of UN push in Kansong area, *New Jersey*'s guns hit enemy mortar emplacements, supply and ammunition dumps and personnel concentrations.
18 July 1951	At Wonsan hit five enemy gun emplacements with five direct hits.
17 August 1951	Bombarded Kansong area inflicting heavy toll on enemy troops.
29 August 1951	Involved in support of ROK troops, again at Kansong.
30 August 1951	Began three-day saturation shelling of Changjon area inflicting severe widespread damage to enemy facilities.
23 September 1951	Bombarded Kansong area in support of US X Corps, destroying a bridge, a dam, several gun emplacements, mortar positions, pillboxes, bunkers and two ammunition dumps.
1–6 October 1951	In action against Kansong, Hamhung, Hungnam, Tanchon and Songjin firing on railroad tunnels, bridges, an oil refinery, trains, enemy bunkers and supply areas.
16 October 1951	Active in gunstrikes in Kojo area.
1–6 November 1951	Raided transportation facilities along North Korean coast, striking bridges, and road and rail installations at Wonsan, Hungnam, Tanchon, Iowon, Songjin and Chongjin.
13 November 1951	Completed two-day attack on Kansong and Chang-San-Got Peninsula.
14 November 1951	Relieved by *Wisconsin* and underway for United States.
20 December 1951	Arrived at Norfolk for six month overhaul.
19 July 1952	Became flagship of Rear-Admiral H. R. Thurber for NROTC training cruise to Cherbourg, Lisbon and Caribbean which lasted until 5 September.
5 March 1953	Departed Norfolk for second Korean tour.
5 April 1953	Arrived Yokosuka and relieved *Missouri* as flagship of Vice-Admiral Joseph H. Clark, Commander Seventh Fleet.
12 April 1953	Saw her first action in shelling of Chongjin achieving seven direct hits in as many minutes.
16 April 1953	Fired upon coastal batteries and buildings at Kojo.
18 April 1953	Gunstrikes on railway track and tunnels near Hungnam.
20 April 1953	Attacked gun emplacements in Wonsan Harbor.
23 April 1953	Took Songjin under fire with six direct 16in hits on a railroad tunnel and two bridges.
1–6 May 1953	Hit targets at Wonsan, Hodo Pando Island and Kalmagak.
23 May 1953	At Inchon with President and Madame Rhee and Lieutenant-General Maxwell Taylor and other dignitaries aboard.
25 May 1953	Bombarded harbor defense positions at Chinampo.
27–29 May 1953	Under fire at Wonsan before destroying five gun emplacements, four gun caves and a fuel storage area or ammunition dump at Wonsan.
7 June 1953	In support of troops at Kosong *New Jersey* destroyed two gun positions.

24 June 1953	Bombarded Wonsan then returned to support troops at Kosong until 10 July.	20 October 1968	Bombarded Viet Cong command posts in Nha Trang area in support of Army 173rd Airborne Brigade.
11–12 July 1953	Concentrated bombardment of gun positions and bunkers on Hodo Pando.	25 October 1968	Provided support to 5th Infantry Division, firing on Viet Cong stronghold at Kinh Mon.
13 July 1953	Smashed radar control positions and bridges at Kojo and her gunners continued shelling along east coast with devastating accuracy until 24 July.	October 1968	*New Jersey* finished month at DMZ. Destroyed North Vietnamese anti-aircraft batteries, bunkers and gun emplacements.
25 July 1953	Bombarded coastal guns, bridges, a factory area and oil storage tanks at Hungnam, a major rail and communications center.	2 November 1968	In support of American units at Phan Thiet.
		Mid-November 1968	Two weeks at Subic Bay for replenishment.
		23 November 1968	Relieved cruiser *Galveston* at Da Nang.
26 July 1953	Destroyed guns, bunkers, caves and trenches at Wonsan.	25 November 1968	Destroyed thirty-two bunkers, two storage areas and inflicted extensive damage on Viet Cong positions and troops. Her bombardment was similarly effective next day.
28 July 1953	Word of truce received aboard the *New Jersey*.		
20 August 1953	Anchored off Hong Kong where crew celebrated with leave ashore.	7 December 1968	Successful strike against Da Nang.
16 September 1953	In Pusan where President Rhee came aboard to present Korean Presidential Unit Citation to Seventh Fleet.	9 December 1968	To Subic Bay for reprovisioning, then four days of R & R in Singapore.
		22 December 1968	Returned to bombline.
14 October 1953	Relieved as flagship by *Wisconsin* and set sail for home from Yokosuka the following day.	26 December 1968	Supported ARVN troops, striking caves and bunkers.
14 November 1953	Arrived in Norfolk.	December 1968	Turret No. I fired its 1,000th combat round.
1954–1955	Took midshipmen on summer cruises and during rest of the year took part in exercises and training maneuvers along Atlantic Coast and in Caribbean.	3 January 1969	Supported 1st Marine Division at Da Nang.
		7 January 1969	Fired 16in and 5in guns, destroying four enemy bunkers in spite of heavy fog.
		14 February 1969	On bombline off DMZ. Fired on communist forces attacking 3rd Marine Division. Remained on station until 9 March. *New Jersey* saved Marine outpost Oceanview from being overrun by North Vietnamese.
7 September 1955	Put out from Norfolk for her first tour of duty with Sixth Fleet in Mediterranean.		
17 January 1956	In Norfolk for training operations.		
31 July 1956	Returned midshipmen to Annapolis from summer training cruise to Northern Europe.	10 March 1969	Supported ARVN troops at Quang Ngai, destroying twenty-two enemy bunkers during her shelling.
27 August 1956	Underway for Europe as flagship of Second Fleet. Visited Lisbon and participated in NATO exercises off Scotland. Paid an official visit to Norway.	21 March 1969	Underway to Cam Ranh Bay to support ROK troops.
		26 March 1969	Destroyed seventy-two enemy bunkers in area of Phan Thiet.
15 October 1956	Returned to Norfolk.	28 March 1969	Returned to DMZ.
14 December 1956	Arrived New York Navy Yard for inactivation.	31 March 1969	Fired last rounds against enemy in Vietnam, making total expenditure of ammunition nearly equal to that of World War II and Korea.
21 August 1957	Decommissioned and placed in reserve at Bayonne, New Jersey.		
6 April 1968	Recommissioned at Philadelphia Navy Yard. Fitted with improved electronics and helicopter landing pad and 40mm battery was removed. Destined to be used as a heavy bombardment ship in Vietnam.	9 April 1969	*En route* to Long Beach when ordered back to Far East following downing of unarmed US reconnaissance plane over international waters by North Koreans.
		22 April 1969	Arrived off Japan and took on 837 tons of ammunition. *En route* to join carrier task force formed to meet crisis *New Jersey* ordered back to United States.
16 May 1968	Departed Philadelphia for West Coast.		
11 June 1968	Arrived at Long Beach, California where training operations were conducted off Southern California.		
		5 May 1969	Arrived at Long Beach.
3 September 1968	Underway to Vietnam.	Summer 1969	Training cruise as flagship of Rear-Admiral Lloyd Vasey in command of a fifteen-ship force.
30 September 1968	Fired her first shots against communist targets in area of so-called Demilitarized Zone (DMZ). Destroyed five enemy bunkers, two gun positions and two supply areas.		
		12 August 1969	Received Navy unit commendation for 'exceptionally meritorious service'.
1 October 1968	Struck six bunkers, a flak site and a truck.	20 August 1969	Pre-deployment ordnance review completed preparatory to scheduled tour of duty in Vietnam to begin 5 September.
2 October 1968	Hit enemy ammunition caches and during next week destroyed enemy bunkers and an observation post.		
		22 August 1969	Defense Department announcement received stating that *New Jersey* would be deactivated in coming fall.
7 October 1968	Destroyed eleven enemy supply boats on the Song Giang River.		
October 1968	Engaged in 'Operation Hilton', giving Marine and air units an opportunity to take showers, get hair cuts, do their laundry and enjoy a few creature comforts lacking ashore.	6 September 1969	Left Long beach for Puget Sound Naval Shipyard and deactivation.
		17 December 1969	*New Jersey* was decommissioned at Puget Sound.
14 October 1968	Attacked caves, coastal artillery emplacements and enemy convoy in areas of Nha Ky and Hon Matt island.	Spring 1981	Congress voted money necessary to start work on reactivation of *New Jersey*.

27 July 1981	Left Bremerton in tow on way to Long Beach.
28 December 1982	Recommissioned at Long Beach Naval Shipyard. Ceremony attended by President Reagan.
10 May 1983	Fired her first test rounds of Tomahawk missiles.
June 1983	Joined Pacific Fleet with stops at Pearl Harbor, Manila and Subic Bay.
July 1983	Diverted to Central America due to situation in Nicaragua.
September 1983	Ordered to Mediterranean.
14 December 1983	Opened fire on Syrian anti-aircraft batteries in Lebanon.
8 February 1984	Fired again on Syrian batteries.
Spring 1984	In port for lengthy refit.
January 1985	Ran her final acceptance trials.
5 February 1985	Refresher training and independent ship exercises.
6 May 1985	Began OPPE (Operational Proficiency Evaluation).
14 August 1985	In San Francisco for VJ Day Ceremony.
21 January 1986	Participated in exercise Computex 86-2.
18 February 1986	Participated in exercise Readiex 86-2.
28 May 1986	Participated in exercise RIMPAC 86.
5 August 1986	Participated in exercise Cobra Gold 86 in Gulf of Thailand.
11 December 1986	Arrived Long Beach Naval Shipyard.
February 1987	In port for refit and service restricted availability.
November 1987	Sea trials, refresher training and independent ship exercises.
April 1988	Independent ship exercises.

USS *Missouri* (BB 63)

6 July 1939	Congress authorized construction of second pair of *Iowa* class battleships, USS *Missouri* and USS *Wisconsin*.
6 January 1941	Laid down at New York Navy Yard.
29 January 1944	Launched at New York Navy Yard, sponsored by Margaret Truman, daughter of then Senator Harry Truman of Missouri.
11 June 1944	Commissioned.
11 November 1944	Following trials and shakedown, left Norfolk for Pacific and passed through Panama Canal on 18th bound for San Francisco.
14 December 1944	After final fitting out as fleet flagship at San Francisco *Missouri* departed for Far East.
13 January 1945	Arrived Ulithi where she became flagship of Admiral Marc Mitscher.
27 January 1945	Served to screen Admiral Mitscher's carrier Task Force 58 as it proceeded to carry out first air strikes against Japan since Doolittle raid of 1942.
19 February 1945	First enemy contact during bombardment in support of Marine landing on Iwo Jima. *Missouri* brought down enemy plane in night attack off Iwo.
5 March 1945	Returned to Ulithi and there was reassigned to *Yorktown* carrier task force.
14 March 1945	Left Ulithi with fast carrier task force headed for Japanese mainland and targets along coast of Inland Sea of Japan.
18 March 1945	During strikes against Japanese coastal installations *Missouri* brought down four enemy raiders. Also covered severely damaged carrier *Franklin* until she was safely on her way to Ulithi until 22 March.

24 March 1945	*Missouri*, *New Jersey* and *Wisconsin* took part in sledgehammer pre-invasion bombardment of southeastern coast of Okinawa. Scored hit against enemy ammunition dump.
1 April 1945	Rejoined screen of carriers as Marine and Army invasion of Okinawa began.
11 April 1945	Japanese kamikaze attacker crashed into starboard side, causing fire and minor damage.
16 April 1945	Suicide plane attempted to crash *Missouri*, but only wing of enemy plane clipped battleship's stern crane before it crashed astern and exploded. *Missouri* received little damage.
17 April 1945	Detected submarine twelve miles from her formation and her report resulted in eventual sinking of Japanese I-56 by carrier *Bataan* and four accompanying destroyers.
5 May 1945	Detached from carrier task force after scoring five kills, one probable, six assists against enemy aircraft. Helped to repel twelve daylight and four night raids.
18 May 1945	*Missouri* became flagship of Admiral William F. Halsey, Jr., upon his assumption of command of Third Fleet prior to its assault on Japanese home islands.
27–28 May 1945	Admiral Halsey took command of all units of Fifth Fleet and Vice-Admiral Marc A. Mitscher boarded *Missouri* to lead Third Fleet in strikes against airfields and installations on Kyushu, Japan.
2–3 June 1945	Struck targets on Kyushu.
5–6 June 1945	Rode out fierce storm, suffering only slight damage to some of her topside fittings.
8 June 1945	Second strike against Kyushu. Then retired to Leyte in Philippines.
13 June 1945	Arrived San Pedro, Leyte to prepare for further strikes against Japanese home islands.
8 July 1945	Led Third Fleet into enemy's home waters.
10 July 1945	Surprise raids on Tokyo.
15 July 1945	Joined in bombardment of Nihon Steel Company and Wanishi Ironworks at Muroran on Hokkaido, Japan.
17–18 July 1945	Bombarded industrial targets in Hichiti area of Honshu.
25 July 1945	Screening carriers during their strikes on Tokyo.
9 August 1945	*Missouri* was with fleet striking against Hokkaido and Northern Honshu when second atomic bomb was dropped. Had last encounter with enemy planes.
10 August 1945	Unofficial reports reached fleet that Japanese were prepared to surrender.
15 August 1945	Word of surrender became official with an announcement by President Truman.
16 August 1945	Admiral Halsey received order Knight of the British Empire from commander of British Fleet aboard *Missouri*.
21 August 1945	Transferred 200 officers and men to *Iowa* for temporary duty with initial occupation force bound for Tokyo.
29 August 1945	Entered Tokyo Bay to prepare for surrender ceremony.
2 September 1945	High-ranking military officials of all Allied Powers received aboard, including Admiral Nimitz and General MacArthur. Japanese representatives followed and in ceremony lasting twenty-three minutes surrender was concluded.

5 September 1945	Admiral Halsey transferred his flag to battleship *South Dakota*.
6 September 1945	*Missouri* left Tokyo for Guam to pick up passengers bound for home.
20 September 1945	Arrived Pearl Harbor.
29 September 1945	Departed Pearl Harbor for United States.
23 October 1945	Arrived New York City.
27 October 1945	President Truman aboard for Navy Day ceremonies.
November 1945–March 1946	Overhaul in New York Navy Yard followed by training cruise to Cuba.
21 March 1946	Received remains of Turkish Ambassador to United States.
22 March 1946	Departed for Gibraltar.
4 April 1946	Anchored in Bosphorus off Istanbul to transfer Ambassador's remains to shore.
9 April 1946	Departed Istanbul for Piraeus, Greece. *Missouri's* presence in eastern Mediterranean gave support to Greece and Turkey in face of pressure from Soviets.
26 April 1946	Left Greece to stop at Algiers and Tangiers before returning to Norfolk.
9 May 1946	Arrived Norfolk.
12 May 1946	Left Norfolk for Culebra Island to join Admiral Mitscher's Eighth Fleet in Navy's first large-scale post-war Atlantic training maneuvers.
27 May 1946	Returned to New York and spent year along Atlantic Coast participating in Atlantic command training exercises.
30 August 1947	Arrived Rio de Janeiro for Inter-American Conference for Maintenance of Hemisphere Peace and Security.
2 September 1947	President Truman aboard to celebrate signing of Rio Treaty.
7 September 1947	Truman family boarded *Missouri* for return trip to United States
19 September 1947	Arrived Norfolk.
23 September 1947–10 March 1948	Overhaul in New York followed by training at Guantanamo Bay, Cuba.
Summer 1948	Engaged in midshipmen and reserve training cruises.
1 November 1948	Departed Norfolk for three-week Arctic cold weather training cruise to Davis Straits.
23 September 1949	Overhauled at Norfolk Navy Yard.
17 January 1950	Overhaul completed, *Missouri* headed to sea when ran aground 1.6 miles from Thimble Shoals Light, near Old Point Comfort. Finally refloated 1 February.
Mid-February–15 August 1950	Conducted midshipmen and reserve training cruises out of Norfolk.
19 August 1950	Departed Norfolk to become first American battleship to reach Korean waters.
14 September 1950	Arrived Kyushu to become flagship of Rear-Admiral A. E. Smith.
15 September 1950	Bombarded Samchok in diversionary move coordinated with Inchon landings. Helped prepare way for 8th Army offensive.
19 September 1950	Arrived Inchon.
10 October 1950	Became flagship of Rear-Admiral J. M. Higgins, commander, Cruiser Division 5.
14 October 1950	Arrived Sasebo and there became flagship of Vice-Admiral A. D. Struble, Commander , Seventh Fleet.
12–26 October 1950	Bombarded Chonjin, Tanchon and Wonsan along east coast of Korea.
November 1950	Screening carriers east of Wonsan.
23 December 1950	Arrived Hungnam to provide support for evacuation of UN troops.
January – 19 March 1951	Conducted carrier operations and shore bombardments off east coast of Korea.
24 March 1951	Arrived Yokosuka and four days later was relieved of duty in Far East.
28 March 1951	Departed Yokosuka for United States.
27 April 1951	Arrived Norfolk and became flagship of Rear-Admiral J. L. Holloway, Jr., Commander, Cruiser Force, Atlantic Fleet.
Summer 1951	Midshipman cruises to Northern Europe.
18 October 1951	Entered Norfolk Navy Yard for overhaul until 30 January 1952.
February–June 1952	Training cruises operating out of Guantanamo Bay.
4 August 1952	Entered Norfolk Navy Yard to prepare for second tour in Korean Combat Zone.
11 September 1952	Departed Hampton Roads for Far East.
17 October 1952	Arrived Yokosuka and became flagship of Seventh Fleet 19 October.
25 October 1952	On 'Cobra Patrol' along east coast of Korea.
17 November 1952	Participated in combined air-gunstrike at Chongjin.
8 December 1952	Bombarded Tanchon-Songjin area.
9–10 December 1952	Continued coastal bombardment at Chaho and Wonsan.
21 December 1952	*Missouri's* spotter helicopter crashed with three men lost at sea.
5 January 1953	Arrived Inchon and then sailed from there to Sasebo, Japan.
23 January 1953	Resumed 'Cobra Patrol' along east coast of Korea with strikes against Wonsan, Tanchon, Hungnam and Kojo.
25 March 1953	Last fighting mission of the Korean War was bombardment of Kojo.
6 April 1953	Relieved as flagship of Seventh Fleet by *New Jersey*.
7 April 1953	Departed Yokosuka for United States.
4 May 1953	Arrived Norfolk.
14 May 1953	Flagship of Rear-Admiral E. T. Woolridge, Commander, Battleships-Cruisers, Atlantic Fleet.
8 June 1953	Departed Norfolk for midshipman training cruise and returned 4 August.
20 November 1953	Entered Norfolk Navy Yard for overhaul until 2 April 1954.
7 June 1954	Departed Norfolk for midshipman training cruise to Lisbon and Cherbourg.
3 August 1954	Returned to Norfolk.
23 August 1954	Departed Norfolk for inactivation on West Coast.
15 September 1954	Arrived Seattle and three days later entered Puget Sound Naval Shipyard.
26 February 1955	Decommissioned and entered Bremerton Group, Pacific Reserve Fleet. There, served as headquarters ship of Group and was open year around to visitors.
14 May 1985	Left Bremerton for Long Beach Naval Shipyard for modernization and reactivation.
25 May 1984	Arrived Long Beach Naval Shipyard.
29 January 1986	Engineering portion of builder's trials.
10 May 1986	Recommissioned at San Francisco.
14–25 May 1986	Ship Qualification Trials in Southern California operations area.
4–14 August 1986	Refresher training.

10 September 1986	Departed Long Beach to begin three-month around the world shakedown cruise.
16–18 September 1986	Pearl Harbor.
1–5 October 1986	Sydney, Australia.
26 October 1986	Diego Garcia.
7 November 1986	Transited Suez Canal.
11–14 November 1986	Istanbul, Turkey.
25–28 November 1986	Lisbon, Portugal.
9 December 1986	Transited Panama Canal.
19 December 1986	Returned to Long Beach.
December 1986	In port for refit and service restricted availability.
June 1987	Sea trials, refresher training and independent ship exercises.
July 1987	Post-shakedown overhaul.
27 July 1987	Departed Long Beach for North Arabian Sea.
30 August 1987	Arrived in North Arabian Sea to begin Persian Gulf presence operations.
2 December 1987	Departed North Arabian Sea.
19 January 1988	Returned to Long Beach.
April 1988	Independent ship exercises.

USS Wisconsin (BB 64)

6 July 1939	Congress authorized construction of second pair of Iowa class battleships, USS Missouri and USS Wisconsin.
25 January 1941	Laid down at Philadelphia Navy Yard.
7 December 1943	Launched under sponsorship of Mrs Walter S. Goodland.
16 April 1944	Commissioned.
7 July 1944	Departed Norfolk for Trinidad on shakedown cruise followed by post-shakedown period in Philadelphia Navy Yard for repairs and alterations.
24 September 1944	Sailed for West Coast.
2 October 1944	Reported for duty with Pacific Fleet.
9 December 1944	Arrived Ulithi to join Admiral William F. Halsey's Third Fleet.
17 December 1944	Lost plane swept from port catapult during typhoon. A second OS2U Kingfisher was severely damaged along with anti-aircraft mounts and both whaleboats.
3 January 1944	Covered carriers during air strikes against Formosa, Luzon and Nansei Shoto with thrust into South China Sea.
21 January 1945	Received seventeen wounded men from destroyer Maddox.
16 February 1945	With Admiral Spruance's Task Force 58 to cover carriers as their aircraft struck at Japanese coast.
17 February 1945	With Task Force 58 off Iwo Jima.
19 February 1945	In support of landings on Iwo Jima, Wisconsin saw her first combat of the war.
25 February 1945	Again off Japanese coast screening carriers.
14 March 1945	Left Ulithi for Japan with carrier task force.
19 March 1945	Retired with task force from attack on Kyushu to screen disabled carrier Franklin.
24 March 1945	Wisconsin, Missouri and New Jersey took part in bombardment of Okinawa. This was first bombardment experience for Wisconsin.
28 May 1945	Escorting carriers during air attacks on Japanese mainland which continued into June.
8 June 1945	During final air assault on Kyushu, Wisconsin's float plane landed and rescued downed pilot from carrier Shangri-La.

13 June 1945	At anchor in Leyte Gulf for replenishment and repairs.
1 July 1945	Underway with carrier task force for Japanese waters.
15 July 1945	Bombarded steel mills and oil refineries at Muroran, Hokkaido.
17 July 1945	Wrecked industrial site in Hitachi Miro area northeast of Tokyo.
13 August 1945	Screened carriers in final air strike on Tokyo.
15 August 1945	Word of Japanese surrender reached Wisconsin.
5 September 1945	Arrived Tokyo Bay as part of occupying force.
23 September 1945	Homeward bound from Okinawa, participating in operation 'Magic Carpet' to bring men home from war.
4 October 1945	Arrived at Pearl Harbor.
15 October 1945	Arrived at San Francisco.
11–13 January 1946	Transited Panama Canal.
18 January 1946	Arrived at Hampton Roads, Virginia.
Summer 1946	At Norfolk Naval Shipyard for overhaul.
1–26 November 1946	Cruised South American waters.
Spring 1947	Engaged in two-week training cruises for naval reservists.
June–July 1947	Midshipmen cruise to northern European waters.
January 1948	Joined Atlantic Reserve Fleet at Norfolk for inactivation.
1 July 1948	Placed out of commission, in reserve, assigned to Norfolk Group of Atlantic Reserve Fleet.
3 March 1951	Recommissioned.
25 October 1951	Following shakedown and midshipmen and reserve training cruises to England, Europe, New York and Cuba, Wisconsin left Norfolk for Pacific.
29 October 1951	Transited Panama Canal.
21 November 1951	Arrived Yokosuka, Japan to relieve New Jersey as flagship for Vice-Admiral H. M. Martin, Commander, Seventh Fleet.
26 November 1951	Departed Yokosuka for Korean waters to support fast carrier operations of Task Force 77.
2 December 1951	Provided gunfire support for Republic of Korea Corps in Kasong-Donsong area.
3–6 December 1951	Returned to bombline in support of 1st Marine Division. Destroyed a tank, two gun emplacements, a building, enemy bunkers, artillery positions and troop concentrations.
6 December 1951	Relieved by heavy cruiser St Paul for brief period.
11 December 1951	Returned to bombline in Kasong-Kosong area, shelling enemy bunkers, command posts, artillery positions and trench systems.
14 December 1951	Left bombline to provide gunfire support in Kojo area in support of UN troops.
16 December 1951	Left for Sasebo to rearm.
18 December 1951	In support of 11th ROK Division with night illumination fire enabling Korean forces to repulse an enemy attack.
20–22 December 1951	Bombarded targets ashore and in harbor at Wonsan. Moved north to shell boat concentrations and provided support for UN troops ashore.
22 December 1951	Rejoined carrier task force.
31 December 1951	Arrived Yokosuka.
8 January 1952	Left Yokosuka.
9 January 1952	Arrived Pusan and entertained South Korean President and Mrs Rhee on the 10th.
11 January 1952	Returned to bombline in support of 1st Marine Division and 1st ROK Corps, firing on command

	posts, shelters, bunkers, troop concentrations and mortar positions.
23 January 1952	After rearming at Sasebo and a brief time with Task Force 77, returned to the bombline.
26 January 1952	Participated in coordinated air and gun strike in Kojo area, served on bombline again and returned to bombard enemy gun sites at Hodo Pando.
2 February 1952	After rearming at Sasebo, rejoined Task Force 77 and then went on for replenishment at Yokosuka. Returned to gun support in the Kosong area.
25 February 1952	Arrived at Pusan.
2 March 1952	Arrived Yokosuka and then a week later went on to Sasebo.
15 March 1952	Fired on enemy railway at Songjin destroying troop train. She received first direct hit when starboard 40mm mount struck by shell from 155mm gun battery. Battery was subsequently destroyed by *Wisconsin*'s 16in guns.
19 March 1952	Returned to Japan.
1 April 1952	Relieved as flagship of Seventh Fleet by *Iowa* and left Yokosuka for United States.
4–5 April 1952	Took part in test of Navy's largest floating drydock at Guam, marking first time an *Iowa* class battleship had ever used such a facility.
19 April 1952	Arrived at Long Beach and subsequently set sail for Norfolk.
June 1952	Midshipman training cruise to Scotland, France and Cuba.
25 August 1952	Left Hampton Roads to participate in NATO exercise, Operation Mainbrace in North Atlantic.
Fall 1952	In Norfolk Navy Yard for overhaul.
11 February 1953	Underway for Cuba and refresher training.
April 1953	Returned to Norfolk.
Summer 1953	Midshipman training cruise to Brazil, Trinidad and Cuba.
4 August 1953	Into Norfolk for short overhaul.
9 September 1953	Departed Norfolk for Far East.
12 October 1953	Relieved *New Jersey* as flagship of Seventh Fleet.
Winter 1953	Visited Japanese ports of Kobe, Sasebo, Yokosuka, Otaru and Nagasaki.
25 December 1953	In Hong Kong.
1 April 1954	Relieved of flagship duties and returned to United States.
4 May 1954	Arrived Norfolk.
11 June 1954	Entered Norfolk Navy Yard for brief overhaul.
12 July 1954	Midshipman training cruise to Scotland, France and Cuba.
Fall 1954	In Norfolk for repairs.
January 1955	Took part in Operation Springboard which took her to Haiti.
Summer 1955	Midshipman cruise to Scotland, Denmark and Cuba
Fall 1955	Major overhaul at New York Navy Yard.
Winter 1955–56	In Caribbean for refresher training and another Springboard exercise with visits to Haiti, Mexico and Colombia.
31 March 1956	Returned to Norfolk for local operations through April and May.
6 May 1956	Collided with destroyer *Eaton* in heavy fog.
13 May 1956	Entered drydock at Norfolk Navy Yard to repair extensive damage to her bow. Bow replaced with 68ft long section of bow of uncompleted battleship *Kentucky* which was transported by barge from Newport News Shipbuilding and Drydock Corp.
28 June 1956	Repaired in record time and ready for sea.
9 July 1956	NROTC training cruise to Spain, Scotland and Cuba.
31 August 1956	Arrived back at Norfolk.
Fall 1956	Participated in Atlantic Fleet exercises off coast of Carolinas.
8 November 1956	Arrived in Norfolk.
15 November 1956	Entered Norfolk Navy Yard for major repairs. Work complete 2 January 1957.
3–11 January 1957	Local operations off Virginia Capes.
15 January 1957	Left Norfolk for Guantanamo Bay, Cuba.
2–4 February 1957	Shore bombardment practise off Isle of Culebra, Puerto Rico.
7 February 1957	Arrived Norfolk.
27 March 1957	Sailed for Mediterranean.
5 April 1957	Arrived Gibraltar and subsequently joined Task Force 60 in Aegean Sea.
11 April 1957	Arrived with task force in Xeros Bay, Turkey for NATO exercise Red Pivot.
14 April 1957	Departed Xeros Bay.
18 April 1957	Arrived Naples for a week's visit followed by exercises in eastern Mediterranean. Rescued pilot and crewman who survived crash of their plane from carrier *Forrestal*.
10 May 1957	Arrived Valencia, Spain.
17 May 1957	Left Valencia for Norfolk.
27 May 1957	Arrived Norfolk.
19 June 1957	Conducted mishipman training cruise through Panama Canal and in South American waters.
3 July 1957	In Valparaiso, Chile.
11 July 1957	On way back to Atlantic through Panama Canal.
5 August 1957	Arrived Norfolk and conducted local operations into September.
14 September 1957	In England for NATO exercises in North Atlantic.
22 October 1957	Back in Norfolk.
4 November 1957	Departed Norfolk on her last cruise.
6 November 1957	Arrived in New York City.
8 November 1957	Underway for Bayonne, New Jersey, to begin pre-inactivation overhaul.
8 March 1958	Placed out of commission at Bayonne leaving America without an active battleship for first time since 1895. *Wisconsin*, with *New Jersey*, was subsequently towed to Philadephia when Bayonne facility closed.
8 August 1986	In tow from Philadelphia to New Orleans and the Avondale Shipyard, Inc. for modernization and reactivation.
16 August 1986	Arrived Avondale Shipyard, Inc. and subsequently towed to Ingalls Shipbuilding, Pascagoula, Missouri, for completion of work.
22 October 1988	Scheduled recommissioning at Ingalls Shipbuilding.

APPENDIX D

SOURCE MATERIAL

Nearly all of the material for this publication was taken from official sources, primarily in the repositories at: the Naval Historical Center, Washington Navy Yard; US Naval Academy Library, Annapolis, Maryland; US National Archives, Washington, DC; and Federal Records Center, Suitland, Maryland.

Much first-hand experiences and information was gained while I served aboard the USS *Iowa* (BB 61) in 1986. During that time, I had the opportunity to work with FCCM (SW) Stephen Skelley, USNR, who directed me to many of the manuals, reports and drawings that provided much of the detailed information for this book.

In the case of publications which have several issues and/or revisions, such as the OPs (Ordnance Pamphlets), usually more than one was used for reference and updating information on equipment. The date given is for the earliest issue researched.

All material used and cited was unclassified or had been declassified as of the date of this publication.

SOURCES

Books

Dulin, R., Garzke, W. and Sumrall, R.: *Battleships; U.S. Battleships in World War II*, US Naval Institute Press, 1976.

Friedman, N: *Naval Radar*, US Naval Institute Press, 1981.

Friedman, N: *U.S. Battleships; an Illustrated Design History*, US Naval Institute Press, 1985.

Friedman, N: *U.S. Naval Weapons*, US Naval Institute Press, 1985.

Leifer, Neil: *Dreadnought Returns*, Baum Printing House, 1969.

Leifer, Neil: *Dreadnought Farewell*, Kay Publications, Inc., Philadelphia, 1970.

Muir, Malcolm: *The IOWA Class Battleships: IOWA, NEW JERSEY, MISSOURI & WISCONSIN*, Blandford Press, Poole, Dorset, 1987.

Wiseman, C.: *The International Countermeasures Handbook*, EW Communications, Inc., Palo Alto, California, 1986.

Articles

Bell, G. R.: 'The NEW JERSEY—Tomahawk Story', Naval Engineers Journal, May 1984.

Friedman, Norman: 'The Reborn Battleships', Warship No. 31, Conway Maritime Press, July 1984.

Lewis, E. R.: 'American Battleships Main Battery Armament: The Final Generation', *Warship International*, No. 4, 1976.

Myers, C. E., Jr.: 'A Sea-based Interdiction for Power Projection', USNI *Proceedings*, November 1979.

Pineda, R.: 'Battleship Gunners Tackle Turrets', *Surface Warfare*, November/December 1954

Serig, Howard W., Jr.: 'The IOWA Class: Needed Once Again', USNI *Proceedings, Naval Review*, 1982.

Sims, P. J., Edwards, J. R., Sr., Dickey, R. L., LCDR, USN, and Shull, H. S.: 'Design for NEW JERSEY, IOWA and DES MOINES Modernization', *Naval Engineers' Journal*, May 1984.

US Navy, Bureau of Ordnance (Bu Ord)

'Armament Summaries of the Bureau of Naval Ordnance, 1943 through 1955'. Copies held in the Operational Archives, Naval Historical Center.

'Catapults, Type P, MK VI, With Catapult-Gun, MK VI', 10/1/42.

'History of the Bureau of Ordnance, World War II', Part II, Vol. 1–5, first draft narrative, 1946.

Naval Ordnance: A Textbook, USNI, US Naval Academy, 1939.

NAVORD OS 751, Ordnance Specifications: Steel Armor for the US Navy, Naval Proving Ground, Dahlgren, 11/17/47.

Principles of Naval Weapons Systems, Frieden, D. R., LCDR USN, USNI Press, US Naval Academy, 1984.

Range and Ballistic Tables, 1946, USNI, US Naval Academy, 7/1/46.

Report No. 10–48, Definitions of the Terms Used in the Ballistic Testing of Armor, Naval Proving Ground, Dahlgren, in about 1945.

Shipboard Weapons Systems, Course Book for EW-301, Fox, J. R. Lt. USN, US Naval Academy, 1963.

The Manufacture of Armor Plate and Armor Piercing Projectiles, Naval Proving Ground, Dahlgren, 4/19/42.

OD No. 4166 Dummy Director, MK 1 and Error Recorder MK 1, 10/41.

OP No. 4, Ammunition, Instructions for the Naval Service 5/43.

OP No. 657, Fire Control Radars MK 3 (FC) and MK 4 (FD), 4/43.

OP No. 658 , Fire Control Radar, MK 8, 1/43.

OP No. 769, 16-Inch Three Gun Turrets: 16-inch/50 caliber MK 7 Gun 6/43.

OP No. 805, 5-Inch/38 Cal. Twin Gun Mounts, MK 28, MK 32, Mk 38, 8/14/53.

OP No. 810, Gun Directors, MK 38 and Mods., 10/42.

OP No. 812, Gun Director MK 40, 3/43.

OP No. 909, 20-mm A.A. Assemblies (single) MK 2, MK 4, MK 5, MK 6, MK 10, 3/43.

OP No. 1007, Radar Equipment MK 19, 9/9/43.

OP No. 1040, Gun Sight MK 14, 3/4/46.

OP No. 1060, Gun Director MK 37 and Mods., 3/31/45.

OP No. 1068, Range Keeper MK 8, 4/49.

OP No. 1076, Radar Equipment, MK 12, 4/44.

OP No. 1098, Gun Sight MK 15, 4/7/50.

OP No. 1112, Gun Mount and Turret Catalog 3/45.

OP No. 1153, Radar Equipment, MK 22, 6/44.

OP No. 1154, Radar Equipment, MK 26, 8/44.

OP No. 1155, Radar Equipment, MK 27, 8/44.

OP No. 1172, Performance of Bombs and Projectiles, 5/9/44.

OP No. 1188, Abridged Range Tables for US Naval Guns, 6/13/44.

OP No. 1297, Radar Equipment MK 13, 7/30/45.

OP No. 1301, Radar Equipment MK 34, 2/12/46.

OP No. 1407, Anti-Jamming Operation of Fire Control Radar, 5/45.

OP No. 1439, 20-mm A.A. Assemblies (twin) MK 20, MK 24, 4/28/45.

OP No. 1507, Japanese Underwater Ordnance, 4/20/45.

OP No. 1545, Target Designation Transmitter and Receiver MK 1, 1945.

OP No. 1664, United States Ordnance, 5/46.

OP No. 1714, Projectiles and Fuzes for Ship and Shore Targets.

OP No. 1773, Radar Equipment MK 13, 8/68.

ORD 653, Armor: Armor Penetration Curves, Naval Proving Ground, Dahlgren, 1/42.

US Navy, Bureau of Naval Personnel (Nav Pers)

Nav Pers 10783, Principles of Naval Ordnance and Gunnery 1965.

Nav Pers 10797, Naval Ordnance and Gunnery 1955.

Nav Pers 16116, Naval Ordnance and Gunnery 1944.

Nav Pers 16116-B, Naval Ordnance and Gunnery, 1952.

US Navy, Bureau of Ships (Bu Ships)

C & R Bulletin No. 13-A, Structural Models Part II: Model Investigations of Armored Structures, Conrad, R. D., Lt. USN, 6/1/39.

Eng. 167, Navy Model SG, 7/1/44.

NAVSHIPS 900, Radar Installation Plan; Allowances and Installations.

NAVSHIPS 900, 342 (A) Navy Model TDY-1, 9/7/45.

NAVSHIPS 900, 551 (A) Navy Model TDYa/TDY-1, 8/1/45.

NAVSHIPS 900, 861 (A), Radar Set Model SG-6.

NAVSHIPS 91522 (A), Radar Set AN/SPS-8.

NAVSHIPS 91620 (A), Radar Set AN/SPS-6C, 7/21/52.

NAVSHIPS 91949 (A), Radar Set AN/SPS-12.

NAVSHIPS 982, Radar Installation Plan; Instructions and ICDs.

NAVSHIPS, Technical Manual Chapt. 9720, Turrets and Gun Mounts 9/67.

Ships' Data US Naval Vessels, numerous volumes 1920–1945.

Ships 265, Radar Equipment MK 8, Mod 2, 6/31/44.

US Navy, Naval Historical Center

Reilly, J. C., Jr.: *Operational Experience of Fast Battleships World War II, Korea, Vietnam*, US Navy, Naval Historical Center.

US Navy, Naval Sea Systems Command (NAVSEA)

USS IOWA BB 61 Propulsion Operating Guide, 4/28/44.

OP 2173, Vol. I, Nav Air 19–100–1.1, Carrier, 16-Inch Projectile, MK 3.

Plans; hull, mechanical and electrical on microfilm. BB 61, Reel No. D79 and BB 62 Reel No. 5482. Copies held in the Portsmouth Naval Shipyard, Portsmouth, New Hampshire.

Ships' Characteristics Board records. Copies held at NAVSEA.

US Navy, US Fleet – Commander in Chief (COMINCH)

COMINCH P-08, Radar Bulletin No. 1 A (RADONE-A), 7/45.

US Navy, Chief of Naval Operations

Command History, Narrative '1968' History of the USS NEW JERSEY (BB62).

OPNAV – 16 V, A 43, Striking Power of Airborne Weapons.

US Navy, Office of the Secretary of the Navy

Bureau of Construction and Repair records. The National Archives.

Bureau of Ships records. The National Archives and Federal Records Center, Suitland, Maryland.

General Board records. Copies held in the Operational Archives, Naval Historical Center.

USS Iowa (BB 61)

IOWAINST 1040.1, Enlisted Surface Warfare Specialist Lesson Plans, 5/13/84.

GLOSSARY

AA – Anti-aircraft.

AAC – Anti-aircraft Common type projectile.

AAW – Anti-air Warfare.

A–4 – Skyhawk series attack aircraft.

ABL – Armored Box Launcher.

ADF – Auxiliary Detonating Fuze.

ADT – Automatic Detection and Tracking.

AIMS – A – ATCRBS (Air Traffic Control Radar Beacon System)
I – IFF (Identification Friend or Foe)
M – Mark XII Identification System
S – Systems (reflecting many configurations).

AN/SRA-57 – conical portion of discone/cage array of NTDS antenna.

AN/SRA-58 – disc portion of discone/cage array of NTDS antenna.

AN/VPS-2 – fire control pulsed doppler type radar used with 20mm Mk 15 Phalanx CIWS.

AN/WCS-3 – dish antenna used with OE-82 satellite communication relay system.

AOE – Fast Combat Support Ship (supermarket).

AP – Armor Piercing projectile.

APT – Armor Piercing Target projectile.

Armor, Class A – forged face hardened armor, 4in thick and over.

Armor, Class B – forged homogenous armor, 4in thick and over.

Armor, STS – special treatment steel, rolled homogenous armor under 4in thick.

Armor, cast – usually homogenous; can be face hardened.

Armor, splinter protection – rolled light STS plate.

Armored box – armored citadel protecting the vitals of the ship.

Arrow Shell – 4in fin-stabilized sabot shell fired from an 8-in/55 cal smooth bore gun. (See gun launched guided projectile and Zeus.)

ARVN – Army of the Republic of Vietnam.

AS-37 – ECM antenna, intercept receiving, referred to as a 'wagon wheel'.

AS-56 – ECM antenna, intercept receiving, in the form of a long, heavy dipole.

AS-57 – ECM antenna, intercept receiving, in the form of encased double cones resembling a field drum.

AS-177/UPX-23 – IFF antenna, interrogator-responsor.

AS-177/UPX-27 – IFF antenna, interrogator-responsor.

AS-177/UPX-72 – IFF antenna, transponder.

AS-177/UPM-137 – IFF antenna, interrogator.

AS-570/SLR – ECM antenna, RDF.

AS-571/SLR – ECM antenna, RDF.

AS-1341/ULO – ECM antenna, jammer.

AS-1735/SRC – antenna, radio transmitter.

AS-1750/SL – ECM antenna, transmitter-receiver.

AS-1751/SLA – ECM antenna, receiver.

AS-2188/UPX-23 – IFF antenna, interrogator-responsor.

AS-3240/URN-25 – antenna, TACAN.

ASW – Anti-Submarine Warfare.

ATCRBS – Air Traffic control Radar Beacon System.

AUR – All-Up-Round

Bag gun – any gun in which the propellant charge is contained in bags which are loaded separately from the projectiles.

Barbette – armoured enclosure protecting the elements of the turret below the gunhouse.

BBG – guided missile battleship.

BBBG – Battleship Battle Group.

BGM-109 series – Tomahawk Cruise Missiles.

BDF – Base Detonating Fuze.

BK – IFF transponder/antenna.

BI – IFF interrogator-responsor/antenna.

BL-PT – Blind Loaded and Plugged Tracer.

Blanket defense – a barrage.

BM – IFF interrogator-responsor/antenna.

BMG – Browning Machine Gun, 0.50 cal.

BN – IFF interrogator-responsor/antenna.

BO – IFF interrogator-responsor/antenna.

Bofors – Swedish ordnance manufacturer.

BOL – Bearing Only Launch mode.

Broadway – main fore-and-aft passageway on the third deck within the armor citadel.

Bu C & R – Bureau of Construction and Repair.

Bu Eng – Bureau of Engineering.

Bu Ord – Bureau of Ordnance.

Bu Ships – Bureau of Ships.

Bu Weps – Bureau of Weapons.

CAGW-66131 – ECM antenna, replacement for AS-57 antenna, referred to as a 'derby'.

CAGW-66132 – ECM antenna, replacement for AS-56 antenna, referred to as a 'sword'.

Chaff – strips of aluminum foil dispensed to change the electrical properties of the air between a missile and its target to cause the missile to be diverted.

CHAFF – chaff dispensing 5in projectile.

CHT – Collection, Holding and Transfer system.

CIPS – Class Improvement Plans.

Citadel – armoured box protecting the vitals of the ship.

CIWS – Close-In Weapons System.

CNO – Chief of Naval Operations.

COM – common type projectile for pentrating light armor.

CVBG – Carrier Battle Group.

CVT – Controlled Variable Time Fuze.

D839 propellant – original 16in/50 cal granulation.

D840 propellant – original 8in/55 cal granulation.

D845 propellant – original 8in/55 cal granulation (reduced flashless).

D846 propellant – original 16in/45 cal granulation.

DASH – Drone Anti-Submarine Helicopter.

DBA – radio direction finder.

DBM – radar direction finder.

De-capping plate – armor designed to have enough resistance to initiate fuze action and dislodge or knock off the AP cap of a projectile.

Deflection – lateral angular correction of the target angle at right angles to the line of fire.

Destex HE – warhead explosive.

DFM – Diesel Fuel Marine.

Discone/cage antenna – NTDS dual communications antenna stacking the AN/SRA-57 and AN/SRA-58 antennas.

Dispersion – distance of the point of impact of a shot from the mean point of impact of the salvo.

DOD – Department of Defense.

DR-810 – radar velocimeter for measuring initial velocity and tracking the trajectory of 16in shells.

DRB – radio direction finder.

Dummy – drill projectile.

ECM – Electronic countermeasures.

ECCM – Electronic counter-countermeasures.

ESM – Electronic Support Measures.

ESR – Equivalent Service Rounds.
ETF – Electronic Time Fuze.
EW – Electronic Warfare.
EX-1 – original experimental designation for the 1,900 pound Mk 13 HC projectile.

FER – Fatigue Equivalent Rounds.
FIM-92 – Stinger Surface-to-Air Missile.

General Board – a group of senior naval officers that advised the Secretary of the Navy on fundamental naval policy rearding strategy, tactics and the shipbuilding program.
GFCS – Gun Fire Control System.
GP bomb – high explosive load, not armor piercing.
Gun launched Guided Projectile. (See Arrow Shell and Zeus.)

Harpoon – RGM-84 cruise missile.
H-1 – 'Huey' series helicopter.
HC – high capacity load.
HC/PD – high capacity, point detonating projectile.
HE – high explosive load.
HE-CVT – high explosive, controlled variable time projectile.
HE-MTF – high explosive, mechanical time projectile.
HE-MT/PD – high explosive, mechanical time/point detonating projectile.
HE-PD – high explosive, point detonating projectile.
HE-IR – high explosive, infrared projectile.
HE-VT – high explosive, variable time projectile.
HP-85 – digital IBC used with Mk 38 GFCS.
Huey – H-1 series helicopter.

IBC – Initial Ballistic Computer.
ICM – Improved Conventional Munition.
IFF – Identification Friend or Foe.
ILLUM – illuminating projectile.
Immune Zone – The inner and outer distance at which the armored citadel of the ship cannot be penetrated.
IRBM – Intermediate Range Ballistic Missile.

Kingfisher – OS2U observation aircraft.

LINK 11 – crypto-secure weapons direction system link to non-NTDS equipped ships.
LINK 14 – crypto-secure one-way data link to non-NTDS equipped ships.
Loading machine – 5in, for loading drills and practise.
LROG – Long-Range Objectives Group.
LST – Landing Ship Tank.

Mean point of impact – geometrical center of all points of impact of a salvo.
M43A1 – wedge grenade.
M61 – USAF Vulcan gun used with 20mm Mk 15 Phalanx CIWS.
M564 MTF – Mechanical Time Fuze.
M724 ETF – Electronic Time Fuze.
M732 CVT – Controlled Variable Time Fuze.
Mark A – 18in/47 cal gun.
Mark II – 16in/50 cal gun.
Mark III IFF – recognition system.
Mark X IFF – recognition system.
Mark XII IFF – recognition system.

Mark 1 – 18in/48 cal gun.
Mark 1 – starshell computer used with Mark 37 GFCS.
Mark 1/1A – computer used with Mark 37 GFCS.
Mark 2 – 40mm quadruple gun mount.
Mark 3 – fire control radar used with Mark 40 director.
Mark 3 – mechanical analog computer used in 16in turrets.
Mark 3 – target designation transmitter and receiver used with Mark 37 GFCS.
Mark 4 – fire control radar used with Mark 37 GFCS.
Mark 4 – rangefinder stabilizer used with Mark 52 and Mark 53 turret rangefinders.
Mark 4 – 20mm single gun mount.
Mark 5 AP – 16in, 2,240 pound projectile.
Mark 5 – target designation transmitter used with Mark 37 GFCS.
Mark 6 – 16in/45 cal gun.
Mark 6 – stable element used with Mark 37 GFCS.
Mark 6 – target designation transmitter used with Mark 37 GFCS.
Mark 7 – 16in/50 cal gun.
Mark 8 AP – 16in 2,700 pound projectile.
Mark 8 – fire control radar used with Mark 38 GFCS.
Mark 8 – rangekeeper used with Mark 38 GFCS.
Mark 9 – spotting glass used with Mark 40 director.
Mark 10 – 20mm twin gun mount.
Mark 12/2 – fire control radar used with Mark 37 GFCS.
Mark 12 – 5in/38 cal double purpose gun.
Mark 13 – fire control radar used with Mark 38 GFCS.
Mark 13 HC – 16in 1,900 pound projectile.
Mark 13 HE – 16in 1,900 pound projectile.
Mark 14 – gun sight used with 20mm single gun mount and Mark 51 director.
Mark 15 – gun sight used with Mark 51 director and Mark 63 director.
Mark 15 – 20mm Phalanx CIWS.
Mark 16 – computer used with Mark 57 GFCS.
Mark 17 – computer used with Mark 57 GFCS.
Mark 19 – fire control radar used with Mark 49 director.
Mark 21 BDF – Base Detonating Fuze.
Mark 23 – 16in, 1,900 pound nuclear projectile nicknamed 'Katie'.
Mark 24 – 16in, 1,900 pound practice projectile for the Mark 23 round.
Mark 25 – fire control radar used with Mark 37 GFCS.
Mark 27 – fire control radar used with Mark 40 director.
Mark 28 – periscope used with 16in main battery turret.
Mark 28 – 5in/38 cal twin gun mount.
Mark 29 PDF – Point Detonating Fuze.
Mark 29 – periscope used with Mark 38 director and main battery turret.
Mark 29 – gun sight used with Mark 51 director and Mark 63 director.
Mark 30 – gun order converter used with Mark 56 GFCS.
Mark 30 – periscope used with Mark 40 director.
Mark 32 – periscope used with Mark 40 director.
Mark 34 – fire control radar used with Mark 57 director and Mark 63 director.
Mark 35 – fire control radar used with Mark 56 director.
Mark 36 – sight assembly used with Mark 28 5in/38 cal twin gun mount.
Mark 36 – Super RBOC Launcher.
Mark 37 – secondary battery director used with Mark 37 GFCS.
Mark 37 – GFCS for control of the secondary 5in/38 cal battery.
Mark 38 – GFCS for control of the main 16in/50 cal battery.
Mark 38 – main battery director used with Mark 38 GFCS.
Mark 39 – sight assembly used with Mark 28 5in/38 cal twin gun mount.
Mark 40 – main battery director used with Mark 38 GFCS.
Mark 41 – stable vertical used with Mark 38 GFCS and is the firing station for the plotting rooms.
Mark 42 – ballistic computer used with Mark 56 GFCS.
Mark 42 – rangefinder used with Mark 37 director.
Mark 48 BDF – base detonating fuze.
Mark 48 – shore bombardment computer used with Mark 38 GFCS.

Mark 48 – stereoscopic rangefinder used with Mark 38 director.
Mark 49 – director used with 40mm battery.
Mark 51 – director used with 40mm battery.
Mark 52 – stereoscopic rangefinder used in 16in Turrets No. II and No. III.
Mark 53 – coincidence rangefinder used in 16in Turret No. I.
Mark 55 ADF – auxiliary detonating fuze.
Mark 56 – director used with Mark 56 GFCS.
Mark 56 – GFCS for control of the 40mm and 5in batteries.
Mark 56 – telescope used with Mark 38 director.
Mark 57 – director used with Mark 57 GFCS for 40mm battery.
Mark 57 – GFCS for control of the 40mm battery.
Mark 60 – telescope used with Mark 37 director.
Mark 62 – 45-second time fuze.
Mark 63 – GFCS for control of the 40mm battery.
Mark 66 – telescope used in 16in turrets.
Mark 68 – telescope used with Mark 36 sight assembly.
Mark 69 – telescope used with Mark 38 director.
Mark 137 – SRBOC Launcher.
Mark 141 – launcher for RGM-84 Harpoon cruise missile.
Mark 143 ABL – launcher for BGM-109 series Tomahawk cruise missile.
Mark 143 HE/CVT – 16in 1,900 pound projectile.
Mark 144 ICM/ETF – 16in 1,900 pound projectile.
Mark 145 HE/ET – 16in 1,900 pound projectile.
Mark 146 ICM/ETF – 16in 1,900 pound projectile.
Mark 149 – 20mm projectile used with Mark 15 Phalanx CIWS.
MTF – Mechanical Time Fuze.

NALC/DODIC – Naval Ammunition Logistics Code/Department of Defense Inventory Code.
NAVSEA – Naval Sea Systems Command.
NavSea 03D – Surface Combatant Design Directorate.
NGFS – Naval Gun Fire Support.
NTDS – Naval Tactical Data System.

OE-82 – satellite communication relay system which uses a pair of AN/WCS-3 dish antennas.
Oerlikon – Swiss ordnance manufacturer.
OS2U – Kingfisher observation aircraft.
PDF – Point Detonating Fuze.
Phalanx – 20mm Mark 15 CIWS.
Pioneer – RPV used for observation.
Pocket battleship – German armored ship (Panzerschiffe).
PDF – Point Detonating Fuze.
Polaris – IRBM.
Proximity fuze – VT fuze, carries a self-contained radio transmitter-receiver so that when the projectile comes within effective fragmentation range of the target an echo of the transmission is reflected back to the receiver causing detonation.

Radar – acronym for RAdio Detection And Ranging.
Rangefinder – instrument to determine target distance.
Range/Ranging – to determine target distance along the line of fire.
RAP – Rocket Assisted Projectile.
RBL – Range and Bearing Launch mode.
RBOC – Rapid Bloom Offboard Chaff.
RDF – Radio Direction Finder.
Regulus II – RGM-15 (SSM-N-9) Surface-to-Surface nuclear missile.
RGM-84 – Harpoon Cruise Missile.
RPV – Remotely Piloted Vehicle.

Salvo – two or more shots fired simultaneously.
SC-1 – Seahawk observation aircraft.
SCB – Ship's Characteristics Board.

Seahawk – SC-1 observation aircraft.
SecNav – Secretary of the Navy.
SG – surface search radar.
SG-6 – surface/zenith search radar.
SK – air search radar.
SK 2 – air search radar.
Skyhawk – A-4 series attack aircraft.
SLQ-32 (V) 3 – ECM system.
SLQ 25 – NIXIE Torpedo Countermeasures System.
Snoopy – DASH helicopter used for observation.
SP – smokeless powder, a uniform ether-alcohol colloid of purified nitrocellulose with a quantity of diphenylamine or ethyl centralite added for stability.
SP Index:
    SP – Smokeless Powder.
    B – Blended.
    C – Stabilized by Ethyl Centralite.
    D – Stabilized by Diphenylamine.
    F – Flashless Powder.
    G – Includes Nitroglycerin and Nitroguanidine.
    N – Nonhygroscopic.
    W – Reworked by grinding.
    X – Water-drying process.
SP – height-finding/low angle search radar.
Splash colors – assigned to identify shell splashes by individual ship when concentrating fire on a target. The void space between the ballistic cap and the windshield in AP and APT projectiles is filled with color dye.
Splash color index:
    IOWA – Orange
    NEW JERSEY – Blue
    MISSOURI – Red
    WISCONSIN – Green
Spot/Spotting – observation of the fall of shot in relation to the target in order to correct for range, deflection or fuze settings of future salvos or bursts.
SPS-6 – air search radar.
SPS-8 – height-finding/low-angle search radar.
SPS-10 – surface search radar.
SPS-12 – air search radar.
SPS-49 – 2-D air search radar.
SPS-67 – surface search radar (solid state version of SPS-10).
SPT-1 – ECM signal jamming system.
SPT-4 – ECM signal jamming system.
SQ – portable, emergency surface search radar.
SR – air search radar.
SRBOC – Super Rapid Bloom Offboard Chaff.
SR-3 – air search radar.
SR-3c – modification of SR-3 air search radar.
SS-N-2 – STYX series Soviet Surface-to-Surface missile.
Stinger – FIM-92 Surface-to-Air Missile.
STS – Special Treatment Steel.
STYX – SS-N-2 series Soviet Surface-to-Surface missile.
SU – surface search radar.
Supermarket – Fast Combat Support Ship (AOE)
SupShip – Supervisor of Shipbuilding.
Surgical strike – a controlled, precision gun strike.
SWC – Strike Warfare Center.

TACAN – Tactical Air Navigation.
TACU – Target Acquisition Unit.
Talos – RIM-8 Surface-to-Air missile.
Tartar – RIM-24 Surface-to-Air missile.
TASM – Tomahawk Anti-Ship Missile.
TDY/TDY-1a – ECM antenna, jammer.
TERCOM – terrain contour matching.

Terrier – RIM-2 Surface-to-Air missile.
TLAM-C – Tomahawk Land-Attack Missile – Conventional.
TLAM-N – Tomahawk Land-Attack Missile – Nuclear.
Tomahawk – BGM-109 series cruise missile.
TP PUFF-PDF – target (puff), point detonating projectile.
TP PUFF-MTF – target (puff), mechanical time projectile.

UHF – Ultra High Frequency.
ULQ-6 – ECM system.
UNREP – Underway Replenishment.

VT – Variable Time Fuze.

VT-NONFRAG – target, nonfragmenting, variable time projectile.

W 23 – nuclear warhead for the 16in 1,900 pound Mark 23 'Katie' projectile.
Waveguide – rectangular tube used to transmit radar signals.
WP-MTF – white phosphorus (smoke), mechanical time projectile.
WP-PD – white phosphorus (smoke), point detonating projectile.

Zeus/Zeus II – XSAM-N-8 gun launched guided projectile. (See Arrow Shell.)
Zuni – 5in folding-fin rocket adapted for chaff delivery.

INDEX